Managing Service Quality

STANDARD

Paul Chapman Publishing Ltd distributes exclusively in the UK, and Republic of Ireland, Australia, New Zealand, South Africa, Hong Kong, China, Japan, Philippines, South Korea, Thailand, Burma, Indonesia, Malaysia, Singapore.

Paul Chapman Publishing can be contacted at:
    144 Liverpool Road
    London N1 1LA
    United Kingdom

CIP-data Koninklijke Bibliotheek, Den Haag /
British Library Cataloguing in Publication Data

Managing Service Quality
I. Kunst, Paul II. Lemmink, Jos
658.562

ISBN 90-802322-1-1 (The Netherlands)
ISBN 1-85396-293-7 (United Kingdom)

Production: Datawyse, Maastricht, The Netherlands

MANAGING
SERVICE
QUALITY

Edited by:

Paul Kunst
Jos Lemmink

P·C·P
Paul Chapman
Publishing Ltd

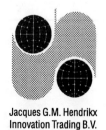

Jacques G.M. Hendrikx
Innovation Trading B.V.

Preface

When we edited the first book on *Quality Management in Services* (Kunst & Lemmink 1992), our aim was, at least to some extent, to close the gap between research and practice. Additionally, we attempted to create a platform for multi-disciplinary studies. These objectives are still worthwhile to pursue. Once again, this book includes examples that fit both objectives. At the same time, we must admit that some of the contributions may not fit the objectives, although they are certainly not less interesting. In recent years, the interest in the topic has proved to be overwhelming, and has resulted in numerous new approaches and challenges in the area of services management. Therefore, we must broaden our perspective in order to continue to offer an overview of what is going on in research and practice.

The interest in the topic has consequences for the editors as well. We are now confident that what started as a single book will evolve into a series on quality management in services. This would have been impossible without the assistance of the European Institute for Advanced Studies in Management (EIASM) in Brussels, which, in conjunction with other academic institutes, organized a number of workshops on Quality Management in Services. The first workshop was co-organized by the Strategic Quality Institute of the Erasmus University of Rotterdam and the Maastricht Economic Research Institute on Innovation and Technology (MERIT). The second was hosted by MERIT, and the third by the Swedish School of Economics and Business Administration. More workshops have been planned for future years.

Our work as editors has been made considerably easier by a number of persons, and this is the perfect place to extend our gratitude to them. First of all, Gerry van Dyck, programme director of the EIASM; her continuous interest in the topic and her efforts to make the workshops successful have been of great value for the publication of this book. Christian Grönroos, Veronica Liljander and Tore Strandvik of the Swedish School of Economics organized the third workshop on Quality Management in Services, which provided the first drafts of the majority of the papers in this book. Furthermore, Christian and Tore assisted us in making the final selection of the papers to be included. To publish this second volume would not have been possible without sponsoring. Heineken Breweries in Amsterdam have recognized the importance of service quality and showed this by generously providing us with the necessary funds.

Finally, we thank Corien Gijsbers at MERIT for her valuable assistance in editing the book. It can be certified that her assistance level is of outstanding quality.

Paul Kunst and Jos Lemmink

Maastricht, April 1994

Table of Contents

PART II: MANAGERIAL CONSEQUENCES

CHAPTER 5.
Quality Marks: Prospective Tools in Managing Service Quality Perceptions
Henk Roest and Theo Verhallen

CHAPTER 6.
The Impact of Cross-Cultural Dimensions on the Management of Service Quality
Audrey Gilmore and David Carson

CHAPTER 7.
Managing Service Recovery
Colin G. Armistead, Graham Clark and Paula Stanley

CHAPTER 8.
Service Performances as Drama: Quality Implications and Measurement
Raymond P. Fisk and Stephen J. Grove

Table of Contents

1

Quality Positioning in the Austrian Banking Industry: A Benchmark Case Study

Gerhard A. Wührer

Problem Situation: The Case Setting

The Kärntner Sparkasse is a major bank in Carinthia and belongs to an Austrian-wide banking group. During the last years the bank has worked intensively on strengthening its marketplace profile, strategic competencies and upgrading its capabilities with a view to expansion and intensification of sales within the existing customer base. This is due to the intensified competition in the Austrian market with its strong concentration tendency of anticipating changes that will facilitate the unification of Europe and Austria's integration in the European Community. The Kärntner Sparkasse has been a successful bank in recent years, with the Raiffeisenbank, the Bank für Kärnten und Steiermark and other regional banking institutions being the main competitors at the marketplace in Carinthia. During the last years the Kärntner Sparkasse in Carinthia has been working on some strategic issues dealing with the assessment of enterprise culture and customer satisfaction. The quality benchmark case study should provide information and orientation for future strategic competencies and operational actions, i.e., internal marketing within the banking institution (see Figure 1).

Up until now, the banking institutions have used the "Finanzmarkt-Datenservice" (FMDS) as a marketing research instrument. This tracking device is a multi-client study offered by a major Austrian marketing research institute, bought by most of the banking institutions and mainly based on image criteria, which have limited power for positioning a bank as a service-oriented enterprise. In addition, as data are not exclusively provided, any move can be traced by the competitors,

1

which might lead to a "zero-sum game". In fact, the perceptual map of the image positions shows only some minor differences between the major banking institutions. For the reasons mentioned above it seems necessary to develop a research instrument measuring service quality, providing information about the service orientation of competitors, making representative figures about nation-wide key-benchmarks on the subject of quality with breakdown by banks available, allowing comparisons of the quality standards in the country of Carinthia and helping to develop a programme for a stronger quality-oriented strategy in services.

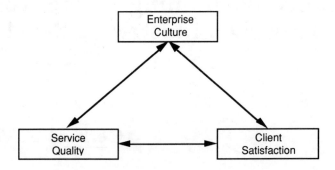

Figure 1. Internal project contingencies of the quality benchmark study

The Development of Instruments: A Process View

A literature review of theoretical and empirical sources (e.g., Bruhn and Stauss 1991) led to the consideration of using the SERVQUAL questionnaire, but some in-depth interviews with marketing and human resource managers showed that the original version in its German translation (Zeithaml, Parasuraman and Berry 1992) was too general to offer substantial information for further managerial decisions in these case contingencies. It can also be argued that the questionnaire is culture-bound and must be adapted accordingly. It was decided to use the framework of the SERVQUAL model with its original, more explicated 10 dimensions with the content of the questionnaire being tailored towards the underlying problem situation.

Explorative-Qualitative Study

To operationalize the variables of the measurement instrument we followed the procedure recommended by Churchill (1979). The domain of the constructs was based on the SERVQUAL model with its 10 dimensions. To generate a sample of items for each construct we used the critical incident approach (Flanagan 1954, Koelemeijer 1992). Sixty in-depth interviews with a partly structured questionnaire were performed in three customer segments: commercial clients, youth segment, private consumer. The aim was to discuss typical incidents that led to low or high quality in delivering service, explaining the contents of different dimensions such as tangibles ("äußeres Erscheinungsbild"), reliability ("Zuverlässig-keit"), competence ("Kompetenz"), responsiveness ("Entgegenkommen"), com-munication ("Kommunikation"), credibility ("Glaubwürdigkeit"), security ("Si-cherheit"), courtesy ("Höflichkeit"), understanding/knowing customers ("Kun-denverständnis") and access ("Erreichbarkeit") (Parasuraman, Zeithaml and Berry 1988, Zeithaml *et al.* 1992).

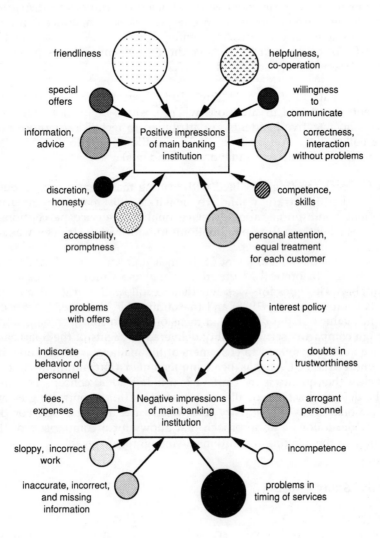

Figure 2. Problem patterns in delivering quality service in banking institutions (n = 60, explorative study)

The answers to the questions regarding critical incidents have been transcribed, analyzed as to content, and clustered by eyeballing. A summary of the preliminary results of this part of the study showed that positive incidents are based mainly on personal factors such as friendliness, helpfulness and co-operation, correctness and interaction without problems, personal attention and fair equal treatment for each customer. Incidents that are connected with technical and procedural episodes (see Figure 2) play a relatively minor role. Incidents that led to a negative impression of one's main bank may be summarized as "disappointed" expectations in relation to offers, procedures and information. Of course, interest rate policies of banks are a permanent source of negative attitudes towards these institutions, and these are enforced when changes are not announced in advance or explained on request afterwards. Apparently, major sources of discontent are a delayed transfer of an amount to one's credit, or —from a client's point of view— other delayed services and actions of a bank.

Looking at the pattern of the qualitative study it seems quite interesting that positive incidents developed in situations where positive interactions with the clerks took place and negative incidents are attributed to technical or procedural problems (see Folkes 1988, Weiner 1985, Mohr and Bitner 1991 for assumptions about attributions for favorable and unfavorable incidents).

The first feedback meeting was held with leading managers to give inputs for the internal marketing strategy and to sensitize the management for gap 2 (management assumptions about service quality - service perceptions of customers). Consequently, a top-down, bottom-up information strategy was followed.

The next step was the development of the measurement model based on the qualitative study and theoretical assumptions about the validity of measurements in service quality. The question was whether to follow the original model as outlined by Parasuraman *et al.* (1988) and to examine the "delivered", "expected" and "important" values of the different dimensions, or to follow a more straightforward design comparing service quality delivered to clients of the Sparkassensektor and service quality delivered to customers of the main competitors. Looking at the models where SERVQUAL has been implemented (Parasuraman *et al.* , 1988) it becomes clear that quality is measured as an independent concept, i.e., not in relation to the delivered service quality of competitors (for a contrasting example, see the international study on industry level of Ernst & Young 1992). For these reasons the model followed an approach that allows for a comparison of the delivered services of the banking institutions on an aggregate level.

Quantitative Study - Austria

Methodological Issues
The measurement model developed (BDQU = **B**anken-**D**ienstleistungs**q**ualität) comprised the quality of delivered services of banks of the Sparkassensektor and the main competitors and the importance of several indices as expected to be delivered by an excellent banking institution. In total the developed items based on the qualitative study amounted to 51 covering 10 dimensions (see Figure 3) and were displayed to the interviewee by means of cards and then sorted on a Likert scale ranging from 1 ("does not exist at all") to 7 ("does strongly exist"). The scale of importance of quality delivered by an excellent bank ranged from 1 ("is not important at all") to 7 ("is very important"). Some additional questions have been

added, for example, self-image of interviewee, image of main bank, future importance of main bank, overall satisfaction with main bank and demographic variables to relate the variables of service quality with them.

Main Features:
"Dienstleistungsqualität" ("Service Quality")
Number of dimensions: 10
Number of items: 51
Scale type: Likert (scaling 1 to 7)
Expressions: "does not exist at all"/"does strongly exist"
"is not important at all"/"is very important"
Breaks: By main banking institution (14 banks)
Weight of dimensions: Percentage

Additional features :
"Self-image of interviewee"
Number of items: 61
Scale type: Likert (scaling 1 to 7)
Expressions: "does not exist at all"/"does strongly exist"
"Image of main bank"
Number of items: 26
Scale type: Likert (scaling 1 to 7)
Expressions: "does not exist at all"/"does strongly exist"
"is not important at all"/"is very important"

"Overall satisfaction with service quality of main bank"
Number of items: 1
Scale type: Likert (scaling 1 to 7)
Expressions: "not satisfied at all"/"very satisfied"
"Future importance of main bank"
Number of items: 1
Scale type: Semantic-differential
Expressions: "less", "equal", "more"
Socio-demographic Variables:
Country, size of city, sex, age, life stage, religion, education, occupation, household size, net household income, persons with income in household, voting behavior, politics

Figure 3. Main characteristics of measurement model and questionnaire

A quota sample (n = 1000) was drawn from the Austrian population. The main structures of the sample correspond to the results of the last available national census. The 1,000 cases have been used for reliability analysis. The results of the reliability test using Cronbach's Alpha are shown in Table 1. The values of Cronbach's Alpha are sufficient (Henerson, Morris and Fitz-Gibbon 1987) improved reliability was achieved in the Carinthian sample and questionnaire, where some items have been deleted. The dimension of credibility could have been measured with fewer items, but it was decided to include them all to comprise more information on improvement of credibility. The number of items not only seems to be a matter of theoretical considerations but should also be treated from a pragmatical point of view. Having more items provides additional information on the strategies to improve credibility.

5

Table 1. Reliability tests of the questionnaire for measuring service quality[1]

English	German	# of items	# of items del.	Cronbach's Alpha (n = 1000) "Austria"	Cronbach's Alpha (n = 400) "Carinthia"
Compatibles	Erscheinungsbild	3	0	0.71	0.81
Reliability	Zuverlässigkeit	5	2	0.63	0.72
Responsiveness	Entgegenkommen	5	1	0.73	0.81
Competence	Kompetenz	3	0	0.74	0.78
Courtesy	Höflichkeit	5	1	0.59	0.70
Credibility	Vertrauen	11	2	0.84	0.84
Security	Sicherheit	3	1	0.67	0.56
Accessibility	Erreichbarkeit	8	2	0.78	0.78
Communication	Kommunikation	5	1	0.71	0.82
Understanding/ Knowing customers	Kundenverständnis	3	0	0.63	0.71
Total		51	10		

With respect to the question of validity, one may refer to the procedure used as outlined by Churchill (1979). Hentschel (1991) argues about the reliability and validity of quality dimensions of SERVQUAL and states that the concept with five dimensions is fuzzy. A factor analysis (see Table 3) revealed five complex factors. Factor I is the most complex and contains reliability, security, credibility and responsiveness items. Factor II is primarily based on items expressing communication and tangibles. Factor III could be labeled technical accessibility, factor IV contains understanding/knowing customer items and factor V is also courtesy-related.

---

1   The German questionnaire and the detailed measurement model (BDQU = Banken-Dienst-leistungsqualität) are available from the author upon request.

Table 2. Quality patterns - strengths and weaknesses [a]

Factor I	Factor-loading	Importance %[2]	Sparkasse %[3]	Raiffeisenbank %[4]
Reliability				
Item 11...............	0.71	59	34	**39**
Item 28...............	0.69	53	**40**	38
Item 29...............	0.66	61	39	**40**
Σ		**173**	113	117
Security				
Item 32...............	0,52	54	**53**	47
Responsiveness				
Item 37...............	0,63	45	**37**	36
Item 30...............	0,46	42	**39**	32
Σ		87	76	68
Credibility				
Item 27...............	0,70	56	49	**51**
Item 26...............	0,68	65	**47**	42
Item 22...............	0,64	53	40	**42**
Item 3...............	0,57	43	31	**39**
Item 13...............	0,53	44	35	**43**
Σ		**261**	202	217
Courtesy-Processing				
Item 16...............	0,54	46	35	**42**
Item 20...............	0,50	51	39	**43**
Item 44...............	0,49	48	26	**29**
Σ		145	100	114
Factor II				
Communication / Tangibles				
Item 41...............	0,60	18	**33**	28
Item 24...............	0,53	38	**51**	41
Item 40...............	0,52	38	**47**	38
Item 33...............	0,62	38	**36**	35
Item 34...............	0,60	25	**34**	28
Item 25...............	0,55	38	**31**	28
Item 21...............	0,48	38	**28**	24
Σ		233	260	222
Factor III				
Technical Accessibility				
Item 6...............	0,83	38	**39**	39
Item 5...............	0,81	28	**31**	30
Item 17...............	0,67	25	**30**	26
Item 7...............	0,47	37	**30**	26
Σ		128	130	121
Factor IV				
Understanding / Knowing Customers				
Item 46...............	0,47	48	18	19
Item 47...............	0,60	39	25	23
Item 48...............	0,58	46	24	25
Item 49...............	0,47	45	16	16
Σ		**178**	83	83
Factor V				
Courtesy Clerks				
Item 9...............	0,75	20	14	18
Item 8...............	0,61	22	37	47
Item 45...............	0,54	31	30	**30**
Item 18...............	0,51	25	30	**36**
Item 16...............	0,50	35	39	**40**
Σ		133	150	171

(a) The German version of the items is available from the author upon request

2   The percentages are "extremely" values (i.e., "1" or "7") of **important** service qualities of excellent banking institutions.
3   The percentages are "extremely" values (i.e., "1" or "7") of **perceived** service quality.
4   The percentages are "extremely" values (i.e., "1" or "7") of **perceived** service quality.

The Positions of Banking Institutions in Austria. A Factor-Analytical Approach

Relative quality competitiveness
The table of the factor pattern[5] clearly shows that Sparkasse[6] and its major competitor Raiffeisenbank are positioned on different areas of service quality. In total, Sparkasse is slightly superior (when also taking into account the **importance** of the different items) to Raiffeisenbank. But we realize weak positions in regard to item 11 and 29, which indicate some problems by delivering correct and promised service. The next weakness of Sparkasse is a discrete, undisturbed contact with customers and interaction, which is also connected to courtesy during processing orders and counselling customers. The advantage of Raiffeisen in handling clients is the so-called "one-point system". In this system the bank counter clerk is responsible for all transactions, so that the customer will not be sent around to different persons or other counters in the bank. Strong competitive positions of the Sparkasse are the responsiveness offered, the bankers' discretion, security aspects regarding no risky investments, etc. Factor II expresses a strong position in communicating with the customers, the external appearance and generally good performance of the bank.

General quality competitiveness
The importance of the different items expected to be typical of an excellent bank shows that both banking institutions lack considerable understanding and knowledge of customers (factor IV). Customers are under the impression that interest rates are changed without notice, that one has to argue intensively for higher interest rates, and that both banks operate for their very own profit. Even in the quality dimensions, both institutions are under expectancy pressure of their clients in terms of correct and accurate delivery of service and keeping promises on the advantages of different services and products. In addition, some credibility traits should also be improved.

A summary (see Figure 4) of the different quality positions from an input-output perspective shows the main sources of quality competence. Sparkasse is strong on the input side of services, where it beats its competitor. Raiffeisen has some strengths on the output side that are connected to the organization of services leading to some advantages in perceived courtesy and reliability at the 'frontier line'. Here the management of service quality should start at Sparkasse. Input factors are factors that are especially objective and controllable by the provider (Roest and Verhallen 1992). Output factors are more subjective and customer-dependent. They develop with the interactive contact between provider and client and are less controllable and manageable by the provider alone.

---

5   PCF, eigen value criteria, varimax rotation, explained variance 48%.
6   The following discussion only compares Sparkasse and its main competitor Raiffeisenbank.

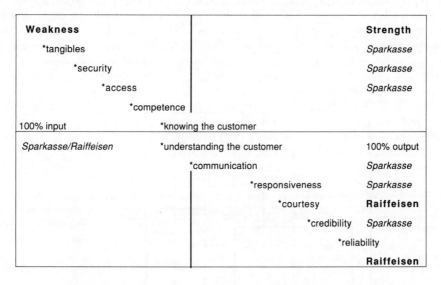

Weakness		Strength
*tangibles		*Sparkasse*
*security		*Sparkasse*
*access		*Sparkasse*
*competence		
100% input	*knowing the customer	
Sparkasse/Raiffeisen	*understanding the customer	100% output
	*communication	*Sparkasse*
	*responsiveness	*Sparkasse*
	*courtesy	**Raiffeisen**
	*credibility	*Sparkasse*
	*reliability	
		Raiffeisen

Figure 4. Input-output connectivity of service quality
(Source: Roest and Verhallen, 1992)

The Concept of Value-Added Quality Chain and Partnership

The research findings in all stages (i.e., explorative study, Austrian study, and Carinthian Study, with the latter being of strategic interest and not explained here) have been presented to managers of different levels of the Sparkasse. The final meeting has been held with the board of directors. Parallel to the Austrian study the bank institution started a strategy of internal marketing by combining these results with an in-house cultural and client satisfaction study to create and increase strategic awareness (Hambrick 1981) of gaps 2 and 3 (Zeithaml *et al.* 1992) and to give momentum to the importance of quality issues on a corporate-wide level. One concept and project developed (see Figure 5) is the "Concept of Value-Added Quality Chain and Partnership", because traditional measures of TQM in industrial management could not be applied (Kerfoot and Knights 1992).

The principle of the "Value-Added Quality Chain and Partnership Concept" states that from transaction to transaction the overall quality of a service should be planned, managed and controlled. The benefits of quality offered in one transaction should be mandated to the next one. This requires the identification and analysis of typical transactions and possible critical incidents (for example, advice on a specific service and delivery of service) along the service line (Rafiq and Ahmed 1992), involved partners (customers and co-workers), and the most concerned quality dimensions in delivering the service. The partners should be aware of the quality ("selling the quality") added in the distinct stages (and not only at the point of sale, see Kerfoot and Knights (1992)) in the delivery to the partner/customer.

At the present stage, the process of development and implementation of the project implies (Parasuraman *et al.*, 1988) the introduction of building on teamwork, assessment of positions, techniques and roles in the service line and a continuous control system.

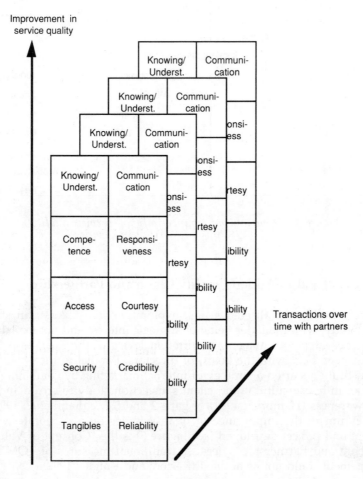

Figure 5. Value-Added Quality Chain and Partnership Concept

Conclusions and Outlook

The case study offers different perspectives and conclusions on the research and management of quality in services:

1. The development of problem-tailored research instruments is highly recommended. It should be done in a systematic procedure and begin with a qualitative study. This part provides insight into the problem situation and leads to the construction of situation-based measurement instruments to be used in the

second stage. The uncritical transfer of already used concepts which have their value in a certain (maybe culture-bound) situation could lead to counterproductive decisions. Thus, SERVQUAL offers only a theoretical reference frame for developing these instruments.

2. The nation-wide study offers information about the quality position among competitors on an aggregate and strategic level. The individual branch managers and clerks dealing with their clientele at the local bank can make only limited use of the information gathered from the market study. More information may become available when one uses a benefit segmentation approach, which is allowed by the model (see Figure 3). A service quality-based typology of clients could be developed, thus offering a richer description.

3. The transfer of research findings, the development and implementation of a concept of quality management is a very critical issue. The whole process should be planned carefully and take into account the contingencies of the different functions and branches of the enterprise. The CEO and his staff members of the Carinthian branch of Sparkasse have assumed responsibility for the project and therefore emphasized the importance of the research and development programme to the members of the organization. The success of a quality management programme also depends on the internal marketing of the issue. 'Labelling' of the project plays an important role (e.g., "Partnership and Quality Chain"). Marketing functions and human resource management departments have been involved in the project from the beginning. The marketing research results will be used for training and as a basis for directions of organizational development within the quality management programme "quality goals ==> planning ==> delivery ==> controlling".

4. Tracking the changes in delivering quality and results caused by organizational programmes will be an important future issue for feedback actions to management. Control could be established by periodic updating of research. Internal means could be the analysis of customer complaints reports and other direct or indirect information sources. This task also needs systematical development of measures which could help to detect discrepancies. Overall, quality programmes cost money and need budgets. The return on investment in software and hardware for improving service quality will also be a guideline.

4. Tracking the changes in delivering quality and results caused by organizational programmes will be an important future issue for feedback actions to management. Control could be established by periodic updating of research. Internal means could be the analysis of customer complaints reports and other direct or indirect information sources. This task also needs systematical development of measures which could help to detect discrepancies. Overall, quality programmes cost money and need budgets. The return on investment in software and hardware for improving service quality will also be a guideline.

References

Bruhn, M. and B. Stauss (eds.), *Dienstleistungsqualität*. Konzepte-Methoden-Erfahrungen, Wiesbaden, 1991.

Churchill, G.A. Jr., A Paradigm for Developing Better Measures of Marketing Constructs, *Journal of Marketing Research*, 16, 1979, pp. 64-73.

Flanagan, J.C., The critical incident technique, *Psychological Bulletin*, 51, 1954, pp. 327-357.

Folkes, V.S., Recent Attribution Research in Consumer Behavior: A Review and New Directions, *Journal of Consumer Research*, 14, 1988, pp. 548-656.

Hambrick, D.C., Strategic Awareness within Top Management Teams, *Strategic Management Journal*, 2, 1981, pp. 263-279.

Henerson, M.E., Morris, L.L. and C.T. Fitz-Gibbon, *How to Measure Attitudes*, 2nd ed., Newbury Park/Beverly Hills/London/New Delhi, 1987.

Hentschel, B., Multiattributive Messung von Dienstleistungsqualität, in: M. Bruhn and B. Stauss (eds.), *Dienstleistungsqualität. Konzepte-Methoden-Erfahrungen*, Wiesbaden, 1991, pp. 312-343.

International Quality Study. A Definitive Report on International Industry-Specific Quality Management Practices, Cleveland, Ohio, Ernst & Young, 1992.

Kerfoot, D. and D. Knights, Managerial Evangelism? - Planning for Quality in Financial Services, in: J. Lemmink and P. Kunst (eds.), Proceedings 2nd Workshop on Quality Management in Services, 19-22, May, Maastricht, 1992, pp. 137-152.

Koelemeijer, K., Consumer (Dis)satisfaction with Retail Services: A Critical Incident Approach, in: J. Lemmink and P. Kunst (eds.), Proceedings 2nd Workshop on Quality Management in Services, 19-22 May, Maastricht, 1992, pp. 46-60.

Mohr, L.A. and M.J. Bitner, Mutual Understanding between Customers and Employees in Service Encounters, in: R.H. Holman and M.R. Solomon (eds.), *Advances in Consumer Research*, 18 ed., Provo, 1991, pp. 611-617.

Parasuraman, A., Zeithaml, V.A. and L.L. Berry, A Multiple-Item Scale for Measuring Consumer Perceptions of Service Quality, *Journal of Retailing*, 64 (Spring), 1988, pp. 12-40.

Rafiq, M. and P.K. Ahmed, The Limits of Internal Marketing, In: J. Lemmink and P. Kunst (eds.), Proceedings 2nd Workshop on Quality Management in Services, 19-22 May, Maastricht, 1992, pp. 184-198.

Roest, H. and Th. Verhallen, Managing Service Quality Perceptions by Quality Marks, in: J. Lemmink and P. Kunst (ed.), Proceedings 2nd Workshop on Quality Management in Services, 19-22 May, Maastricht, 1992, pp. 97-114.

Weiner, B., An Attributional Theory of Achievement Motivation and Emotion, *Psychological Review*, 92 (4), 1985, pp. 548-573.

Zeithaml, V.A., Parasuraman, A. and L.L. Berry, *Qualitätsservice. Was Ihre Kunden erwarten - was Sie leisten müssen*, Frankfurt/New York, 1992.

2

Measuring Service Quality: The Results of a Longitudinal Study in Further Education

Sabine Haller

The Development of Service Quality during the Service Process

In the typical service process the following phases have been identified: Based on the model by Donabedian (1980, p. 81) global quality perceptions are a result of three components: structure, process and outcome. Structure, later defined as "potential-oriented phase" (Hilke 1989, p. 11; Engelhardt, Kleinaltenkamp and Reckenfelderbäumer 1992, p. 10) consists of the service supplier's stable characteristics. These include professionalism, equipment, personal, organizational context and access. The process implies all activities that are directly connected to the process of service delivery. The outcome refers to the results of the services at the end of the process.

Meyer and Mattmüller (1987, p. 79) added a fourth phase to this model: The ultimate outcome of a service that in certain sectors can only be judged some time after the service process ended (for example, the quality of an operation).

According to this model, it can be assumed that the customer's choice of important criteria and his perception of the process change in the course of service.

In the first phase, which ends with signing the contract, the customer tries to evaluate quality by means of indicators: These consist mainly of reputation, information and occasionally guaranties (Kleinaltenkamp 1992, p. 817). His reaction is such because service quality is primarily composed of experience quality dimensions rather than search quality dimensions. At the start of the process and throughout the period of service delivery, different criteria may become more important. These can vary again when the performance ends. Finally, there is a fourth point in time where the quality judgment can differ: The ultimate quality evaluation that often becomes apparent after a certain time period has passed.

Assuming that the customer's judgment varies over time, the following hypotheses have been formulated to be tested in the empirical study for the sector of further education:

Hypothesis 1: The importance of the criteria that build the customer's judgment of quality varies throughout the process of service delivery.

Hypothesis 2: During the process of service delivery the focus of the customer's evaluation is on process-oriented criteria.

Hypothesis 3: At the end of the process the focus shifts to outcome-oriented criteria.

The service quality model developed by Grönroos (1982, p. 79) emphasizes two different dimensions of service quality: technical and functional quality. Technical quality expresses **What** the customer receives (Grönroos 1982, pp. 61-63) whereas functional quality refers to **How** he receives a service. In the global quality judgment both dimensions are important.

In selecting categories of evaluations for the attribute-oriented methods of measurement, it is necessary to combine the two models (the phases of the service process and the dimensions of service quality) (Meyer 1991, p. 201).

Methods of Measuring Service Quality

Several methods of measuring service quality have been developed and discussed over the last few years. Reviewing the service quality literature, most of these models work with expectations (Parasuraman, Zeithaml and Berry 1988, Buswell 1986, Liljander and Strandvik 1992, 1993).

The customer compares his expectations towards a certain service with its perceived performance. The judgment of quality is built up on the basis of this theoretical construct. Good service quality evaluation develops when perceptions exceed/are equal to expectations. Consequently, most approaches try to measure direct or indirect disconfirmation (Liljander and Strandvik 1993). Because there are different kinds of expectations —such as ideal, predictive, minimal, product-type and brand-oriented —different methods lead to different results.

On the other hand, the models explaining product quality use the concept of importance (Kawlath 1969, Hüttenrauch 1973, Behrens, Schneider and Weinberg 1978, p. 135). The customer determines all characteristics he expects the ideal product to show. Because not all of them are equally important, he weighs the importance of each. He builds his quality judgment on his perception of each characteristic multiplied with its specific significance. Summing up all evaluated criteria gives the total quality score.

$$\text{Quality Judgment} = \sum wjcj \text{ (where } j = 1,...,i)$$

(Behrens, Schneider and Weinberg 1978, p. 135)

Expectations are already integrated in the evaluation of the perception. When a customer judges a certain characteristic to be "very good", he expresses that it exceeds either his predictive or his product type-oriented expectations. There is the possibility that the performance matches his ideal expectations. However, the customer often has only a vague idea about the latter. For this reason, the measurement of expectations had been rejected. Instead, the author decided to ask for perceptions and the importance of the attributes. This method of measurement corresponds with the underlying model of product quality as described above.

The Results of the Empirical Study

Design

The empirical study was performed in the sector of further education. The research object was a course offered by the Freie Universität Berlin, "Weiterbildendes Studium Technischer Vertrieb". The course was targeted towards engineers working in sales positions. Its aim is to provide this group with marketing and managerial skills. The duration of the course is one year. The course originated in the form of a correspondence course that includes four seminars. All students work full-time during their studies; this means that they carry the double burden of working and studying throughout the period of one year. The mailed study units are equipped with exercises that must be completed and sent to Berlin. Tutors review and comment on these exercises and return them to the students for feedback. The course ends with a comprehensive assignment and final examinations.

From November 1991 to September 1992 the participants were asked to complete three mail interviews. The first took place in November 1991, approximately four weeks after the course began. The second interview was conducted in May 1992 during the third seminar, and the final one took place in September 1992 during the final seminar. From the 39 students who registered in October 1991, 36 completed the first questionnaire, 33 the second and 30 the final one. These figures correspond with the number of students who actively participated in the course on a continuous basis. The others appeared to have dropped out of the course.

The main part of the three questionnaires was identical. The participants were first asked to rate the actual perception of service quality on a 5-Point Likert Scale with 1= "very good", 2= "good", 3="satisfying", 4="sufficient" and 5="poor, insufficient". This scale corresponds with the German grading system used in education. They had to evaluate twenty-three criteria. Furthermore, an evaluation of the global quality of the course had to be given using the same scale.

The students were then asked to allocate a hundred points among the 23 criteria according to their importance. This constant sum rating scale was used to show distances in the relevance of the attributes. As many empirical studies show, people tend to choose the second highest score —here "important"— when rating the importance on a Likert scale (Dichtl and Müller 1986, p. 233). As a result, a limit was set that would force the students to decide among the criteria. Giving more points to one attribute meant that they had to give less to another. Although this method is complicated and requires some calculations, pretests showed that the participants dealt satisfactorily with this matter. In other circumstances a Likert scale would be more adequate in spite of the apparent deficiencies.

Besides the rating of attributes the students were asked to describe critical incidents occurring during the programme. Other studies show that attribute ratings and the critical incident technique arrive at different results (Buchanan 1979, Stauss and Hentschel 1991a). Taking both methods into account when interpreting the results can provide a broader picture of the construct of quality.

When selecting the criteria for the questionnaires the three main phases of the service process were taken into consideration. It was necessary that potential orientation, process orientation and outcome orientation as well as the technical and the functional dimensions of quality (referred to as "tech" and "touch" dimensions by Meyer (1991, p. 201)) were integrated into the questionnaire. The small number of participants and the chosen method of measurement required a limited amount of items. The following items were chosen:

"TECH"

Predominantly potential-oriented criteria:
Costs of course
Structure/Timing of course
Name recognition of institute offering course
Professional competence of tutors/leader

Predominantly process oriented criteria:
Access to seminar locations and equipment
Organizational realization of seminars
Structure and contents of seminars
Performance of guest lecturers
Content focus of study units
Systematical structure of study units
Detailed reviews of/comments on mailed exercises
Promptness of reviews of mailed exercises

Predominantly outcome-oriented criteria:
Usefulness of final certificate concerning further career

"TOUCH"

Image/respectability of institute offering course
Willingness of tutors to deal intensively with participants' problems

Possibility to contact tutors easily
Motivation by tutors
Practical orientation of case studies
Possibility of exchanging informal contacts with participants/tutors
Design of study units (layout, practical examples, motivation to continue)

Practical orientation of course
Personal development of managerial skills
Relationship between personal effort and utility

Changes in Importance of the Criteria

As Table 1 shows, the relevance of several criteria changed significantly during the process of service delivery.

Table 1.   Changes in importance during the study

Criteria	Changes 1.- 2.	Changes 2.- 3.	Changes 1.- 3.
Potential-oriented criteria:			
Costs of course	−		
Structure/timing of course			
Image/respectability			
Name recognition of institute			
Tutors deal intensively with problems			
Professional competence of staff	−		
Process-oriented criteria:			
Easy contact to tutors		+	
Motivation by tutors	+	−	
Seminar locations		−	−
Organization of seminars			
Contents of seminars		−	
Guest lecturers			
Case study work		+	
Contact with participants/tutors			
Contents of study units	+		
Systematical structure of study units	+	−	
Layout/examples/motivation of study units	+		
Detailed review of exercises		−	−
Promptness of review of exercises	−		−
Outcome-oriented criteria:			
Practical orientation of course		+	+
Usefulness of certificate	−	+	
Personal development			
Effort/utility relationship			

P < 0.1

Comparing the first and second series of interviews regarding significant changes, items that gained importance belong to the process-oriented criteria. Between the second and the third survey most items losing relevance fall into this category. One exception, *easy contact to tutors,* can be explained by the specific circumstances. At the time of the last interview many participants had not yet finished their assignment and frequently required help and information from the tutors. It is possible that the criterion *practical orientation of case study work* is indirectly influenced by the item *practical orientation of course* that gained importance during the second half year.

Taking a closer look at the different kinds of criteria, one can see that there were hardly any significant changes in the items concerning the potential-oriented phase (with two exceptions!). However, it must be noted that *professional competence of tutors* was judged to be very good and, therefore, became less important.

Another interesting fact is that a comparison between the beginning and the end of the course reveals only a few significant changes. Only when integrating the second series of interviews does it become obvious that a changing picture of the service delivery process has occurred.

With respect to the hypotheses as mentioned above, it can be said that the results confirm Hypothesis 1. However, Hypothesis 2 and Hypothesis 3 must be rejected. Process-oriented criteria gained importance during the service process, but they still remained less important than the outcome-oriented items. The outcome-oriented criteria belonged to the most important criteria in the last series of interviews. However, this cannot be considered a confirmation of Hypothesis 3, because these items were important to the participants throughout the course (see the importance-performance-analysis below). Only the item practical orientation of the course shows an increase in importance during the second half year of the course.

Importance-Performance-Analysis

The importance-performance-analysis (Martilla and James 1977, Hentschel 1991) shows the results of the study. The median was chosen to separate the very important from the less important variables. The items with an arithmetical average between "good" and "very good" are located on the right side; those evaluated with less than "good" are placed on the left side.

In order to obtain four equally sized quadrants, the scales used are not proportionally linear. On the horizontal performance axis, distances on the right side are twice the size as those on the left. On the vertical importance axis, the scale intervals of the lower quadrant are larger than those of the upper one.

Figure 1. Importance-Performance analysis

Figure 2 shows the results of the first survey one month after the course began. Students see strengths indicating very good performance in the *practical orientation, image/respectability of the institute offering the course, the structure and contents of the first seminar* and *the professional competence of the staff.*

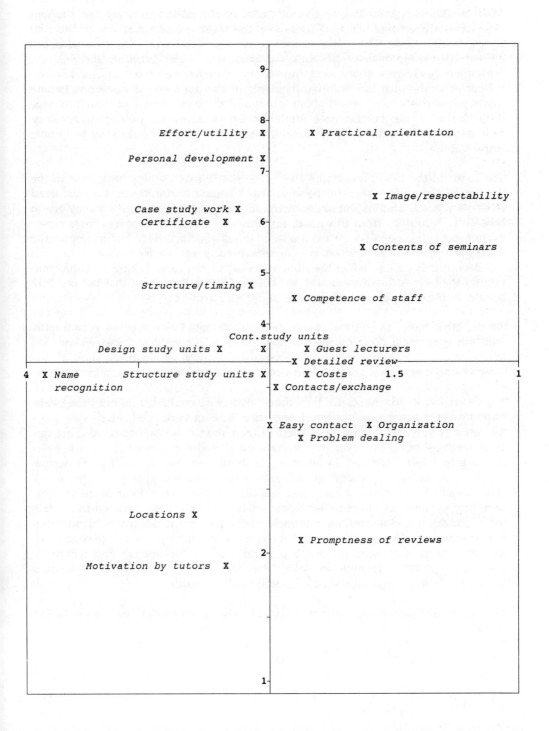

Figure 2. Importance-Performance analysis: Results of the first survey

Main weaknesses according to the judgment of the participants are the *relationship between effort and utility*. This is also the most important factor in the first series of interviews. Other dimensions to be improved were the *personal development concerning managerial skills, the usefulness of the certificate, the practical orientation of the case study work* and *the structure/timing of the course*. The latter corresponds with the negative incidents in the open-ended questions, where many participants complained about stress and the lack of time in which to cope with all their tasks. Furthermore, students also criticized the mailed study units. This indicates the main problem areas where the institute should start to initiate improvements.

The items in the lower quadrants show the criteria that are less important in the opinion of the participants. In the lower right square performance was evaluated to be very good. The institute administrators must analyse carefully if they are to take away resources from this quadrant to improve the weaknesses. For a closer examination, the penalty-reward analysis should be included. For example, the *willingness of tutors to deal intensively with participants' problems* is a factor that has been highly rewarded in the dimension of *tutorial care*. Taking this information on the two different measures, the conclusion can be drawn that the institute should maintain its good performance under all circumstances.

On the other hand, the *costs of the course* were evaluated as not being very important, but very good. This means that the course was considered inexpensive. As the price did not appear in the penalty-reward-factors, the institute should consider raising it to a level where it still would not be evaluated as a penalty factor.

The lower left quadrant shows the criteria that were evaluated as not being very important and perception of performance as not being very good. As service quality depends very much on details, these criteria should not be neglected. First improvements should, however, concentrate on the elimination of the weaknesses in the upper left quadrant. In addition, it should be considered if poor performance is punished in the critical-incident analysis. For example, the criterion *access to seminar locations and equipment* belongs to this sector. Poor seminar locations are punished as the critical-incident analysis shows (here included in the factor organization). However, an extremely well-equipped location would probably not be rewarded. Our conclusion is that the institute offering the course should try to find a functional location, where participants can concentrate and where all necessary equipment is made available. They should not invest in more resources to find the best seminar location as this will not be rewarded.

The results of the second survey conducted six months after the course began (Figure 3) shows changes in the evaluation of some criteria. The *personal development* was now regarded as a strength (in the first survey it showed up as a weakness). In the middle of the course many process-oriented items gained importance. *Contents, systematical structure and layout/examples of the mailed study units* were perceived as a weakness. In the lower quadrants some changes can also be observed.

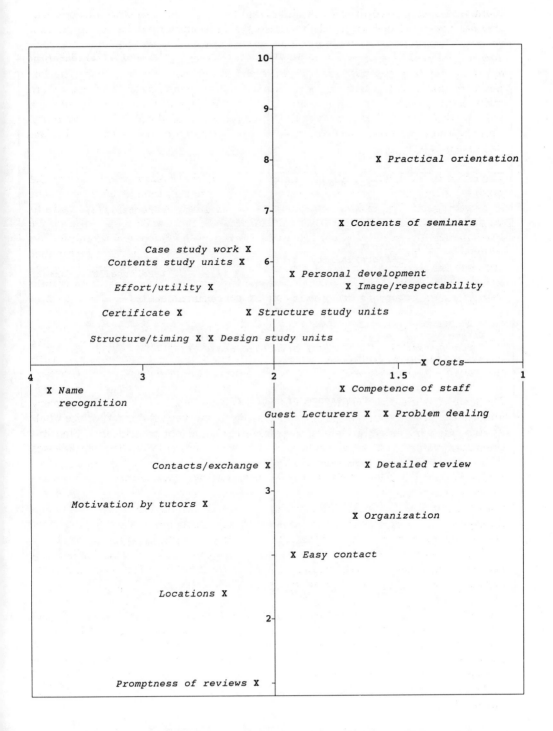

Figure 3. Importance-Performance analysis: Results of the second survey

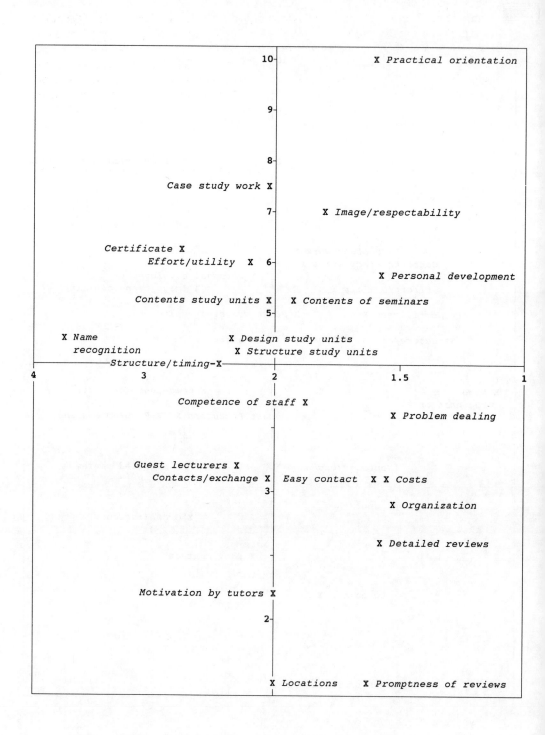

Figure 4. Importance-Performance analysis: Results of the third survey

The importance-performance analysis of the third survey in September 1992 confirms some trends that already started developing in the second survey (Figure 4). Strengths here include the *relationship between effort and utility*. Weaknesses are reduced to two complexes: *the study units* and *the usefulness of the course concerning the participants' further career*. A new criterion entered the quadrant of weaknesses: *Name recognition* of the institute offering the course. This corresponds with the evaluation of the usefulness of the certificate. Since little is known about the institute by the industry, participation in the course is not acknowledged by many companies.

Figure 5 gives an overview of the above-mentioned findings, showing the changes in selected criteria over time.

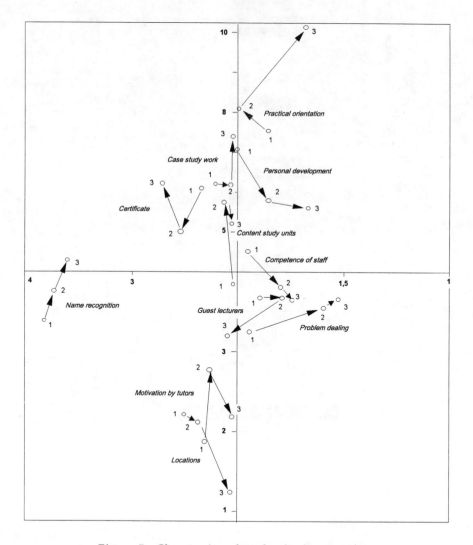

Figure 5. Changes in selected criteria over time

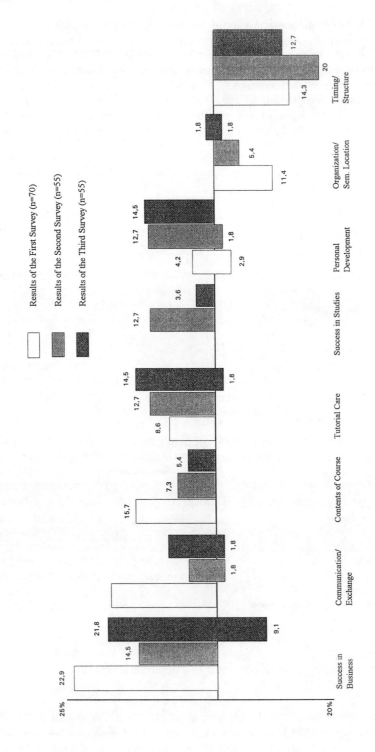

Figure 6. Results of the critical-incident analysis

Penalty-Reward-Factors

With the evaluation of performance and importance, the participants were asked to tell about critical incidents. All three questionnaires included two open-ended questions: "Were there any positive incidents you remember in the context of the course?" and "Were there any negative incidents you remember in the context of the course?". By the evaluation of the answers the total number of incidents was counted and the reports were classified into factors, where incidents with the same or similar contents were combined into one factor. If mostly positive events were described, the dimension would be regarded as a reward factor; if it contained mainly negative incidents it would be considered as a penalty factor (Brandt 1987, 1988, Stauss and Hentschel 1991a).

Figure 6 shows the percentage output of eight factors derived from 70 (55 in the second survey; 55 in the third survey) incidents that were classified as positive or negative.

Eight different types of incidents were identified. The most frequently reported positive events throughout the period of study can be related to the successful transfer of newly acquired knowledge into business situations. The negative incidents in this category mainly concerned external resistance during the process of implementation. The individuals in the company or the company structure proved to be too inflexible for proposed changes. The factor *communication/exchange* was rewarded highly only at the beginning of the course; later it lost its importance. A similar development can be noted with events of the factor *contents of course*. On the other hand, positive events dealing with *tutorial care* gained importance throughout the period of study.

Positive reports about *success in studies* appeared mainly in the second series of interviews and can be related to passed examinations etc. *Personal Development* integrates all reported incidents about broadened horizons, better understanding of the decisions of the board and the constant effort of participants to act more economically. This factor gained importance throughout the questioning period.

In addition, two factors can be regarded as penalties. The first factor concerned organization-related incidents, for example an exhausting journey to Berlin, difficulties with hotel rooms and seminar locations. Most of the negative incidents dealt with the timing of the course. The students complained about lack of time, a permanent bad conscious towards their families, problems with the partner, etc. Such situations obviously worsened with time. It was only at the very end of the programme that the number of such reports diminished.

Measuring Service Quality with Two Different Methods: A Comparison of the Results

Both methods show similar results regarding certain strengths and problem areas. In the importance-performance analysis, the *practical orientation of the course* was seen as the most important strength throughout the studies. This corresponds with the strongest reward-factor *success in business*. The students evaluated the criterion *personal development* as important and good in the attribute-oriented method. In the incident-oriented analysis it was regarded as a reward factor.

Especially during the first half year of the course, the *timing/relationship of personal effort and utility* were regarded as being the weakest area. Again the results of both methods match concerning this dimension, but only the critical-incident analysis revealed the extent of this problem.

At the end of the course, the participants considered the *usefulness of the certificate* as the main weakness. However, in the critical-incident analysis not a single event concerning this focus had been reported. Here the results of both methods do not match at all. This might be explained by the expectations of the students: They knew from the very beginning that the institute and the course were hardly known. Therefore they did not expect the certificate to be very useful when applying for a new job. The performance met their expectations.

On the other hand, a factor that was highly rewarded by the students in the critical incident analysis, *tutorial care*, could not be found among the strengths in the importance-performance analysis. The reason might be that this dimension had been split up into several criteria.

Outlook

In this study the quality of the service process and the quality of outcome were measured. The results of the study show that the students' evaluated importance of the criteria, as well as their perceptions, changed during the period of the service process. Owing to the small number of cases, it is not possible to generalize these results. However, the hypothesis can be generated that service quality is evaluated dynamically and changes throughout the period of service delivery. One interesting finding of the study was that mainly process-oriented criteria gained importance during the service process and lost it towards the end. On the other hand outcome-oriented items were evaluated as being more relevant at this point in time. On the basis of these results the assumption can be made that especially in sectors of long-term services, evaluation must take place dynamically. This means that it must be measured at several points in time instead of just one.

Expectations as a concept of measurement turned out to be problematic as they deal with different meanings of the expression such as ideal, predictive, product type oriented or minimal expectations. Therefore the author hypothesizes to measure importance (together with the perceptions) instead. The presentation of the results in the importance-performance-analysis diagram seems to be an adequate instrument to identify strengths and weaknesses and helps to set priorities for improvements in the service quality process.

With the attribute ratings students were asked to report about critical incidents. Grouping these into several factors revealed penalty and reward dimensions. When it comes to improvements, this information seems to be vital for servicers.

After eliminating the highest penalty factors they should concentrate on the reward dimensions as this raises quality perceptions. Furthermore, the study shows that the results using attribute ratings and incident collection differ. Instead of the decision to use only one method, the servicer should consider a combination of two methods of measuring service quality, as this can provide additional information. This knowledge seems to be very valuable as a broader picture of the concept of service quality develops.

References

Behrens, G., R. Schneider and P. Weinberg, Messung der Qualität von Produkten —eine empirische Studie, in: E. Topritzhofer (Hrsg.), *Marketing —Neue Ergebnisse aus Forschung und Praxis*, Wiesbaden 1978, 1978, pp. 131-143.

Brandt, D.R., A Procedure for Identifying Value-Enhancing Service Components using Customer Satisfaction Survey Data, in: C. Surprenant (ed.), *Add Value to Your Service*, Chicago, 1987, pp. 61-65.

Brandt, D.R., How Service Marketers can Identify Value-Enhancing Service Elements, *The Journal of Services Marketing*, 2, 3, Summer 1988, pp. 35-41.

Buchanan, D., *Development of Job Design Theories*, 1979.

Buswell, D., The Development of a Quality Measurement System for a UK Bank, in: B. Moores (ed.), *Are They Being Served?*, Oxford, 1986, pp. 141-155.

Dichtl, E. and S. Müller, Anspruchsinflation und Nivellierungstendenz als me·technische Probleme in der Absatzforschung, *Marketing -ZFP*, Heft 4, November 1986, pp. 233-236.

Donabedian, A.,*The Definition of Quality and Approaches to its Assessment, Explorations in Quality, Assessment and Monitoring, Volume I*, Ann Arbor, Michigan, 1980.

Engelhardt, W.H., M. Kleinaltenkamp and M. Reckenfelderbäumer, *Dienstleistungen als Absatzobjekt*, Arbeitsbericht Nr. 52 der Ruhr-Universität Bochum, May, 1992.

Grönroos, C., *Strategic Management and Marketing in the Service Sector*, Helsingfors, 1982.

Hentschel, B., Die Messung wahrgenommener Dienstleistungsqualität mit SERVQUAL; Eine kritische Auseinandersetzung, *Marketing ZFP*, Heft 4, IV. Quartal 1990, pp. 230-240.

Hentschel, B., Multiattributive Messung von Dienstleistungsqualität, in: M. Bruhn and B. Stauss (Hrsg.), *Dienstleistungsqualität; Konzepte - Methoden - Erfahrungen*, Wiesbaden, 1991, pp. 311-344.

Hilke, W., *Dienstleistungs-Marketing*, Wiesbaden, 1989.

Hüttenrauch, R., Probleme um Qualität und Preis beim Warentest, *Markenartikel 9*, 1973, pp. 434-444.

Kawlath, A., *Theoretische Grundlagen der Qualitätspolitik*, Wiesbaden, 1969.

Kleinaltenkamp, M., InvestitionsgüterMarketing aus informationsökonomischer Sicht, *Schmalenbachs Zeitschrift für betriebswirtschaftliche Forschung*, Heft 9, September 1992, pp. 809-829.

Liljander, V. and T. Strandvik, Estimating Zones of Tolerance in Perceived Service Quality and Perceived Value, Working Paper 247, Swedish School of Economics and Business Administration, 1992.

Liljander, V. and T. Strandvik, Different Comparison Standards as Determinants of Service Quality, Working Paper presented at "Zweiter Dienstleistungsworkshop Innsbruck", 18.-19. Feb. 1993.

Martilla, J.A. and J.C. James, J.C., Importance-Performance Analysis, *Journal of Marketing*, 41, January 1977, pp. 77-79.

Meyer, A., Dienstleistungs-Marketing, *Die Betriebswirtschaft*, Heft 2, 1991, pp. 195-209.

Meyer, A. and R. Mattmüller, Qualität von Dienstleistungen. Entwurf eines praxisorientierten Qualitätsmodells, *Marketing ZFP*, Heft 3, Aug. 1987, pp. 187-195.

Parasuraman, A., V. Zeithaml, and L.L. Berry, SERVQUAL: A Multiple-Item Scale for Measuring Consumer Perceptions of Service Quality, *Journal of Retailing*, 64, 1, Spring 1988, pp. 5-37.

Stauss, B. and B. Hentschel, Attribute-Based Versus Incident-Based Measurement of Service Quality: Results of an Empirical Study in the German Car Service Industry, in: T. van der Wiele and J. Timmers (eds.), *EIASM Workshop: Proceedings of the "Workshop on Quality Management in Services"*, Brussels, 1991, pp. 27-46.

3

The Retail Service Encounter: Identifying Critical Service Experiences

Kitty Koelemeijer

Introduction[1]

During the last decade much research has been done on consumer perceptions of so-called pure services and resulting cognitive, affective, and behavioral consequences (e.g., Bitner 1990; Bolton and Drew 1991, Grönroos 1990, Nyquist and Booms 1987, Parasuraman, Zeithaml and Berry 1985, 1988). Less attention has been devoted to the analysis of retail services associated with the marketing of goods, also known as customer services (Grönroos 1983). These services will, at least to some extent, be evaluated on the quality dimensions found for pure services, like those identified by Parasuraman *et al.* (1985) —tangibles, reliability, responsiveness, assurance, and empathy. In addition, one may argue the existence of other evaluative dimensions. Customer services facilitate goods distribution and have a close relationship to the physical product. The development of a scale for measuring perceived quality of customer services should begin with additional exploratory research, little of which was done in the past.

Although it is an important aspect of a retailer's offerings, the service may not be central to the consumer's buying process. This is especially true for fast-moving, standardized, consumer goods. When buying these goods consumer interaction with service personnel does not only take place in a later stage of the buying process, but is also relatively less involving than interaction in a pure services con-

1   The author wishes to thank Theo M.M. Verhallen for his valuable comments on an earlier version of this paper. Linda Koning and Lucille Rameckers are acknowledged for their help in collection and categorizing the data.

text. Consequently, consumers may more easily switch stores or change their minds with respect to buying goods than with respect to buying pure services. For example, when the merchandise presented is not appealing, or when the customer disapproves of an employee's behavior. Furthermore, retailers may influence the quality of goods sold, for example, by storage and handling activities. In the case of perishable goods, quality maintenance becomes an important aspect in both pre- and post-transaction stages of the consumer buying process. It may induce or prevent occurrence of a transaction, and in the post-transaction stage it may affect consumer complaining and ultimately repurchase behavior.

In this chapter retail encounters with respect to both pure services and services associated with the marketing of consumer goods are considered. Both types of services are referred to as retail services in the rest of this chapter. The present study employs the critical incident technique to explore the nature of a variety of retail services. The study offers insights into the causes of favorable and unfavorable consumer experiences across different retail service encounters, different store types and product categories. In addition attribution processes are investigated in order to assess whether the technique uncovers the full range of causes of (dis)satisfying service encounters. If so, the technique can be used as an exploratory method for generating items from the domain of a concept for which a measurement instrument is developed. Finally, a measure for the degree of understanding between both parties to the encounter, a concept called mutual understanding, defined by Mohr and Bitner (1991) as "between two people, the messages received equal the messages sent, with no distortion", was compared across consumer experiences with retail services.

Analyzing Retail Services Using The Critical Incident Technique

For the development of an instrument for measuring perceived service quality that is valid across a variety of retail contexts research that compares different retail settings is needed. In the exploratory research phase preceding the development of the instrument for measuring perceived service quality —SERVQUAL— Parasuraman *et al.* (1985) conducted focus group interviews with consumers where attention was focused solely on the encounter regarding pure services. Although the instrument is reliable, it does not appear to be generalizable across a variety of retail settings (Finn and Lamb 1991, Koelemeijer 1992), once more suggesting that additional exploratory research on retail services is needed.

On the basis of Grönroos' (1983) classification of perceived service quality dimensions into an instrumental or technical component and an expressive or interaction component, we argue that in addition to a general retail service encounter dimension of perceived service quality, one or more specific dimensions may exist. For example, a technical or logistics dimension may be distinguished, operationalization of which may vary among different store types, for example, a supermarket encounter as opposed to a restaurant encounter. Another, product-specific, dimension that can be distinguished is quality maintenance. Thus, operationalization of perceived retail service quality may require domain-specific constructs.

The Critical Incident Technique reveals sources or "fundamentally necessary factors" (Bitner, Booms and Tetreault 1990) leading to extreme satisfaction/dissatisfaction, which will ultimately determine quality perceptions. The idea underlying the use of the Critical Incident Technique for analyzing retail services is that events inducing extreme affective reactions have more impact on the consumer's attitude and behavior than transactions that are followed by low or moderate affective reactions. Also, these incidents will typically represent good or bad service quality from the consumer's perspective. The Critical Incident Technique will enable us to uncover some 'generic' events and behaviors across retail settings, for which the underlying causes of satisfactory and dissatisfactory encounters may be similar. This does not imply the underlying events and behaviors that lead to satisfactory and dissatisfactory encounters to be similar. In addition, specific, non-generic events may be mentioned.

The Critical Incident Technique

The Critical Incident Technique (CIT) is a method by which specific events and behaviors can be identified that result in satisfaction/dissatisfaction. Bitner *et al.* (1990) define critical incidents as "specific interactions between customers and service firm employees that are especially satisfying or especially dissatisfying". More specifically, a critical incident is described as "an observable human activity that is complete enough in itself to permit inferences and predictions to be made about the person performing the act (incident) that contributes to or detracts from the general aim of the activity in a significant way (is critical)". CIT, which was introduced by Flanagan (1954), provides insight into the fundamentally necessary factors leading to customers' satisfactory/dissatisfactory evaluations.

CIT yields results similar to indirect observation, it does not necessitate artificial control over the environment as in laboratory research or field experiments, and avoids the problem of asking respondents for generalized information (Bitner, Nyquist and Booms 1985). In addition, it does not rely on a small number of predetermined components and allows for interaction among all possible components of the product. Several advantages and criticisms of the critical incident technique are reported in the literature. Among the advantages are (Viney 1983): "its capacity to provide accurate and consistent interpretations of people's accounts of events without depriving these accounts of their power or eloquence", and usage of both qualitative and quantitative techniques for analysis. In general, reliability and validity of the collected information seems good (Anderson and Nilsson 1964, Ronan and Latham 1974, White and Locke 1981). Criticisms attribute reliability and validity problems to the ambiguity of word meanings, category labels, and coding rules in a particular study (Kassarjian 1977, Weber 1985). All of the advantages and disadvantages that apply to exploratory methods are also shared by the CIT. However, CIT is particularly well suited to increase knowledge of a phenomenon about which relatively little has been documented and/or to describe a real-world phenomenon based on thorough understanding (Bitner *et al.* 1990).

Bitner *et al.* (1990), in a pure services context, explored events and contact employee behavior causing consumers' experiences with the service encounter to be very satisfactory or very dissatisfactory (see also Nyquist, Bitner and Booms 1985). When analyzing retail services not only the employee-customer interaction should be considered, but also, for example, physical distribution issues, among which the degree of quality maintenance of the physical product. Therefore, we extended their approach to include both pure and customer services. In our study we require an incident to meet the following criteria: (1) involving firm-customer interaction, including the role of human and nonhuman (e.g., goods, atmosphere) service elements during pre-transaction, transaction, or post-transaction stages of the buying process, (2) being very satisfying or dissatisfying from the customer's point of view, (3) being a discrete episode, and (4) having sufficient detail to be visualized by the interviewer.

The following research questions were formulated to which our study attempts to find answers:

- Do differences exist between the nature of critical incidents reported with respect to pure retail services as compared to services associated with the marketing of goods?
- Do critical incidents reported with respect to retail services match previously formulated classification schemes of perceived service quality dimensions?
- Does the CIT result in identification of clear attributes from which scales may be developed?
- Do differences exist between the nature of critical incidents among different types of retail settings? Retail settings will vary in the degree to which different types of attributes such as search, experience, and credence attributes (e.g., Darby and Karni 1973) are available and will be involved in consumer evaluation processes. The degree of intangibility (Shostack 1977), for example, and the proportion of experience and credence attributes, of the product offered has consequences for consumer evaluation processes (Zeithaml 1981). On the basis of differences in the relative availability of search and experience attributes associated with different retail settings we expect the nature of the critical incidents to vary across store types.

Attributions for Favorable and Unfavorable Incidents

Attribution theory views people as rational information processors whose actions are influenced by their causal inferences (Folkes 1988). People engage in so-called "spontaneous causal thinking", particularly in cases of unexpected or negative events (Weiner, 1985). An interesting question is whether critical incidents are accompanied by particular consumer attributions. For an incident to be critical, extreme satisfaction or dissatisfaction must be experienced by the customer that is important enough to be remembered. Mohr and Bitner (1991) found that all consumers they interviewed blamed external causes for dissatisfying incidents, although employees occasionally perceived the customer's own behavior as being the source of dissatisfaction. This can be explained by the results of previous research (e.g., Folkes 1988, Folkes and Kotsos 1986, Weiner 1985) which revealed that satisfaction or dissatisfaction with a supplier is unlikely to occur when the customer attributes the cause of the experience to him/herself. The same body of research showed empirically that extreme affective reactions coincide with relatively more stable and controllable attributions.

From the literature on consumer attribution processes previously mentioned, and the nature of critical incidents, we expect to find that consumers will attribute the causes of critical incidents (1) more to an external cause than to themselves, (2) to a relatively stable cause, and (3) to a relatively controllable cause. Weiner (1985) stated that consumers engage less in causal thinking in case of favorable events than in case of unfavorable events. By making causal inferences consumers try to find explanations for certain events. In this way attribution processes may serve as a mechanism for reducing negative disconfirmation of expectations. In case of extremely favorable events, consumers will find it less necessary to search for causes, so their attributions will be relatively more 'neutral'. For critical incidents this means that in the case of favorable experiences consumers will form less extreme (4) locus, (5) control, and (6) stability attributions than in case of unfavorable experiences.

Mutual Understanding

Mutual understanding between the customer contact employee and the customer depends on the degree of cognitive similarity between them. According to Mohr and Bitner (1991) cognitive similarity may imply people using the same underlying attribute or dimension in forming judgments, and/or accurate role behavior by the employee. They suggested a hypothesis that they did not test, but that will be considered in this study: the degree of mutual understanding between contact employee and customer will be higher in case of favorable events than in case of unfavorable events.

Methodology

Data Collection

Four different retail settings were selected on the basis of the varying degree of search and experience attributes that were thought to be part of their total offerings: supermarkets, florists, clothing stores, and hairdressers. On a continuum ranging from solely supporting customer services to pure services —for example, pure tangibles to pure intangibles— we may put supermarkets near the pure tangibles end, florists somewhere near the pure tangibles end, clothing stores somewhere in the middle between both ends, and hairdressers near the pure intangibles end.

A randomly drawn sample of 360 consumers was interviewed over a period of four weeks. Before being asked to recall critical incidents, respondents were selected on the basis of the frequency with which they purchased items at a particular type of retail store before they were asked to recall critical incidents concerning that store type. In accordance with Bitner *et al.* (1990) the interviewers received detailed training and written instructions to conduct the interviews; they practised the procedure by role-playing and during pretesting of the questionnaires. For each store type, the frequent customers were interviewed about the following questions:

- What specific events lead to satisfying service encounters in retailing from the customer's point of view? What did contact employees do, if anything, that caused these events to be remembered favorably?
- What specific events lead to dissatisfying service encounters in retailing from the customer's point of view? What did contact employees do, if anything, that caused these events to be remembered with such unpleasantness?

After correcting for (1) respondents that did not want to participate in the study, (2) respondents whose shopping frequency was less than required for each of the four store types, and (3) respondents who were unable to recall a critical incident during the interview (less than 10% of the remaining respondents), a total of 158 respondents (107 women and 51 men) generated descriptions of one or more critical incidents that were suitable for further analysis.

Measures

After a detailed description of the critical incident had been given, each respondent answered specific questions regarding attribution processes and the degree of mutual understanding associated with the particular incident. On the basis of Wimer and Kelley's (1982) classification of attributions, one measure of locus attributions, two measures of stability attributions, and two measures of control attributions were developed using Russell's (1982) 7-point semantic differential scale. In our study mutual understanding is conceptualized as the degree to which a customer perceives mutual understanding during the service encounter. Mutual understanding was measured on a 5-item 7-point Likert-type scale ranging from "Strongly disagree" (1) to "Strongly agree" (7). Items were: "Salesperson understood me", "I felt at ease in this store", "Salesperson tried to meet my desires", "Salesperson tried to think with me", and "Salesperson imagined my situation".

Classification of Incidents

After the data collection, the process of incident classification began. Most respondents experienced one or more critical incidents. A total of 245 critical incidents were collected of which 214 incidents dealt with one of the four store types selected, and the remaining 31 concerned a variety of other stores. The first step in the inductive clustering procedure was the development of categories in which the incidents were more similar to one another than to those in another category. The categories resulted from sorting, combining, and resorting iterations. Categories were developed by two judges. First, major groupings were identified that could collectively account for all of the incidents and made the data useful for answering the research questions. After consensus was reached on the major groups, the process of delineating categories within the groups was initiated. Finally, consensus was achieved on category labels and the assignment of each incident into one of the six resulting categories. A third judge allocated the critical incidents to the groups. Interjudge agreement, as an indication of reliability, was assessed as the percentage of incidents classified "correctly", which was 89%.

Results

Classification of Critical Retail Service Incidents

The sorting of the incidents resulted in two major groups that could account for all but one incident. As it was the only incident concerning other customers as participants in the service encounter it was not considered in further analysis. In table 1. the groups and categories that emerged from the classification process are shown. The two main groups distinguished are physical product/instrumental service performance and general employee-customer interactions.

Group 1. Physical product/instrumental service performance

The incidents in the first group were all triggered by performance of the good or "technical" (instrumental) service offered. Three categories are distinguished by the question: Was there an employee reaction which mainly determined the experience? If the answer is "no" the incident belongs to category A within the group, if the answer is "yes" it belongs to category B or C. In case the interaction concerns the physical product or core service it belongs to category B, when the interaction concerns supporting services it belongs to category C.

1A. Superior or inferior performance
All incidents in this category relate to performance of the product bought in case of physical product failure experienced some period of time after the transaction. Examples of dissatisfactory incidents include "The expensive, branded pair of trousers I bought were already worn out after a very short time" and "I had a permanent wave in view of a special occasion, but it was spoiled completely and it couldn't be made right". An example of a satisfactory incident in this category was "My hair was done just perfectly".

1B. Employee response to product failure
In this category, contrary to the incidents in the former category, employee response to product failure is determinant for consumers' affective reactions. Examples of satisfactory incidents in this category are "The flowers I bought perished after only a few days. When I returned to the store they gave me new flowers and apologized" or "The bottle of milk I bought at the supermarket had turned sour. When I told this at my next visit to the store, they offered me a new bottle for free". An example of a dissatisfactory incident is "After the girl at the hairdresser's ruined my hair, she and her supervisor told me I just had the worst hair they had ever seen".

1C. Employee response to supporting service failure
Supporting services which are delivered with respect to the core service or good may also give rise to both satisfactory and unsatisfactory incidents. Many times bad planning of service delivery triggers an incident. These incidents generally correspond with those mentioned in Bitner *et al.*'s (1990) "Response to unreasonably

slow service" category. When the service delivery system fails, employees involved will exhibit behavior in reaction to this failure. Most incidents in this category are dissatisfactory. For example "The cashier in the supermarket made a mistake. When I tried to have her correct it, her supervisor told me not to make such a fuss over such a small amount of money", or "I had to wait a long time at the hairdresser's. When my turn finally came up they asked what treatment I needed, and then told me it was too late to do this". The nature of the product failure experienced by the consumer seems to vary over retail settings. They mainly concerned quality deterioration of goods, bad technical expertise, waiting time, and billing. We decided not to split category 1C into two new categories "Response to unreasonable slow service", and "Response to cashier failure" because waiting mainly concerned the hairdresser's, which is a relatively pure retail service.

Group 2. General employee-customer interactions
The contact between a customer and employee(s) during the service encounter may cause both satisfactory, and dissatisfactory incidents, without reference to the physical product or core service bought. In this group the triggering event is not the good or core service bought. It is the employee-customer interaction that determines the extreme affective reaction experienced by the consumer. In the case where the response was triggered by the employee the incident belongs to categories A (attention paid to the customer), or category B (truly out-of-the-ordinary employee behavior), depending on the nature of the interactions. These categories strongly resemble the categories distinguished by Bitner et al. (1990) between the group "Unprompted and unsolicited employee behaviors". An incident describing a reactive employee response which was induced by customer behavior belongs to category C (employee response to customer error), which resembles the category in Bitner et al.'s group "Employee response to customer needs and requests" after which it has been named.

2A. Attention paid to customer
The incidents in this category concern the level of attention paid to the customer, that can be viewed as very favorably or very negatively (compare the relevant category in Bitner *et al.*). Examples are: "I walked around in the clothing store, wanting to ask something to a saleslady, but they just continued talking, pretending not to see me" and "I doubted whether I should buy this pair of trousers. When I came in for the third time that day, just before closing time, I was encountered in a very friendly manner and they let me try the trousers on once more". Trust is often mentioned with respect to the incidents represented in this category. Another aspect heavily represented here is obtrusive selling behavior; employees' behavior may be very clearly directed at just selling a product instead of at meeting customers' desires.

2B. Truly out-of-the-ordinary employee behavior
In this category incidents are represented that concern extraordinary employee behavior and extra efforts, exceeding the level of attention or actions one could hope to receive. An example of an incident in this category is "The girl at the counter remembered my son was allergic to cow-milk cheese, so she offered him goat-milk cheese".

2C. Employee response to admitted customer error

Customer error that triggers employee reactions characterize the incidents in the last category of the second group. For example: "After I pushed down a pile of cans the employee told me to contact my insurance company in order to arrange for payment of the damage", or "One Saturday I left my wallet on the counter. When I phoned the store after closing time, the owner trusted me immediately and told me I could come and get it".

Table 1. Group and category CI classification by (dis)satisfaction

	Type of incident outcome					
	Satisfactory		Dissatisfactory		Total	
	No.	%	No.	%	No.	%
Group 1. **Physical product/instrumental** **service performance**						
A: Superior/inferior performance	6	6.8	41	26.3	47	19.3
B: Employee response to product failure	16	18.2	19	12.2	35	14.3
C: Employee response to supporting service failure	1	1.1	29	18.6	30	12.3
Subtotal, group 1	23	26.1	89	57.1	112	45.9
Group 2. **Employee-customer interactions**						
A: Attention paid to customer	25	28.4	52	33.3	77	31.6
B: Truly out-of-the-ordinary employee behavior	32	36.4	2	1.3	34	13.9
C: Employee response to customer error	8	9.1	13	8.3	21	8.6
Subtotal, group 2	65	73.9	67	42.9	132	54.1
Total	88	36.1	156	63.9	244	100.0

Table 1 summarizes the results of the data collection. Most incidents refer to dissatisfactory experiences. In the group "employee-customer interactions" satisfactory incidents are relatively well represented. Although the number of critical incidents collected in this study is limited, comparison of our classification with the one obtained by Bitner *et al.* reveals some interesting similarities and dissimilarities. As stated earlier, the degree of involvement of consumers with the transactions may be lower for packaged fast-moving consumer goods as relatively low amounts of money are involved for the separate goods and consumers are less involved in the 'production processes'. With the exception of most supermarket incidents many incidents were concerned with purchases for special occasions. With respect to purchase of consumer goods the degree of employee-customer interaction is generally lower than that associated with the purchase of pure services, which creates the possibility for suggesting that the classification of incidents relating to these dimensions of retail services in general will be less detailed than for pure services. Furthermore, consumers have the possibility to leave a store selling goods before making a purchase, which is not so easy when visiting a restaurant, hotel, or travelling by airplane. Also, interaction with other customers as a source of (dis)satisfaction is virtually absent. Product quality maintenance is a very important source of satisfaction/dissatisfaction, which does not necessarily imply employee reactions, as is the case for branded goods. In general, many unprompted and unsolicited employee actions were mentioned. Little evidence of employee response to customer needs and desires was generated as being the cause of consumer satisfaction/dissatisfaction. Finally, the presence of trust, or the lack thereof, as shown by employees appeared to be very important to customers.

Table 2. Incident classification by retail setting

	Store type									
	Supermarket		Florist		Clothing		Hairdresser		Total	
	No.	%	No.	%	No.	%	No.	%	No.	%
Satisfactory incidents										
Product performance	2	9.1	9	32.1	4	23.5	5	35.7	20	24.7
Employee-customer interactions	20	90.9	19	67.9	13	76.5	9	64.3	61	75.3
Total	22	27.2	28	34.6	17	21.0	14	70.3	81	100.0
Dissatisfactory incidents										
Product performance	13	38.2	11	78.6	14	37.8	36	76.6	74	52.1
Employee-customer interactions	21	61.7	3	21.4	23	62.2	11	23.4	58	40.9
Total	34	23.9	14	9.9	37	26.1	47	33.1	132	100.0

Satisfaction/dissatisfaction, incident groups, and incident categories
Table 2 presents the results for the stores that have been distinguished *a priori*. The results of contingency table analysis, based on hierarchical model tests, indicate statistically significant relationships between classification variables in both Tables 1 and 2. For Table 1 significant relationships were found between satisfaction/dissatisfaction and incident category (ΔL.R. χ^2 =22.36, p<.001). A considerably larger proportion of dissatisfactory incidents (57.1%) than satisfactory incidents (26.1%) is found in group 1. Although the incidents in category A include product successes as well as failures, results in category B indicate that employee response can dissipate dissatisfaction in case of product failure. However, conclusions have

to be drawn with care because the possibility exists that some of the product failures in category A caused such dissatisfaction that any contact with employees was avoided. In group 2 the proportion of satisfactory incidents (69.5%) exceeds that of dissatisfactory incidents (41.9%). Attention paid to the customer is a major source of both satisfaction and dissatisfaction.

Satisfaction/dissatisfaction, incident groups, and retail settings

For Table 2, significant relationships were found between (1) satisfaction/dissatisfaction and incident group (ΔL.R. χ^2=21.54, p<.001), (2) store and incident group (ΔL.R. χ^2=23.99, p<.001), and (3) store and satisfaction/dissatisfaction (ΔL.R. χ^2=22.24, p<.001). The three-way interaction between store type, type of outcome and group is not significant (ΔL.R. χ^2=2.23, p>.50). Most incidents were reported in relation to the hairdressers and least in relation to the florists. This could possibly have been caused by relative differences in minimum shopping frequency required, which was highest for supermarkets (at least once every two weeks) and lowest for hairdressers and clothing stores (at least once every six months). The highest proportion of the hairdressers' incidents was in group 1 (67.2%). The highest proportions of incidents in group 2 were found for the supermarkets (73.2%), the clothing stores (66.7%), and the florists (52.4%). This could be partially explained by stating that the goods sold by these outlets are to a relatively large degree standardized; in particular the supermarkets and clothing stores offer mainly branded goods that are not produced or affected intrinsically by the retailer. The latter also applies, although to a lesser degree, to florists. With this in mind, it is not surprising that the largest proportion of incidents reported with regard to these stores concern employee-customer interactions. When the hairdressers, being the only pure service providers, are left out of the table 2 analysis similar significant relationships show between (1) satisfaction/dissatisfaction and incident group (ΔL.R. χ^2=13.89, p<.001), (2) store type and incident group (ΔL.R. χ^2=10.07, p<.01), and (3) store type and satisfaction/dissatisfaction (ΔL.R. χ^2=18.25, p<.001). Again, the three-way interaction was not significant (ΔL.R. χ^2=2.09, p>.30).

Attributions

Cronbach's alpha and Pearson's correlation coefficients were computed for the measures of control and stability attributions. Coefficient alpha estimates were .82 and .67, and Pearson's correlation coefficients were .76 and .49 for the control and stability attribution scores respectively. This indicates the measures used were internally consistent.

Table 3 summarizes the results of tests on attributions for the critical incident outcomes and groups. First, t-tests were done to determine whether critical incidents are attributed to relatively external, stable and controllable causes. For ease of interpretation attribution scores were first re-coded as deviations from the neutral point (which was 4 on the 7-point rating scale). Attributions were found to be significantly external (t=6.53, p<.001) and significantly controllable (t=4.63, p<.001). Consumers attributed the critical incidents to relatively unstable causes (t=–7.37, p<.001). Next, attributions for favorable and unfavorable incidents were compared. In the case of unfavorable incidents respondents attributed the incident more to an external cause than in the case of satisfactory incidents (t=3.54, p<.001), which is in agreement with recent findings on the relationships between consumer attributions and consumer satisfaction/dissatisfaction (e.g., Folkes 1988). Mean scores were 6.09 and 4.94 for the dissatisfactory and satisfactory outcomes respectively. As expected, satisfactory incidents were attributed to less controllable causes than dissatisfactory incidents (t=4.48, p<.001). Mean summated scores were respectively 10.50 and 7.69 for unfavorable and favorable outcomes. No significantly different stability attributions could be detected between satisfactory and unsatisfactory incidents (t=.08, p<.90). This may result from incidents being separate, unique events about which respondents have difficulty stating whether or not they will occur again, triggered by the same cause(s). Finally, attributions for the two major incident groups were compared. Locus attributions differed significantly between "product performance" and "interaction" incidents (t=3.45, p<.001). Mean scores were 6.20 and 5.21 respectively. This finding indicates consumers may hold others (retailers) more responsible for physical product/instrumental service incidents than for customer/employee incidents (see also McGill 1990). Both summated ratings on control (t=−.95, p>.30) and stability attributions (t=1.73, p=.085) were not significantly different across the incident groups.

Table 3. Attributions for critical incidents[1]

Attribution dimension	Incident outcome		Incident group	
	Satisfaction	Dissatisfaction	Product performance	Interaction
Locus			*External*	
	−	+	+	−
Controllability			*Controllable*	
	−	+		n.s.
Stability			*Unstable*	
	n.s.		n.s.	

1   Significant differences (p<.001) are indicated by + and − for, respectively, more and less effect in the indicated direction.

Mutual Understanding

Cronbach's coefficient alpha for the five items used to measure the degree of mutual understanding experienced by the customer with respect to the critical incident is .94, indicating high internal consistency. Differences in mean scores of favorable and unfavorable incidents, which equalled 4.59 and 1.82 respectively, differed significantly (t=11.88, p<.001). In addition, differences between the favorable and unfavorable incidents were highly significant as well for each individual item (p<.001) and for each store type (p<.001). No significant differences could be assessed between critical incident groups, which emphasizes the importance of employee behavior directed at meeting individual consumer's needs.

Discussion

Our analysis of critical incidents in retail settings resulted in a classification of events causing extreme consumer satisfaction or dissatisfaction. The nature of the incidents appears to differ between retail settings. The incidents for retail stores selling goods, which offer a high proportion of search attributes, for example supermarkets and clothing stores, and to a lesser degree florists, relatively often concern employee-customer encounters, as opposed to, for example, hairdressers, where technical services relatively often give rise to critical experiences. Consumers may avoid critical incidents with respect to goods or supporting services using information derived or inferred from search attributes. Critical incidents concern relatively high involvement situations (Bitner 1990). In our study, with the exception of most of the supermarket incidents, many critical incidents dealt with purchases for special occasions. Consumers' attributions for critical incidents are mainly external and controllable. Moreover, locus and control attributions for favorable incidents are less extreme than attributions for unfavorable incidents. An in-depth analysis of the possibilities of developing an instrument for measuring perceived service quality across retail settings and products becomes possible by analysis of critical incidents, although (dis)satisfiers with stable causes may be underrepresented. One finding in this respect is that the trust expressed by the seller appeared to be very important from the consumer's point of view. To date, this aspect has been lacking in measures of perceived service quality (e.g., SERVQUAL), where only the amount of trust the consumer places in his or her supplier is considered.

Methodological issues of the study concern first the minimum shopping frequencies with respect to each store type. The incident frequencies presented here might not be fully representative for retail encounter incidents. Relatively 'heavy' shoppers have been interviewed, the degree of required 'heaviness' being different across store types. Second, measurement of hindsight expectations and perceptions of performance with respect to the incidents could have provided insights into their role in formation of extreme satisfaction or dissatisfaction with retail encounters.

Future research may concentrate on personal or situational characteristics that may relate to the nature of critical incidents, such as product involvement. The degree of uncertainty consumers experience in evaluating services is related to the proportion of search, experience, and credence attributes the goods/service combination possesses (Zeithaml 1981), suggesting the degree to which a consumer is risk-seeking or risk-averse (Keeney and Raiffa 1976) may be important with respect to the incidents reported. Furthermore, employee response may overcome failure of the delivery system (Bitner 1990, Bitner *et al.* 1990). In this respect the concept of mutual understanding deserves more attention, especially when analyzing employee-customer interactions, as consumers indicate mutual understanding to be significantly higher for favorable experiences as compared to unfavorable experiences. This suggests that the employees' role in critical incidents experienced by consumers in retail settings can always be determinant.

Managerial implications of our research include the possibility of setting clearer priorities to improve retail services by acquiring quantified insights into strengths and weaknesses on determinant aspects, as opposed to analyzing consumer responses on a predetermined set of general attributes. Events and behaviors causing the consumer to remember them as critical will affect consumers' attitudes most and may have strong implications for their repurchasing behavior.

References

Anderson, B.E. and S.G. Nilsson, Studies in the Reliability and Validity of the Critical Incident Technique, *Journal of Applied Psychology*, 48 (6), 1964, pp. 398-403.

Bitner, M.J., Evaluating Service Encounters: The Effects of Physical Surroundings and Employee Responses, *Journal of Marketing*, 1990.

Bitner, M.J., B.H. Booms and M. Stanfield Tetreault, The service Encounter: Diagnosing Favorable and Unfavorable Incidents, *Journal of Marketing*, 54 (January), 1990, pp. 71- 84.

Bitner, M.J., J.D. Nyquist and B.H. Booms, The Critical Incident as a Technique for Analyzing the Service Encounter, In: T.M. Bloch, G.D. Upah and V.A. Zeithaml (eds.), *Services Marketing in a Changing Environment*, American Marketing Association, Chicago, 1985, pp. 48-51.

Bolton, R.N. and J.H. Drew, A Multistage Model of Customers' Assessments of Service Quality and Value, *Journal of Consumer Research*, 17 (March), 1991, pp. 375-384.

Darby, M.R. and E. Karni, Free Competition and the Optimal Amount of Fraud, *Journal of Law and Economics*, 16, pp. 67-88.

Finn, D.W. and C.W. Lamb, Jr., An Evaluation of the SERVQUAL Scale in a Retail Setting, In: R.H. Holman and M.R. Solomon (eds.), *Advances in Consumer Research*, 18, Association for Consumer Research, Provo (UT), 1991, pp. 483- 490.

Flanagan, J.C., The Critical Incident Technique, *Psychological Bulletin*, 51 (July), 1954, 327-357.

Folkes, V.S., Recent Attribution Research in Consumer Behavior: A Review and New Directions, *Journal of Consumer Research*, 14 (March), 1988, pp. 548-565.

Folkes, V.S. and B. Kotsos, Buyers' and Sellers' Explanations for Product Failure: Who Done It?, *Journal of Marketing*, 50 (April), 1986, pp. 74- 80.

Grönroos, C., Strategic Management and Marketing in the Service Sector, Report no. 83-104, Marketing Science Institute, Cambridge (Mass.), 1983.

Grönroos, C., *Service Management and Marketing*, Lexington Books, Lexington, 1990.

Kassarjian, H.H., Content Analysis in Consumer Research, *Journal of Consumer Research*, 4 (June), 1977, pp. 8-18.

Keeney, R.L. and H. Raiffa, *Decisions with Multiple Objectives: Preferences and Value Tradeoffs*, Wiley, New York, 1976.

Koelemeijer, K., Measuring Perceived Service Quality in Retailing: A Comparison of Methods, In: K. Grunert (ed.), *Marketing for Europe - Marketing for the Future*, Proceedings of the 21th Annual Conference of the European Marketing Academy, Aarhus, Denmark, 1992, pp. 729-744.

McGill, A.L., Predicting Consumers' reactions to Product Failure: Do Responsibility Judgments Follow from Consumers' Causal Explanations?, *Marketing Letters*, 2 (1), 1990, pp. 59-70.

Mohr, L.A. and M.J. Bitner, Mutual Understanding between Customers and Employees in Service Encounters, In: R.H. Holman and M.R. Solomon (eds.), *Advances in Consumer Research*, 18, Association for Consumer Research, Provo (UT.), 1991, pp. 611-617.

Nyquist, J.D., M.J. Bitner, and B.H. Booms, Identifying Communication Difficulties in the Service Encounter: A Critical Incidents Approach, In: J. Czepiel, M. Solomon and C. Surprenant (eds.), *The Service Encounter*, Lexington Books, Lexington, 1985, pp. 195-212.

Nyquist, J.D. and B.H. Booms, Measuring Services Value from the Consumer Perspective, In: C. Surprenant (ed.), *Add Value to Your Service*, American Marketing Association, Chicago, 1987, pp. 13-16.

Olshavsky, R.W., Perceived Quality in Consumer Decision Making: An Integrated Theoretical Perspective, In: J. Jacoby and J. Olson (eds.), *Perceived Quality*, Lexington Books, Lexington, 1985, pp. 3-29.

Parasuraman, A., V.A. Zeithaml and L.L. Berry, A Conceptual Model of service Quality and Its Implications for Future Research, *Journal of Marketing*, 49 (Fall), 1985, pp. 41-50.

Parasuraman, A., V.A. Zeithaml and L.L. Berry, SERVQUAL: A Multiple-Item Scale for Measuring Consumer Perceptions of Service Quality, *Journal of Retailing*, 64 (1), 1988, pp. 12- 40.

Ronan, W.W. and G.P. Latham, The Reliability and Validity of the Critical Incident Technique: A Closer Look, *Studies in Personnel Psychology*, 6 (1), 1974, pp. 53- 64.

Russell, D., The Causal Dimension Scale: A Measure of How Individuals Perceive Causes, *Journal of Personality and Social Psychology*, 42 (6), 1982, pp. 1137- 1145.

Shostack, G.L., Breaking Free from Product Marketing, *Journal of Marketing*, 41 (April), 1977, pp. 73-80.

Viney, L.L., The Assessment of Psychological States through Content Analysis of Verbal Communications, *Psychological Bulletin*, 94 (3), pp. 542-563.

Weber, R.P., *Basic Content Analysis*, Sage University Paper Series on Quantitative Applications in the Social Sciences, 07-049, Sage Publications Inc., London, 1985.

Weiner, B., An Attributional Theory of Achievement Motivation and Emotion, *Psychological Review*, 92 (4), 1985, pp. 548-573.

White, F.M. and E.A. Locke, Perceived Determinants of High and Low Productivity in Three occupational Groups: A Critical Incident Study, *Journal of Management Studies*, 18 (4), 1981, pp. 375-384.

Wimer, S. and H.H. Kelley, An Investigation of the Dimensions of Causal Attribution, *Journal of Personality and Social Psychology*, 39 (2), 1982, pp. 186-200.

Zeithaml, V.A., Do Consumer Evaluation Processes Differ between Goods and Services, In: J.H. Donnelly and W.R. George (eds.), *Marketing of Services*, American Marketing Association, Chicago, 1981, pp. 186-190.

4

The Relation Between Service Quality, Satisfaction and Intentions

Veronica Liljander and Tore Strandvik

Introduction

Perceived service quality has been defined as the difference between expectations and performance of the service (e.g., Grönroos 1982, Parasuraman, Zeithaml and Berry 1988). If performance equals or exceeds expectations, then the perceived service quality is satisfactory, otherwise it is unsatisfactory. Service quality is thus defined in a similar way to satisfaction in the disconfirmation paradigm in consumer behavior studies. The disconfirmation paradigm states that the consumer will feel unsatisfied if the performance is below expectations (negative disconfirmation) and satisfied when expectations are confirmed or exceeded (positive disconfirmation). Satisfaction is expected to increase as positive disconfirmation increases. The best-known instrument for measuring service quality is the SERVQUAL scale, developed by Parasuraman *et al.* (1988), where quality is defined as the difference between what a service company should offer and what it actually offers. Few studies have related this measure to measures of overall satisfaction, overall quality or to behavioral measures.

Purpose of the Study

The purpose of our study is to explore the relation between perceived service quality as measured by SERVQUAL and independent measures of disconfirmation, satisfaction, overall quality, and intention to rebuy.

The study is organized around research on satisfaction and perceived service quality in the following way. To begin with we elaborate on the difference between satisfaction and perceived service quality according to the service quality literature. Different types of expectations in satisfaction and service quality studies have been used and will be presented. However, only 'should' expectations (normal SERVQUAL) are measured in the empirical study. We will then refer to prior research on the relation between disconfirmation of expectations and overall measures of satisfaction/service quality and the possibility that perceived performance alone may be the best predictor of satisfaction. Finally, we will discuss research on the relation between satisfaction/service quality and intentions.

Perceived Service Quality Related to Satisfaction

SERVQUAL is based on the conception of perceived service quality, which is defined as the discrepancy between what the customer feels that a service provider should offer and his perception of what the service provider actually offers (Parasuraman *et al.* 1988). Perceived service quality differs from satisfaction in that service quality is the customers' attitude or global judgement of service superiority over time, while satisfaction is considered to be connected to a specific transaction (Bitner 1990, Bolton and Drew 1991a, Parasuraman *et al.* 1988). In the service quality literature the term "expectations" also differs from the way it is used in the consumer satisfaction literature. According to Parasuraman *et al.*, (1988), expectations in the satisfaction literature have been operationalized as predictions of service performance, while expectations in the service quality literature are viewed in terms of what the service provider should offer. Zeithaml, Berry and Parasuraman (1991) modify this distinction by introducing two different levels of expectations and proposing the existence of a zone of tolerance between these levels. They argue that satisfaction is the function of the difference between predicted service and perceived service, while perceived service quality is the function of the comparison of adequate or desired service with perceived service performance. Woodside, Frey and Daly (1989) also make a distinction between quality and satisfaction but the difference remains unclear as they state that overall satisfaction is a function of overall service quality, which depends on customer satisfaction with service quality of an act.

Parasuraman *et al.* (1985, 1988) do not explicitly discuss whether dis/satisfaction precedes service quality or if the reverse occurs. However, as they argue in favour of the similarity between perceived service quality and the attitude concept (Parasuraman*et al.* 1988), they quote Oliver (1981), according to whom satisfaction with time decays into an overall attitude. This suggest that satisfaction also will decay to form overall perceived service quality, and thus satisfaction precedes perceived service quality. Bolton and Drew (1991a) and Bitner (1990) explicitly argue that dis/satisfaction with specific transactions precede evaluations of overall service quality.

Kasper and Lemmink (1988), on the other hand, suggest that the concepts of satisfaction and quality are different, and that it is the perceived service quality that will affect consumer satisfaction. This is also the perspective of Lewis and Klein (1987).

Some researchers, e.g., Grönroos and Gummesson in their quality model (Gummesson 1991), and Brogowicz, Delene and Lyth (1990), treat service quality and satisfaction as equivalent constructs. This is supported by Nguyen (1991), who reported a strong correlation between satisfaction and perceived service quality, coming to the conclusion that the two concepts measure the same underlying construct.

The question of the difference between satisfaction and service quality, and the relation between them, is problematic as researchers use different definitions and operationalizations of the constructs. One important factor here is if and how expectations are measured. Most studies concerning satisfaction and service quality are based on the disconfirmation paradigm, but there are exceptions where only perceptions of service performance have been measured (e.g., Hedvall and Paltschik 1991, Kasper and Lemmink 1989, Nguyen 1991, Reidenbach and Sandifer-Smallwood 1990).

Different Types of Expectations

The concept of expectations has a different meaning for different authors both between and within satisfaction and service quality studies. Miller (1977) first suggested that there might exist different types of expectations, ideal, expected, deserved and minimally tolerable, stressing the importance of knowing against what type of expectations the consumer compares the performance of the product. Gilly, Cron and Barry (1983) studied these concepts and found moderate support for them as independent constructs. Research has also shown that some types of expectations, or standards, seem to be better than others at explaining satisfaction (Bolfing and Woodruff 1988, Cadotte, Woodruff and Jenkins 1983) and that the relationships between disconfirmation, performance and satisfaction may change depending on the standard used (Bolfing and Woodruff 1988). The consumer may also use several standards simultaneously (Tse and Wilton 1988).

Most of the studies within the disconfirmation paradigm have defined expectations as a prediction of future product performance (Day 1983, Oliver 1980a, 1980b, Swan 1988, 1992). In addition to the indirect effect through disconfirmation, predictive expectations have been found to have a direct positive effect on satisfaction (Bolfing and Woodruff 1988, Churchill and Surprenant 1982, Prakash and Lounsbury 1984, Tse and Wilton 1988). The consumer may also have experience with other brands than the focal brand and this may affect his/her perceptions of the performance of the focal brand. Three types of norms as comparison standards have been suggested in the satisfaction literature: A best brand norm, a product type norm and a brand norm (Cadotte *et al.* 1983, 1987, Woodruff, Clemons, Schumann, Gardial and Burns 1983). Cadotte *et al.* (1983) found these norms to be valid and useful concepts.

Equity theory —Is it a fair deal for both customer and seller?— and deserved standard —Does the customer get what he/she feels he/she deserves?—, have also been suggested as standards of comparison in satisfaction studies (Fisk and Coney 1981, Miller 1977, Liechty and Churchill 1979, Swan and Oliver 1985a, b, Tse and

Wilton 1988, Woodruff *et al.* 1991). Equity as a determinant of satisfaction was supported by Fisk and Coney (1981) and Mowen and Grove (1982).

Zeithaml *et al.* (1991) elaborate on the meaning of expectations within their proposed service quality model and suggest the concepts of desired (excellent) and adequate service. According to the authors, desired service supports the normative standard and is also similar to deserved service. Swan and Trawick (1980) also see similarities between desired expectations and deserved product. If 'deserved service' is interpreted and operationalized as what the service should be like, then it has the same meaning as 'desired' in SERVQUAL. Desired service, however, differs from Miller's (1977) definition of deserved in that it does not consider the efforts and costs associated with obtaining or using the service.

According to Zeithaml *et al.* (1991), adequate service is similar to Miller's (1977) minimum tolerable level and Cadotte *et al.*'s (1983, 1987) experience-based norms. It is, however, unclear which type(s) of experience-based norm(s) Zeithaml *et al.* (1991) compare the adequate service level to. Miller's (1977) minimum tolerable level is not conceptually similar to any of the experience-based norms proposed by Cadotte *et al.* (1983).

Figure 1 shows the difference between satisfaction and SERVQUAL as it is described by Parasuraman *et al.* (1988). According to Parasuraman *et al.*, perceived service quality is good if perceptions of service performance, over all previous encounters, equals or exceeds perceptions of what constitutes excellent service. Satisfaction, on the other hand, is connected to a specific transaction and is considered good if perceptions of service performance of one occasion equals or exceeds predicted expectations.

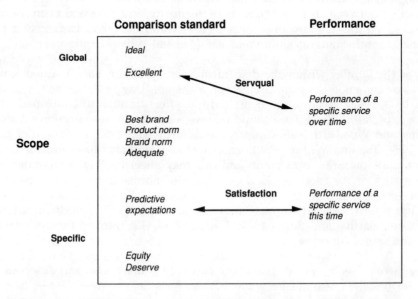

Figure 1. SERVQUAL compared to the classical satisfaction model

Predictive expectations present the narrowest comparison standard in that it concerns one specific service outlet. It is transaction-specific but previous experiences with the outlet will also affect the evaluation. Equity and deserved are also transaction-specific but draw on the consumer's experiences also with other than the focal outlet. Excellent service can be described as industry-specific, which distinguishes it from the transaction-specific standard used in satisfaction studies. This distinction does not, however, recognize that all experience-based norms are, to varying degrees, more global in nature than predictive expectations. The brand norm requires experiences with other outlets of the same brand and the product norm captures the consumer's experience with similar services, or services that fill the same basic need. The best brand norm may be of the best outlet within a brand, the best within a product type or the best at filling consumer needs. This norm will thus also draw upon the consumer's all previous experiences and is a more global comparison standard than predictive expectations.

It is obvious that there is no agreement among researchers about definitions of different types of expectations. As this adds to the difficulties of comparing and interpreting results from different studies it would be beneficial in further research to address the question of different levels of expectations.

Disconfirmation of Expectations Related to Overall Measures of Satisfaction and Perceived Service Quality

Various studies have found disconfirmation to be a good predictor of satisfaction (e.g., Bolfing and Woodruff 1988, Bolton and Drew 1991b, Cadotte *et al.* 1983, Churchill and Surprenant 1982, Oliver 1980a, Oliver and Bearden 1983, Swan 1988). Some studies have compared disconfirmation on different types of expectations and their relation to satisfaction. Although differences have been found, no general pattern can be discerned on the dominance of disconfirmation of any specific type of expectation (Bolfing and Woodruff 1988, Boulding, Kalra, Staelin and Zeithaml 1993, Cadotte *et al.* 1983, Prakash and Lounsbury 1984, Swan and Trawick 1980, 1982, Tse and Wilton 1988). There is clearly a need for more research in this area.

Parasuraman *et al.* (1988, 1990, 1991) studied different types of services and compared the SERVQUAL scores (difference between expectation and performance scores on 22 attributes) with an "overall quality rating" for each service and found them to be associated. It was possible to determine the relative importance of the five SERVQUAL dimensions by regressing the overall score on the SERVQUAL scores for each dimension. In the 1988 and 1990 studies, reliability was consistently found to be the most important dimension and assurance the second most important. The least important dimensions in both studies were empathy and tangibles. The results from the 1991 study, however, are mixed. Boulding *et al.* (1993) found that only reliability and empathy had significant influences on overall quality and that reliability was the most important dimension in overall quality formation.

There are basically two methods of measuring disconfirmation. It can be measured as an inferred measure where the score for the standard of comparison is subtracted from the score for perceptions, as in SERVQUAL, or as a direct measure where the consumer is asked to compare the performance with his/her expectations on a scale from "worse than expected" to "better than expected". In SERVQUAL and some satisfaction studies, expectations have been measured at the same time as perceptions. It is, however, likely that the expectations are affected by the actual offer and do not represent the consumers' expectations before they consumed the product. This way of measuring expectations does not differ much from asking directly about the disconfirmation on each attribute. It is usual in satisfaction studies to measure expectations before the consumption (Cadotte *et al.* 1983, Swan 1977, 1988, Swan and Trawick 1982, Tse and Wilton 1988) and/or a direct disconfirmation measure (Bolfing and Woodruff 1988, Cadotte *et al.* 1983, Churchill and Surprenant 1982, Oliver and Bearden 1983, Tse and Wilton 1988). To date, a direct overall measure of disconfirmation has not been used in service quality studies, although Parasuraman *et al.* (1990) suggest that this should be done. In satisfaction studies this has been the most popular measure since Oliver (1980a) suggested that disconfirmation has an independent additive effect on satisfaction.

The Role of Performance in Satisfaction and Quality Formation

It has been suggested that expectations for a continually consumed product (Oliver 1989) or a product with which the consumer has an abundance of experience (Johnson and Fornell 1991) will equate with perceptions of performance of the product. This has been supported by Bolton and Drew (1991a), who found that consumers who were interviewed in depth about telephone services did not mention expectations, only perceptions about current performance. Prakash and Lounsbury (1984) studied how confirmation of predictive, normative and comparative expectations affected satisfaction and intentions to repurchase. Both satisfaction and repurchase intentions had the highest correlations with perceived performance. Prakash (1984) questions the necessity for marketing managers to go through the lengthy procedure of collecting expectations data as performance data seems to be sufficient. In regard to SERVQUAL studies, Babakus and Boller (1992) reported a stronger correlation between the performance of the service and service quality than between the SERVQUAL score and service quality. Parasuraman *et al.* (1991) also found performance to be a better predictor of overall service quality. They call for comparative studies where the inferred disconfirmation is compared to direct disconfirmation measures.

Some studies have shown that the determinants of satisfaction may be dependent on the situation or the product investigated. In some cases disconfirmation is the best predictor of satisfaction (Bolfing and Woodruff 1988 (low involvement - product norm, focal brand norm, and high involvement - favorite brand norm), Churchill and Surprenant 1982 (flowers), Swan 1988 (service at restaurant)), while in other cases performance alone explains most of the variation in satisfaction (Bolfing and Woodruff 1988 (high involvement-product type norm/focal brand and low involvement - favorite brand), Churchill and Surprenant 1982 (video player), Swan 1988 (food at restaurant)). One explanation for the effect of performance is that if disconfirmation is held constant it is reasonable to assume that a higher level of performance will yield higher satisfaction. In Tse and Wilton's study (1988, miniature record player) performance explained 65 % of the variation in satisfaction. This model explained more of the variance than expectations and disconfirmation (Oliver 1980a), but less than expectations, performance and disconfirmation (Churchill and Surprenant 1982).

The Effect of Satisfaction and Perceived Service Quality on Intentions to Rebuy

Feelings of satisfaction are said to lead to future purchase intentions (Engel, Blackwell and Miniard 1986, Howard 1974, Oliver 1980a, Swan 1983) and intention is the determinant of actual purchase (Engel *et al.* 1986). Dufer and Moulins (1989) and Bloemer, Kasper and Lemmink (1990) argue that behavioral action, like brand loyalty or brand switching, are rarely investigated in satisfaction studies.

Overall, it can be said that those who have studied satisfaction and intentions have found them to be positively correlated. Swan (1977) found satisfaction with a department store to be positively correlated with intentions to re-shop. Oliver and Bearden (1983) reported a significant effect of satisfaction on post-intentions to buy a diet suppressant for the total sample and a high-involvement group. Cadotte *et al.* (1983) found that product norm disconfirmation and best brand norm disconfirmation were better correlated with satisfaction and intentions than the brand norm disconfirmation or predicted brand disconfirmation. All measures of disconfirmation were, however, positively and significantly correlated with satisfaction and behavioral intentions. Prakash (1984) and Prakash and Lounsbury (1984) reported equally good correlations between product performance and intentions, and satisfaction and intentions, for a study on beer and a fast-food hamburger restaurant. Swan (1988) studied the relation between satisfaction with a restaurant and intentions to revisit because of the food/service. Intentions to revisit because of the food were predicted by both satisfaction and performance, while intentions to revisit because of the service were predicted primarily by satisfaction. Swan and Trawick (1981) analysed the same data with an additional variable that compared the service to the respondent's favorite restaurant. In this analysis, satisfaction was the most important predictor of intentions followed by the variable comparing the restaurant to the favorite alternative. Dufer and Moulins (1989) investigated the relationship between satisfaction with a product (coffee, shampoo and detergent), intended loyalty and actual repurchase. Those who expressed an intention to be loyal displayed a higher score for satisfaction than those who intended to change the brand. The satisfaction scores for those who repurchased the same brand were, however, not significantly different from those who bought another brand, except with detergent. According to the authors this seems to suggest that although satisfaction is a good predictor of intended loyalty it is not a good predictor of actual repurchase. The authors acknowledge that external variables and variety seeking may have affected the results. Bloemer *et al.* (1990) reports a study on dealer satisfaction, intended brand loyalty and intended dealer loyalty. The results show that both brand and dealer loyalty are affected by perceptions of dealer service. The better the service of the dealer was judged on an overall satisfaction scale, the greater the intended dealer and brand loyalty became.

Boulding *et al.* (1993) conducted an experimental and field study on the relation of disconfirmation of predictive expectations and a type of 'should' expectations to different types of behavioral intention. They used structural equations modeling in the analysis of the data. In the first study, perceived service quality of a hypothetical visit to a hotel showed a positive influence on intentions to rebuy and recommend. In the second study the five dimensions of SERVQUAL were measured in an educational setting. Six different measures of behavioral intentions (mainly different types of recommendations) were used. Overall, perceived service quality was found to be strongly and positively related to intentions. The data did not, however, support a model including only the overall quality variable in favor of the model including the additional five perceptual dimension variables.

Although a positive effect of satisfaction on intentions has been demonstrated by several studies, there are few studies on the relation between service quality and intentions. However, as many of the studies on satisfaction and intentions have concerned services, similar results can be expected for service quality. None of the studies discussed above compared which of the two constructs, satisfaction or service quality, is better at explaining intentions to repurchase. Is satisfaction with one specific service encounter more important than an overall evaluation of all previous experiences? Direct disconfirmation, which has been shown to have an independent effect on satisfaction has not been included in service quality studies so far. Thus, there is a need for a study that includes all four concepts. Our study is an attempt to fill this gap.

Data Collection Method

Our study using the SERVQUAL questionnaire was done in a newly opened restaurant in Helsinki, Finland[1] . The self-administered questionnaire was given to 100 customers that had eaten dinner at the restaurant during a weekday evening in November, 1991. 22 questionnaires were discarded as not complete.

As is customary with SERVQUAL, the customers filled in both their expectations and perceptions after they had experienced the service, i.e., as they were waiting for their bills. Expectations were operationalized within the SERVQUAL tradition as to how the restaurant 'should' operate. A full description of the questions can be found in Parasuraman *et al.* (1988, pp. 38-40). Aside from the normal SERVQUAL questions a number of different satisfaction measures were included. The measures that were used in the analysis were:

1. A total expectations measure. This measure is the sum of the expectations values on the 22 attributes.
2. A total performance measure. This measure is constructed as the sum of the performance values on 22 attributes.
3. A total performance minus expectations measure. The sum of the differences between performance and expectations on each of the attributes.

---

1   The data was gathered by students, A. Skogster, T. Spring and P. Tuomolin, as part of the requirements in an advanced course on service management.

4. A direct disconfirmation measure. The respondents were asked to compare the performance to their (predictive) expectations on a 5-point scale, ranging from "much worse than I expected" to "much better than I expected". The middle value represents conformance with the respondents' own expectations.

5. A graphical total satisfaction measure. Here the respondents were asked to evaluate their satisfaction with the visit on a commonly used (e.g., Oliver and Westbrooke 1982) 7-point scale where the scale values are faces with expressions displaying different degrees of satisfaction.

6. An overall quality measure. The respondents were asked to rate the overall quality of the restaurant on a scale from 4 to 10. What is known as the 'school scale' has been recommended as a valid scale in Finland as it is the scale used to grade pupils from junior to high school. The scale is easily understood by respondents and has immediate meaning for them. 4 corresponds to 'fail' and 10 to "excel".

7. A rebuy measure. This scale measures the behavioral consequences of this visit at the restaurant on a scale from 5 ("I will definitely visit the restaurant again") to 1 ("I will definitely not visit the restaurant again"). The middle scale value, i.e., 3, implies indifference, uncertainty.

8. Five dimensions of SERVQUAL. The five dimensions are tangibles, reliability, responsiveness, assurance and empathy. They were computed by averaging the means on the attributes that make up each dimension (Zeithaml *et al.* 1991).

Findings

The discussion of the findings is organized in the following way: We will first examine the SERVQUAL dimensions and then proceed to analyzing the relationship between the core concepts of the study.

Quality Dimensions

Parasuraman *et al.* (1988) reported consistent factor structures over several studies for the five quality dimensions. In these earlier findings, factors were only reported for quality scores (performance-expectations) but later (1991) they conducted five new studies and factor-analyzed expectations and performance of the combined data. Structures were found to be similar in reliability, assurance and empathy, while they differed on tangibles and responsiveness. The authors argue that the structures should at least be consistent where expectations are concerned, as these do not vary in the same way as performance. Other researchers who have used the 22 attributes have not found the five dimensions (Babakus and Boller 1992, Finn and Lamb 1991). Many researchers have used modifications of SERVQUAL but most have not measured expectations (e.g., Haywood-Farmer 1988, Hedvall and Paltschik 1991, Reidenbach and Sandifer-Smallwood 1990) or not presented factor solutions on expectations and performance alone (e.g., Brown and Swartz 1989, Cooper 1989). Vogels, Lemmink and Kasper (1989), and Carman (1990) found different factor structures for expectations, performance and the difference between these two. Both studies, however, used modified SERVQUAL questionnaires.

The data from the restaurant was factor-analyzed on PCMDS, with direct quartimin rotation for simple loadings with gamma = 0. Some caution has to be taken when analyzing the results since the sample size is small. Nunnally (1978) recommends a sample size of ten times the attributes to be factor analyzed and a minimum of five times the items. Tabachnick and Fidell (1989, pp. 603) stress that the required sample size also depends on the magnitude of population correlations and the number of factors. A sample size of 50 may be adequate if there are strong, reliable correlations and a few distinct factors. In a SERVQUAL study five factors are expected. Thus, we consider 78 respondents to be enough for a factor analysis. We can see two interesting things from the results that are presented in the appendix: 1) the five dimensions of SERVQUAL are not extracted from either expectations, performance or perceived service quality, and 2) the factor structures are not the same for expectations, performance and service quality. We noted that items 2 and 4, belonging to the tangibles dimension, had a slightly different meaning in the Finnish questionnaire than in the English. This may affect the structure of the tangibles dimension but does not explain why all four items load differently on the three different measures. The alphas for the total scales are quite high (0.82 for expectations, 0.91 for performance and 0.85 for quality) indicating that all the items are highly correlated and seem to measure one underlying structure, i.e., some measure of satisfaction with the service. An alpha value is considered high if it equals or exceeds 0.70 (Nunnally 1978). Since the factors could not be meaningfully interpreted, no alphas were computed for them. We did, however, compute alphas for the items belonging to each original dimension. The results are mixed. There is no pattern of low/high alphas on the same dimensions when one compares the different measures. Only two of the quality dimensions (reliability and empathy) can be considered adequately reliable. This means that one cannot reliably use the five dimensions on this data. Overall, both the factor structure and the reliability coefficients point to the same thing, i.e. that the five SERVQUAL dimensions cannot be extracted from this data. It should be noted that alphas in the study of Parasuraman's *et al.* (1991c) are all very high (0.80-0.93). One could argue, like Parasuraman *et al.* do (1991c), that if the performance on one or some of the items is not up to the standard of the others that should load on the same factor, then this might be the cause of it/them not loading on the same factor. Therefore, they argue that at least expectations should be stable and yield the correct structure. As can be seen from the appendix this is not the case here. Due to the unreliability of the five dimensions we will not present any further analysis on them and their relation to the different dependent measures (the data has been presented in Liljander and Strandvik 1992).

Overall Constructs

It can be concluded that overall satisfaction with the restaurant was good. 91% marked 5 or higher on the graphic 7-point scale and 78% marked that they would probably or definitely revisit the restaurant. Nineteen per cent were unsure about revisiting. Another interesting finding was that, on the 5-point direct disconfirmation scale, 65% of the respondents considered the performance to be as expected and 23% found it to be slightly better than expected. Only 12% thought that the performance was slightly or much worse than expected. This is contradictory to the perceived service quality gaps as measured by SERVQUAL, according to which we seem to have a quality problem on 18 of the 20 attributes.

The same conclusion can be drawn from the difference between the average sum for performance (102.62) and the corresponding value for expectations (123.73), which gives a SERVQUAL score of –21.11. However, the direct overall measures indicate that the customers are quite satisfied. Meeting or exceeding the excellent level is obviously not required for achieving good perceived quality. From a managerial point of view, it would be interesting to find the expectation standard that discriminates between satisfied and dissatisfied customers. This would involve further studies where different expectation standards are compared.

The correlations in Table 1 show that expectations (EXPECT) do not show high correlations with any of the other measures. The highest correlation is with the SERVQUAL score (SSCORE), however, one must keep in mind that expectations are included in this measure. Expectations are also correlated with performance, for which there may be several explanations. It may be due to a measurement effect because respondents made evaluations about expectations and performance at the same time. It may also be due to cognitive dissonance or assimilation effects as found by several authors using experiments (e.g., Olshavsky and Miller 1972, Olson and Dover 1976, Oliver 1977). Another explanation is that the evaluation of performance in itself already contains an evaluation of expectations and deviations from these.

Table 1. Pearson correlation matrix (N=78)

	EXPECT	PERFORM	SSCORE	DISCON	SATIS	QUALITY
EXPECT						
PERFORM	0.293*					
SSCORE	−0.365*	0.783*				
DISCON	−0.064	0.331*	0.364*			
SATIS	0.082	0.634*	0.564*	0.471*		
QUALITY	0.069	0.757*	0.692*	0.469*	0.722*	
REBUY	−0.015	0.584*	0.578*	0.473*	0.766*	0.719*

* p < 0.01,
EXPECT = sum of scores on expectations for each attribute, SSCORE = SERVQUAL Score (inferred disconfirmation), DISCON = direct disconfirmation score, PERFORM = sum of scores on perceptions for each attribute, SATIS = graphic satisfaction score

The correlation matrix shows that what seems to be important is the evaluation of the service performance. The correlations of performance (PERFORM) with the satisfaction scale (SATIS), overall quality scale (QUALITY) and the intentions measure (REBUY) are higher than the correlation between these measures and the SERVQUAL score or the direct disconfirmation measure (DISCON).

The relatively low correlation of the direct disconfirmation measure (DISCON) with satisfaction (0.471) is in itself interesting. This is considerably lower than the correlation between performance and satisfaction (0.634). The SERVQUAL score shows a better correlation (0.564) than the direct disconfirmation measure with satisfaction, though this can be explained by the influence of the performance measure, which alone is highly correlated with satisfaction.

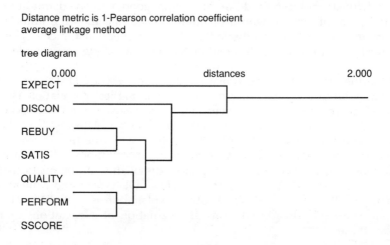

Distance metric is 1-Pearson correlation coefficient
average linkage method

tree diagram

Figure 2. Hierarchical cluster analysis on the main constructs

A hierarchical cluster analysis (run on SYSTAT 5.0 with standardized variables) gives a similar picture of the relations between the different measures. The results of the analysis are displayed in Figure 2. As expected, the sum of the evaluations on attributes (PERFORM) is closely related to the SERVQUAL score. These measures are connected to the quality (QUALITY) variable. This seems to give some support to the SERVQUAL score as a measure or determinant of perceived service quality. We must, however, remember the strong role of performance in the score. It is interesting to note that the performance score is more closely related to overall quality than to satisfaction. This can be explained by the nature of the performance attributes. In SERVQUAL these are not measured on the performance of this particular transaction, as is the satisfaction score, but on the performance of the service over time, such as the overall quality score. Another pair of measures closely connected are total satisfaction (SATIS) and the behavioral measure (REBUY), suggesting that satisfaction with the current service is the best determinant of behavioral intentions. Similar results were obtained by Cronin and Taylor (1992). The implication of this is that it might be more important for managers to measure customers' satisfaction with specific service transactions than to measure perceived service quality over time. Direct disconfirmation and expectations are different from the other measures and enter the group later. This shows that expectations or perceived deviations from expectations do not determine perceived satisfaction or quality.

Regression analysis on different determinants of satisfaction show that performance alone explains 40% of the variation in satisfaction, while performance and direct disconfirmation together explain 48%, (47.9). Expectations, performance and direct disconfirmation also explain 48% (48.2) of the variation. Inferred disconfirmation alone explains 32% of the variation in satisfaction while direct disconfirmation alone explains only 22% of the variation. All R^2 are significant ($p<0.01$). The results resemble those by Tse and Wilton (1988) in that performance alone is a better predictor than inferred disconfirmation alone and that expectations, performance and direct disconfirmation explain most of the variation in satisfaction. Tse and Wilton did not present results for performance and direct disconfirmation. Our results, however, show that this model is to be preferred as the expectations component does not add to the explanation of variation in satisfaction. Performance alone, or together with direct disconfirmation, are thus better measures of satisfaction with the current visit than the inferred disconfirmation, or in other words the SERVQUAL score. The same pattern holds for perceived service quality over time. Performance alone is the best predictor of quality ($R^2=0.57$, $p<0.01$).

Intention to rebuy was best predicted by satisfaction with the current visit ($R^2=0.59$), the perceived service quality over time ($R^2=0.52$), or a combination of these two ($R^2=0.64$). All R^2 are significant ($p<0.01$). Service quality as an inferred measure explained only 33% of the variation in intentions to rebuy.

In another analysis we compared satisfied and dissatisfied customers, based on the direct disconfirmation measure. Differences in expectations were only found on one attribute, but in performance there were significant differences ($p<0.05$) on 13 attributes, where satisfied customers rated performance higher than dissatisfied customers.

Discussion

In the service quality literature the importance of expectations is highlighted. Our results, where expectations were defined in the SERVQUAL tradition as to how a service 'should' be offered, showed that expectations were moderately correlated with how the service performance was perceived and with the SERVQUAL difference score. This would be quite acceptable under the condition that customers are found to be dissatisfied with the service. However, as customers are clearly satisfied on three different overall measures and declare an intention to rebuy on a fourth measure, there seems to be a contradiction. One explanation would be to argue either that expectations generally play a minor role in the determination of service quality, or that this specific type of formulation of expectations (should) does not capture the relevant norm in customers' perception process. It is important that in further research one takes into consideration different types of expectations as suggested in the consumer satisfaction literature and as Zeithaml *et al.* (1991) have recently discussed in the service quality context. It is not clear from a managerial point of view as to why it would be more helpful to relate performance to a 'should' standard rather than to, for example, the best competitor, what is typical of the industry, or the average performance of the firm. These specifications maintain the conception of quality as the accumulated experience rather than the evaluation of a particular event. It must be noted that the operationalization of expectations as a desired level is not implied by the disconfirmation paradigm *per se*; it is a choice made by the SERVQUAL research team.

In our study, performance was a better predictor of satisfaction than either inferred or direct measures of disconfirmation. The strong influence of performance may have implications not only for further research but also for managers. Managerial implications would be that it is beneficial to concentrate on influencing customers' experiences than altering their expectations. Satisfaction was found to have a positive correlation with intentions to rebuy. Service quality, measured as inferred disconfirmation (SERVQUAL score) was also connected to intentions, although perceived performance alone had a higher correlation with intentions. Overall satisfaction was, in this study, a better predictor of intentions to rebuy than overall or inferred service quality. All these findings together suggest that further attention would be needed in scrutinizing the assumed difference/connections between the service quality and satisfaction concept. As service quality is defined as the long run evaluation of a service firm, what is the influence of one bad or one exceptional experience on perceived service quality? Does it effect perceived service quality at all, is it, for example, perceived as an acceptable variation, i.e., do consumers possess some kind of tolerance zone? Exceptional performance, negative and positive, has been studied using the critical incidence method, but in these studies no links have been made to quantitative service quality measures. If it were to be found that certain experiences heavily influence perceived service quality, it might be important to measure performance not as an average over time, as in SERVQUAL, but as performance at this particular point in time.

From a broader perspective, it might be argued that the lack of taking price into consideration in the service quality models might have implications for the correlation between perceived service quality and customer loyalty and retention. In our view, introducing the value concept into the service quality discussion would be important as it indicates that quality is related to costs. Such an approach would be based on a general definition of perceived value as the relation between perceived service quality and perceived price.

References

Babakus, E. and G.W. Boller, An Empirical Assessment of the SERVQUAL Scale, *Journal of Business Research*, Vol. 24, 1992, pp. 253-268.
Bitner, M.J, Evaluating Service Encounters: The Effects of Physical Surroundings and Employee Responses, *Journal of Marketing*, Vol. 54 (April), 1990, pp. 69-82.
Bloemer, J., H. Kasper and J. Lemmink, The Relationship Between Overall Dealer Satisfaction, Satisfaction With the Attributes of Dealer Service, Intended Dealer Loyalty and Intended Brand Loyalty: A Dutch Automobile Case, *Journal of Consumer Satisfaction, Dissatisfaction and Complaining Behavior*, Vol. 3, 1990, pp. 42-47.
Bolfing, C. and R.B. Woodruff Effects of Situational Involvement on Consumers' Use of Standards in Satisfaction/Dissatisfaction Processes, *Journal of Consumer Satisfaction, Dissatisfaction and Complaining Behavior*, Vol. 1, 1988, pp. 16-24.
Bolton, R.N. and J.H. Drew, A Longitudinal Analysis of the Impacts of Service Changes on Customer Attitudes, *Journal of Marketing*, Vol. 55, 1991a, pp. 1-9.
Bolton, R.N. and J.H. Drew, A Multistage Model of Customers' Assessments of Service Quality and Value, *Journal of Consumer Research*, Vol. 17 (March), 1991b, pp. 375-384.

Boulding, W., A. Kalra, R. Staelin, and V.A. Zeithaml, A Dynamic Process Model of Service Quality: From Expectations to Behavioral Intentions, *Journal of Marketing Research*, Vol. XXX (February), 1993, pp. 7-27.

Brogowicz, A.A., L.M. Delene and D.M. Lyth, A Synthesised Service Quality Model with Managerial Implications, *International Journal of Service Industry Management*, Vol. 1, No. 1, 1990, pp. 27-45.

Brown, S.W. and T.A. Swartz, A Gap Analysis of Professional Service Quality, *Journal of Marketing*, Vol. 53, April, 1991, pp. 92-98.

Cadotte, E.R., R.B. Woodruff and R.L. Jenkins, Norms and Expectations: How Different are the Measures?, In: R.L. Day and H.K. Hunt (eds.), *International Fare In Consumer Satisfaction and Complaining Behavior*, Indiana University, Bloomington, IN, 1983, p.49-56.

Cadotte, E.R., R.B. Woodruff and R.L. Jenkins, Expectations and Norms in Models of Consumer Satisfaction, *Journal of Marketing Research*, 24 (August), 1987, pp. 305-314.

Carman, J.M., Consumer Perceptions of Service Quality: An Assessment of the SERVQUAL Dimensions, *Journal of Retailing*, Vol. 66, No. 1, Spring, 1990, pp. 33-55.

Churchill Jr, G.A. and C. Surprenant, An Investigation Into the Determinants of Customer Satisfaction, *Journal of Marketing Research*, Vol. 19 (November), 1982, pp. 491-504.

Cooper, A.R., M.B. Cooper and D.F. Duhan, Measurement instrument development using two competing concepts of customer satisfaction, *Journal of Consumer Satisfaction, Dissatisfaction and Complaining Behavior*, Vol. 2, 1989, pp. 28-35.

Cronin, J.J. and S.A. Taylor, Measuring Service Quality: A Reexamination and Extension, *Journal of Marketing*, Vol. 56 (July), 1992, pp. 55-68.

Day, R.H., The Next Step: Commonly Accepted Constructs for Satisfaction Research, In: R.L. Day and H.K. Hunt (eds.), *International Fare In Consumer Satisfaction and Complaining Behavior*, Indiana University, Bloomington, IN, 1983, pp. 113-117.

Dufer, J. and J.-L. Moulins, La Relation entre la satisfaction du consommateur et sa fidélité à la marque: un examen critique, *Recherche et Application en Marketing*, Vol. IV, No 2, 1989, pp. 21-36.

Engel, J.F., R.D. Blackwell and P.W. Miniard, *Consumer Behavior*, 5th ed. CBS College Publishing, New York, 1986.

Finn, D.W. and Ch.W. Lamb, An Evaluation of the SERVQUAL Scales in a Retailing Setting, In: R.H. Holman and M.R. Solomon (eds.), *Advances in Consumer Research*, Vol. 18, Association for Consumer Research, Provo UT, 1991, pp. 483-490.

Fisk, R.P. and K.A. Coney, Postchoice Evaluation: An Equity Theory Analysis of Consumer Satisfaction/Dissatisfaction With Service Choices, In: H.K. Hunt and R.L. Day (eds.), *Conceptual and Empirical Contributions To Consumer Satisfaction and Complaining Behavior*, Indiana University, Bloomington, IN, 1982, pp. 9-16.

Gilly, M.C., W.L. Cron and Th.E. Barry, The Expectations-Performance Comparison Process: An Investigation of Expectation Types, In: R.L. Day and H.K. Hunt (eds.), *International Fare In Consumer Satisfaction and Complaining Behavior*, Indiana University, Bloomington, IN, 1983, pp. 10-16.

Grönroos, Ch., Strategic Management and Marketing in the Service Sector, Research Reports No 8, Swedish School of Economics and Business Administration, Helsinki, Finland, 1982.

Gummesson, E., Kvalitetsstyrning i tjänste- och serviceverksamheter. Tolkning av fenomenet tjänstekvalitet och syntes av internationell forskning, Forskningsrapport 91:4, Centrum för tjänsteforskning, Högskolan i Karlstad, Karlstad, 1991.

Haywood-Farmer, J. and F.I. Stuart, Measuring the Quality of Professional Services. In: R. Johnston (ed.), *The Management of Service Operations*, Proceedings of the Operations Management Association, 6-7 January 1988, University of Warwick, UK IFS Publicatiuons/Springer-Verlag.

Hedvall, M-B. and M. Paltschik, Intrinsic Service Quality Determinants for Pharmacy Customers, *International Journal of Service Industry Management*, Vol. 2, No. 2, 1991, pp. 38-48.

Howard, J.A., The Structure of Buyer Behavior, In: J.U. Farley, J.A. Howard and L. Winston Ring (eds.), *Consumer Behavior: Theory and Application*, Allyn and Bacon, Boston, 1974.

Johnson, M.D. and C. Fornell, A framework for comparing customer satisfaction across individuals and product categories, *Journal of Economic Psychology*, Vol. 12, 1991, pp. 267-286.

Kasper, H. and J. Lemmink, Perceived, After-Sales Service Quality and Market Segmentation: A Case Study, In: K. Blois and S. Parkinson (eds.), *Innovative Marketing - A European Perspective*,

Proceedings from the XVIIth Annual Conference of the European Marketing Academy, University of Bradford, Bradford, England, 1988, pp. 365-387.

Kasper, H. and J. Lemmink, After Sales Service Quality: Views Between Industrial Customers and Service Managers, *Industrial Marketing Management*, 18, 1989, pp. 199-208.

Lewis, R.C. and D.M. Klein, The Measurements of Gaps in Service Quality, In: Czepiel, J.A. *et al.* (eds.), *Add Value to Your Service: The Key to Success.* American Marketing Association, Chicago, Ill., 1987, pp. 33-38.

Liechty, M. and Gilbert A. Churchill, Jr., Conceptual Insights into Consumer Satisfaction With Services, In: N. Beckwith *et al.* (eds.), *Educator's Conference Proceedings.* American Marketing Association, Chicago, 1979.

Liljander, V. and T. Strandvik, The Relation Between Service Quality, Satisfaction and Intentions, In: J. Lemmink and P. Kunst (eds.), *Proceedings 2nd Workshop on Quality Management in Services*, European Institute for Advanced Studies in Management, Brussels, Belgium, 1992, pp. 77-98.

Miller, J.A., Studying Satisfaction, Modifying Models, Eliciting Expectations, Posing Problems, and Making Meaningful Measurements, In: H.K. Hunt (ed.), *Conceptualization and measurement of consumer satisfaction and dissatisfaction*, Report No. 77-103 (May), Marketing Science Institute, Cambridge, Massachusetts, 1977, pp. 72-91.

Mowen, J.C. and S.J. Grove, Search Behavior, Price Paid, and The 'Comparison Other', In: R.L. Day and H.K. Hunt (eds.), *International Fare In Consumer Satisfaction and Complaining Behavior*, Indiana University, Bloomington, IN, 1982, pp. 57-63.

Nguyen, N., Un modèle explicatif de l'evaluation de la qualité d'un service: une étude empirique, *Recherche et Application en Marketing*, Vol. VI, 2, 1991, pp. 83-97.

Nunnally, J.C., Psychometric Theory, 2nd ed. McGraw-Hill, New York, 1978.

Oliver, R.L., Effect of Expectation and Disconfirmation on Postexposure Product evaluations, An Alternative Interpretation, *Journal of Applied Psychology*, Vol. 62 (August), 1977, pp. 480-486.

Oliver, R.L., A Cognitive Model of the Antecedents and Consequences of Satisfaction Decisions, *Journal of Marketing Research*, Vol. 17 (November), 1980a, pp. 460-469.

Oliver, R.L., Conceptualization and Measurement of Disconfirmation Perceptions in the Prediction of Consumer Satisfaction, In: H.K. Hunt and R.L. Day (eds.), *Refining Concepts and Measures of Consumer Satisfaction and Complaining Behavior*, Indiana University, Bloomington, IN, 1980b, pp. 2-6.

Oliver, R.L., Measurement and Evaluation of Satisfaction Process in Retail Settings, *Journal of Retailing*, 57 (Fall), 1981, pp. 25-48.

Oliver, R.L., Processing of the Satisfaction Response in Consumption: A Suggested Framework and Research Propositions, *Journal of Consumer Satisfaction, Dissatisfaction and Complaining Behavior*, Vol. 2, 1989, pp. 1-16.

Oliver, R.L. and W.O. Bearden, The Role of Involvement in Satisfaction Processes, In: R.P. Bagozzi and A.M. Tybout (eds.), *Advances in Consumer Research*, Vol. 10, Association for Consumer Research, Ann Arbor, 1983, pp. 250-255.

Oliver, R.L. and R.A. Westbrooke, The Factor Structure of Satisfaction and Related Postpurchase Measures, In: R.L. Day and H.K. Hunt (eds.), *New Findings on Consumer Satisfaction and Complaining Behavior*, Indiana University, Bloomington, IN, 1982, pp. 11-14.

Olshavsky, R.W. and J.A. Miller, Consumer Expectations, Product Performance and Perceived Product Quality. *Journal of Marketing Research*, Vol. 9, February, pp. 19-21.

Olson, J.C. and P. Dover, Effects of Expectation Creation and Disconfirmation on Belief Elements of Cognitive Structure, In: B.B. Anderson (ed.), *Advances in Consumer Research*, Vol. 3, Association for Consumer Research, Chicago, 1976, pp. 168-175.

Parasuraman, A., V.A. Zeithaml and L.L. Berry, A conceptual model of service quality and its implications for future research. Journal of Maketing, vol. 49, Fall, 1985, pp. 41-50.

Parasuraman, A., V.A. Zeithaml and L.L. Berry, SERVQUAL: A Multiple-Item Scale for Measuring Consumer Perceptions of Service Quality, *Journal of Retailing*, Vol. 64, No. 1 (Spring), 1988, pp. 12-40.

Parasuraman, A., L.L. Berry and V.A. Zeithaml, An Empirical Examination of Relationships in an Extended Service Quality Model. Report No. 90-122 (December), Marketing Science Institute, Cambridge, Massachusetts, 1990.

Parasuraman, A., L.L. Berry and V.A. Zeithaml, Refinement and Reassessment of the SERVQUAL Scale, *Journal of Retailing*, Volume 67, No. 4 (Winter), 1991, pp. 420-450.

Prakash, V., Validity and Reliability of the Confirmation of Expectations Paradigm As a Determinant of Consumer Satisfaction, *Journal of the Academy of Marketing Science*, Vol. 12, No. 4 (Fall), 1984, pp. 63-76.

Prakash, V. and J.W. Lounsbury, The Role of Expectations in The Determination of Consumer Satisfaction, *Journal of the Academy of Marketing Science*, Vol. 12, No. 4 (Fall), 1984, pp. 1-17.

Reidenbach, R.E. and B. Sandifer-Smallwood, Exploring Perceptions of Hospital Operations by a Modified SERVQUAL Approach, *Journal of Health Care Marketing*, Vol. 10, December, 1990, pp. 47-55.

Swan, J.E., Consumer Satisfaction with a Retail Store Related to the Fulfillment of Expectations on an Initial Shopping Trip, In: R.L. Day (ed.), *Consumer Satisfaction, Dissatisfaction and Complaining Behavior*, Indiana University, Bloomington, IN, 1977, pp. 10-17.

Swan, J.E., Consumer Satisfaction Research and Theory: Current Status and Future Directions, In: R.L. Day and H.K. Hunt (eds.), *International Fare In Consumer Satisfaction and Complaining Behavior*, Indiana University, Bloomington, IN, 1983, pp. 124-129.

Swan, J.E., Consumer Satisfaction Related to Disconfirmation of Expectations and Product Performance, *Journal of Consumer Satisfaction, Dissatisfaction and Complaining Behavior*, Vol. 1, 1988, pp. 40-47.

Swan, J.E., Satisfaction Work: The Joint Production of Patient Satisfaction by Health Care Providers and Patients, *Journal of Consumer Satisfaction, Dissatisfaction and Complaining Behavior*, Vol. 5, 1992, pp. 69-80.

Swan, J.E. and R.L. Oliver, The Factor Structure of Equity and Disconfirmation Measures Within the Satisfaction Process, In: H.K. Hunt and R.L. Day (eds.), *Consumer Satisfaction, Dissatisfaction and Complaining Behavior*, Indiana University, Bloomington, IN, 1985a, pp. 2-9.

Swan, J.E. and R.L. Oliver, Automobile Buyer Satisfaction with the Salesperson Related to Equity and Disconfirmation, In: H.K. Hunt and R.L. Day (eds.), *Consumer Satisfaction, Dissatisfaction and Complaining Behavior*, Indiana University, Bloomington, IN, 1985b, pp. 10-16.

Swan, J.E. and I.F. Trawick, Satisfaction Related to Predictive vs Desired Expectations, In: H.K. Hunt and R.L. Day (eds.), *Refining Concepts and Measures of Consumer Satisfaction and Complaining Behavior*, Indiana University, Bloomington, IN, 1980, pp. 7-12.

Swan, J.E. and I.F. Trawick, Satisfaction, Disconfirmation, and Comparison of Alternatives. In: H.K. Hunt and R.L. Day (eds.), *Conceptual and Empirical Contributions to Consumer Satisfaction and Complaining Behavior*, Indiana University, Bloomington, IN, 1982, pp. 17-24.

Tabachnick, B.G. and L.S. Fidell, *Using Multivariate Statistics*, 2nd ed., Harper & Row, New York, 1989.

Tse, D.K. and P.C. Wilton, Models of Consumer Satisfaction Formation: An Extension, *Journal of Marketing Research*, Vol. 25 (May), 1988, pp. 204-12.

Vogels, R., J. Lemmink and H. Kasper, Some methodological remarks on the SERVQUAL model, In: G.J. Avlonitis, N.K. Papavasiliou and A.G. Kouremenos (eds.), *Marketing Thought and Practice in the 1990s*, Vol.1, European Marketing Academy, Athens, 1989, pp. 789-800.

Woodruff, R.B., D.S. Clemons, D.W. Schumann, S.F. Gardial and M.J. Burns, The Standards Issue in CS/D Research: A Historical Perspective, *Journal of Consumer Satisfaction, Dissatisfaction and Complaining Behavior*, Vol. 4, 1991, pp. 103-110.

Woodside, A.G., L.L. Frey and R.T. Daly, Linking Service Quality, Customer Satisfaction, and Behavioral Intention, *Journal of Health Care Marketing*, Vol. 9, No. 4 (December), 1989, pp. 5-17.

Zeithaml, V., L. Berry and A. Parasuraman, The Nature and Determinants of Customer Expectations of Service, Working Paper, Report No. 91-113 (May), Marketing Science Institute, Cambridge, Massachusetts, 1991.

Appendix: Study on a Tex-Mex restaurant

Expectations (n = 78)

Item	FACTOR	1	2	3	4	5	Alpha
1	Tangibles	−.03728	.26306	−.02603	**.82346**	.03707	**0.82**
2		.26805	−.26042	**.36996**	−.03491	.06103	
3		.06230	−.12745	.13536	**.72675**	.21516	
4		.01648	−.12598	.09613	.26300	**.74319**	
5	Reliability	**.80555**	.02242	.14721	.11019	−.15780	**0.89**
6		**.66625**	−.19099	.07598	−.11323	.16906	
7		**.86078**	−.04721	.04317	−.00731	−.01469	
8		**.84973**	.04443	−.01633	−.01580	−.06923	
9		**.80512**	−.03861	.14157	−.06283	−.04430	
10	Responsiveness	.06071	.36409	.17026	−.38244	.16150	**0.69**
11		−.12532	.05538	**.72148**	−.01260	.15036	
12		.02520	.00989	**.56567**	−.13623	.47471	
13		.01928	.14388	**.79636**	−.00802	.08975	
14	Assurance	**.48732**	.18838	−.33537	−.14597	**.48230**	**0.80**
15		**.55372**	−.09535	−.06304	.08191	.35304	
16		.38498	−.03330	.09297	−.01564	**.53963**	
17		**.65529**	.19323	−.07585	−.01189	.34157	
18	Empathy	.24989	.12150	**.71169**	.09558	−.19442	**0.72**
19		.26000	.06697	**.71846**	.08316	−.25356	
20		−.15305	**.73966**	.22474	−.01241	.12234	
21		.14245	**.71678**	.24837	−.11564	−.04836	
22		−.00525	**.82295**	−.15788	.19800	−.19411	

Performance (n = 78)

Item	FACTOR	1	2	3	4	5	Alpha
1	Tangibles	.09792	−.03547	.13734	−.06904	**.91296**	**0.63**
2		**.73633**	.05122	−.22194	−.09950	.16550	
3		**.69184**	.09709	−.28236	.08532	.18702	
4		**.77617**	.06122	.01530	−.08586	−.12051	
5	Reliability	**.62644**	.09197	.32357	−.01302	−.19693	**0.86**
6		**.67660**	.07049	.37315	.14204	−.07822	
7		**.57026**	.31062	.20737	.19010	.12662	
8		**.51038**	.04048	.45012	−.27887	−.04383	
9		**.52602**	.06155	.29050	.17244	.29261	
10	Responsiveness	.36020	−.03531	**.74536**	−.06079	.09592	**0.61**
11		−.03562	**.63566**	−.06800	.41140	.12602	
12		.42163	.30810	**.46807**	.13881	−.06106	
13		.29092	**.42932**	**.44121**	−.04637	−.08254	
14	Assurance	**.82942**	−.10312	.11816	−.06458	−.00154	**0.78**
15		**.86211**	−.04184	−.16391	.00348	.04385	
16		**.88667**	−.06074	−.04416	−.01267	−.12000	
17		.25307	.03865	.32974	**.51603**	.00960	
18	Empathy	.28508	.27173	.26532	**−.62786**	.12075	**0.81**
19		.45508	.26390	.12270	**−.54124**	−.09889	
20		.14206	**.65598**	.03616	−.06158	−.35090	
21		.10224	**.69263**	.13415	−.06479	−.27127	
22		−.17776	**.77423**	−.09614	−.23752	.11038	

Quality (performance - expectations, n = 78)

Item	FACTOR	1	2	3	4	5	Alpha
1	Tangibles	−.01184	.10318	**.62827**	−.19126	.02023	**0.43**
2		.10966	−.16368	.14011	**.64963**	.14841	
3		.17371	.07266	**.74702**	−.06741	.01426	
4		**.44238**	−.10265	.27499	.21678	.20266	
5	Reliability	**.46900**	.18773	.30485	.05145	.29166	**0.85**
6		**.60229**	.07081	.04731	.09917	.40860	
7		**.74277**	−.08981	.04271	.05125	.23289	
8		.35182	.05531	−.07332	.27173	.33721	
9		**.69322**	−.12215	−.01038	.04404	−.00866	
10	Responsiveness	.23018	.40009	**−.50876**	−.35992	.07030	**0.64**
11		**.62774**	.04407	.03368	−.07411	−.19600	
12		**.65520**	.33220	.05570	.08866	.04464	
13		**.53104**	.31427	.02812	.37704	−.13635	
14	Assurance	.00845	.06047	−.18782	−.19580	**.88704**	**0.64**
15		−.18276	−.03315	.12871	.15548	**.74862**	
16		.18804	.09665	.19830	.17696	**.59910**	
17		**.45711**	−.14419	−.26237	−.01877	.18119	
18	Empathy	.02566	.20074	−.28786	**.78564**	−.00781	**0.76**
19		−.03818	.22639	−.16526	**.85048**	−.00123	
20		.02598	**.72368**	.05626	.20878	.11866	
21		.24857	**.66048**	−.12732	.19308	−.01762	
22		−.26386	**.75983**	.18928	−.04490	.00748	

The variance explained by the 5 factors on expectations, performance and quality are 64.2 %, 67.2 % and 60.5 % for the restaurant study. The reliability coefficients (Cronbach's alpha) are computed on the original 5 dimensions.

5

Quality Marks: Prospective Tools in Managing Service Quality Perceptions

Henk Roest and Theo Verhallen

Introduction

In reaction to the quality sensitivity at the market demand side (e.g., Steenkamp 1989, Zeithaml, Parasuraman and Berry 1990, Parasuraman, Zeithaml and Berry 1985) the supplier side raises quality as a strategic competitive weapon (e.g., Porter 1980, Kotler 1984, Juran 1984). This is particularly true in markets where competition is high (Tettero and Viehoff 1987). If quality is to be an effective marketing instrument, specific attention for and control of perceived quality is indispensable. The technical quality of the product and the production process are dissatisfiers and prerequisites for perceived quality.

Perceived quality literature focuses on the perceived quality delivery. However, perceived quality concerns the matching of quality deliverance and expectations (Parasuraman, Zeithaml and Berry 1985). In their SERVQUAL model, four gaps are distinguished to explain perceived quality problems in services. Three of them are internally oriented (delivery), and one is concerned with external or perceived quality control aspects (expectations). Qualitative research by the same authors provide some indications about the nature and determinants of customer expectations (Zeithaml, Berry and Parasuraman 1991).

This study offers possibilities to improve perceived service quality not only by means of managing service quality delivery but also by managing service quality expectations.

Managing Service Quality

The main reason to devote specific attention to quality of services is the acceptance that services are, as to intrinsic elements, different from goods (e.g., Tettero and Viehoff 1987, Lovelock 1988). These characteristics impede the service provider to gain control of the quality perception process in several ways:

1. The intangibility of services implicates that the product itself offers little for the inference of the quality. This leads to quality unsteadiness;
2. The flexibility and lack of (desired) standardisation of the product and production process offers the service organizations no foothold to communicate the service features unambiguously. "Everything is possible" and "it shows as it shows" fortifies the incertitude and offers little opportunity to attend the quality perception in an adequate manner.
3. Since the customer is part of the service production process, the client not only forms a quality perception of the service (the outcome) but also of the way it is delivered during the production process (Neijzen and Trompetter 1989, Grönroos 1990).

It is evident that in services the assessment of quality by the customer and the control of quality by the service provider is far more difficult than it is in the case of tangible products. Quality formation by the client and quality control by the provider are interactively related. The formation of the quality perception can be simplified when it is made clear to the client what to expect of the service and its provider, and what not to expect. This insecurity reduction places demands on the provider who is responsible for quality control and quality assurance. Although control and guidance of the customers' quality perception process is of vital interest, it is often omitted due to its apparent complexity.

It is said that customers usually don't know what they are getting, until they don't get it (Levitt 1981). To get a grip on the quality perception of services, it is necessary to unfold the quality perception process to see where and how this expectation process can be influenced by the provider (Roest and Frambach 1992).

Service Quality Perception

The literature on the quality perception process emphasises five topics that will be discussed successively:

1. Information collection (e.g., Bettman 1979, Van Raaij 1977, Wilkie 1990, Schiffman and Kanuk 1987);
2. The selection of quality cues (e.g., Miller 1956, Crane and DeYoung 1990, Monroe and Krishnan 1985, Steenkamp 1989);
3. The formation of quality attributes (also when derived from quality cues) (e.g., Juran 1984, Garvin 1987, Van Raaij 1977);
4. The formation of quality expectations (also when derived from quality attributes) (e.g., Holbrook and Corfman 1985, Zeithaml 1988, Parasuraman, Zeithaml and Berry 1985, Zeithaml, Berry and Parasuraman 1991) and

5. Perceived quality evaluation (e.g., perceived differences between desired and adequate expectations and perceived service delivery) (e.g., Kasper and Lemmink 1989, Brown and Swartz 1989, Zeithaml *et al.* 1991).

The consumer needs information to assess the value of an offering that includes the perceived give and get components (e.g., quality) (among others, Van Raaij 1988, Holbrook and Corfman 1985). To serve this purpose, it is of importance to specify the criteria that information must meet. Willenborg (1985), in reference to Weser (1980), shows the requirements for information for optimal usage (see Table 1).

According to Bettman (1979), consumers will first look for internal, passively or actively gathered information, because of its simplicity. However, internal information can be absent, insufficient or in conflict with other information. Dependent on the perceived risk or the level of conflict (Box 1979) the consumer will ignore the lack of (suitable) information and/or search for external information. Desired external information completion, the amount and type of information, will also depend on marginal behavioral costs (time, money, effort) (Verhallen and Van Raaij 1986).

Fishbein and Ajzen (1975), Steenkamp (1988), and others state that quality beliefs and quality attribute beliefs can be formed in several ways:

- Inferential belief formation, in which the consumer forms beliefs about quality attributes from relevant information. Quality cues are, dependent on their predictive and confidence value, used as intermediate variables to infer quality (attributes).
- Descriptive belief formation, in which the customer comes to quality (attribute) beliefs by direct sensory contact, without the use of intermediate cues.
- Informational belief formation, which is influenced by information on quality (attributes) provided by external sources, e.g., experts.

Basic in these processes are the use of search, experience and credence attributes. Search attributes (e.g., style) are product benefits that can be accurately judged prior to consumption. Experience attributes (such as competence) can only be determined during consumption. Credence attributes (e.g., reliability) may never be assessed. Before consumption, experience and credence attributes will be estimated. The actual usage of these three processes to evaluate quality differ.

Due to the absence of readily available search attributes, descriptive attribute belief formation is only possible when a service is tested before it is bought, which is often impossible.

Inferential belief processing, from available information, is the one most commonly used. It also shows several problems: the lack of relevant intrinsic cues (Olson and Jacoby 1972) and purposeful information, the low confidence and predictive values, the presence of *a priori* beliefs (Steenkamp 1989) and the lack of motivation to deduce quality in an intensive and systematic way. Especially in situations of low client involvement, or in situations with high client involvement accompanied by confusion or a lack of personal capacity and/or ability, the transformation process of cues into attribute expectations and of attribute expectations into quality expectations will be superficial and heuristic (Furse, Punj and Stewart 1984, Van Raaij 1977). Before external quality control becomes possible, it is necessary to conduct research on how cues are used and translated into service attributes. Although literature on cues is scarce (see, for example, Crane and DeYoung 1990), literature on attributes is readily available (Garvin 1987, Juran 1984, Morgan 1985, Parasuraman *et al.* 1985).

Informational belief processing, in which consumers depend on external 'expertise', is commonly used (Furse *et al.* 1984). To play a significant role in the quality perception process it is necessary that the information is understood and accepted. Problems can arise from the sender (e.g., incredibility), the receiver (e.g., uncertainty, intelligence) and the attribute information itself (e.g., complexity, ambiguity, availability, completeness).

It is obvious that in services inferential and informational belief processing are used to determine quality (attributes) scores. These attribute expectations are, because of the absence of search attributes in most service environments, experience and credence attributes.

Customer expectations can be defined as pre-trial beliefs about a product that serve as standards or reference points for judging product performances. Judging products on, for example, quality is possible before and after the purchase. The former is related to buying intentions, while the latter relates to (dis)satisfaction and Parasuraman *et al.*'s perceived quality gap. It has been questioned by Cadotte, Woodruff and Jenkins (1987) whether focal brand expectations are used in judging performance after purchase. They state that "experience-based norms" are used in after-purchase evaluations. These norms have two important characteristics: (1) they reflect whether the performance did meet needs and wants; and (2) they are determined by the performance consumers believe to be possible, as indicated by the performance of known brands (see also Jacobs 1987). Qualitative research by Zeithaml *et al.* (1991) shows that the experience-based norms may encompass desired expectations and adequate expectations. The desired expectations can be defined as the level of service the customer hopes to receive; the adequate expectations as the level of service the customer will accept as adequate. The difference between desired and adequate expectations is the tolerance zone. This zone of tolerance can fluctuate as a result of situational, individual and product-typical factors and is attribute-dependent.

Finally, when evaluating service quality, expectations are compared with perceived service delivery. According to Zeithaml *et al.* (1991) the difference between desired expectation level and the perceived delivery is the perceived service superiority, while the difference between adequate expectations and perceived delivery is the perceived service adequacy. The discrepancy between predicted offering and perceived delivery is supposed to determine the satisfaction of the product.

It is evident that the assessment of service quality by customers is a complex task. People do not always have the capacity, the motivation and the ability to make elaborate inferences and will try to escape from doing so. Neutral information seems to be helpful because of its comprehensive and objective nature.

The Role of Neutral Information

Table 1 shows that neutral non-personal information sources, Quality Marks (QM) and Consumer Reports (CR), are very suitable for judging products. A Quality Mark is a mark that appears on the label of a product which guarantees an often unspecified minimal quality for one or more product characteristic controlled by an independent institution (Box 1979). A Consumer Report is a special kind of market research carried out by an independent organisation that is responsible for the selection of the brands within a product class and that also determines the test procedure (Thorelli and Thorelli 1977).

Neutral non-personal information is well suited for consumers in judgemental situations as characterized by one or more of the following (Steenkamp 1989, Willenborg 1985, Wilkie 1990:

- the product is not often purchased;
- the product characteristics are difficult to evaluate;
- the customer has sufficient choice;
- the product is not guaranteed by legal procedures;
- the perceived interest or risk of the purchase is high.

In fact, this holds for most of the services!

It may be concluded that neutral non-personal information can play an important role in the deduction of service quality. From the client's point of view, the service characteristics ambiguity and insecurity are due to the intangibility of a service. The heuristic processing of neutral information may reduce this. Neutral non-personal product information requires less cognitive processing costs (Box 1979) and the structure and standardisation of this kind of information can be helpful.

Neutral non-personal product information also presents several advantages for the service provider. External and internal quality control is made possible because it is now possible to communicate what is to be expected from the service and its provider. The provider knows which attributes are being tested by the independent test organisation and are relevant for the client. Apart from this, a positive test evaluation will stimulate sales and justify higher price levels. Owing to the fragmented and diverse character of the service sector, Quality Marks offer more perspective than Consumer Reports.

As a means of arriving at an effective Quality Mark policy two related questions must be answered:

- From the clients' point of view, what are the requirements for a Quality Mark that will facilitate the quality evaluation of services?
- What are the demands for the service provider that will enable delivery of the service at the required level?

To answer these questions a distinction of quality dimensions has to be made. The quality dimensions differ substantially not only in case of judgment by the customer (search attributes versus experience and credence attributes), but also in controllability by service organizations and Quality Mark institution. By using an input-output continuum, the manageability of quality dimensions can be highlighted. In this perspective, input factors are dimensions that are easily managed because they are more or less objective and customer-independent. Output factors are dimensions that are more difficult to control. They are concerned with the interactive contact between provider and client and are therefore more difficult to manage.

Table 1.
Information criteria scores for types of product information,
according to Willenborg (1985) in reference to Weser (1980) and others

type of information	neutral			non-neutral		
	personal	non-personal		non-personal		personal
info. criteria	observation	CR	QM	mass advertising	brochures	word of mouth
completeness	−	+	?	−	−	−
factual	−	+	+	−	?	−
decision relevancy	+	+	?	+	?	+
structured	−	+	+	?	+	−
insightful	?	+	−	?	+	?
standardised	−	+	+	−	−	−
availability	+	−	+	+	+	+
market coverage	−	−	?	?	−	−
actual	+	?	+	+	+	−
emotional loading	+	−	−	+	+	+
+: is satisfied	CR: Consumer Report					
?: indistinctive	QM: Quality Mark					
−: is not satisfied						

The quality dimensions as provided by Parasuraman, Zeithaml and Berry (1985) can be classified along the input-output axis (see Figure 1).

Research Objective

Using the input and output quality continuum, the objective is to investigate which quality factors are tested and therefore guaranteed by the independent providers (institutions) of Quality Marks and which quality factors are used by customers. Secondly, the factors that are associated with two Quality Marks by customers are assessed. In addition, the actual usage of Quality Marks is examined. This procedure offers possibilities to evaluate the potential of Quality Marks for service quality management. Any differences in actual and perceived quality factors may lead to future changes in Quality Mark procedures or communication thereof.

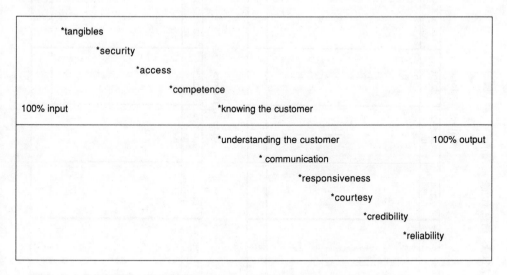

Figure 1. Quality factors along the input-output axis

Method

The assessment of objective, factual Quality Mark characteristics is made on the basis of procedural documents and information gathered from the Quality Mark providers. This factual information was then compared with information provided by a sample of N=200 consumers. The consumer study focused on two different Quality Marks. One Quality Mark, the Benelux hotel star classification, is only concerned with input factors. The other, the Michelin restaurant star classification, incorporates both input and output factors. The sample was randomly selected from the Dutch population. Following a telephone selection, a questionnaire was sent out to assess the following:

- awareness, knowledge and expectations of the quality factors (input and/or output) involved for different service Quality Marks;
- the usage of Quality Marks in the decision and buying process.

Table 2. Input and output quality factors controlled by Quality Marks in service sectors

Roest and Verhallen

Table 2. Input and output quality factors controlled by Quality Marks in service sectors

Business Sector	Quality Marks	Input factors				Output factors			
		tangibles	security	access	competence	communication	responsiveness	courtesy	reliability & credibility
Wholesale and Retail	"Top- en Keurslager" (butchery)	B	B	B	B		B	B	
	"Echte Bakker" (bakery)	B	B		B		B	B	
Hotels, Restaurants Bars	"Benelux hotel classification organization "Horeca""	I	I	I	I	I	I	I	I
	"ANWB hotel acknowledgement"	I	I	I	I	I	I	I	I
	"ANWB restaurant classification"	I	I	I	I	I		I	
	"ANWB restaurant acknowledgement"	I			I			I	B
	"Michelin (restaurants)"	B	B	B	B		I	B	I
	"KNAC (automobile)"								
	"Alliance Gastronomique Néerlandaise (restaurants)"	I	I		I	I	I	I	
	"Lekker '90 (restaurants)"	I			I				
	"Neerlands Dis (restaurants)"				I				
	"Tourist Menu (restaurants)"								
Repair and Service	"Bovag (car repair)"	B	B	B	B				B
	"ANWB acknowledgement"	I	I		I				

Business Sector	Quality Marks	Input factors				Output factors			
		tangibles	security	access	competence	communication	responsiveness	courtesy	reliability & credibility
Professional Service and Rental	"ANWB acknowledgement (bike rental)"		I						
	"Bovag (car rental)"	B	B		B				B
Culture, Sports and Recreation	"ANWB classification campings"	I	I		I				
	"ANWB acknowledgement campings"	I	I						
	"ANWB classification bungalows"	I			I				
	"ANWB acknowledgement group accommodations"	I							
	"ANWB acknowledgement yacht rental"	I						I	I
	ANWB acknowledgement horse sports"	I	I		I	I			
Other Services	"ANWB acknowledgement driving test"	I	I		B				I
	"Bovag driving test"	B	B		B	B			B

Results

The Quality Mark Characteristics Study

In order to be able to determine whether service Quality Marks are tested and controlled on the quality factors, the most important Quality Marks in services were selected across different business branches. Exploratory research showed that some of the eleven service quality factors were judged as being almost identical. "Credibility" and "reliability" were joined because the differences were small. The item "understanding the customer" was combined with "responsiveness" while "knowing the customer" was united with "competence". Thus, a total of eight quality factors were selected, four of them being input and four being output factors. The Quality Mark institutions were divided into independent institutions (I) and business sector organizations (B). In table 2, the input and output factors controlled by Quality Marks are given for the sectors: rental service; sports; hotels etc.

It is clear that most of the Quality Marks do not guarantee full service quality. Especially output factors are neglected in the selection and control processes.

In total, access is taken into account by 5 Quality Marks; competence by 21; security 18 and the fourth input factor "tangibles" by 23 Quality Marks. The output factors score respectively communication 6, courtesy 11, reliability and credibility 9 and responsiveness by 5 Quality Marks. The more objective input quality factors are most often taken into account by the Quality Marks institutions. The quality factors with respect to the interactive way in which service is delivered are less often covered.

Table 3. Information usage in hotel and restaurant selection (N=156)

information (source)	hotel choice in %	restaurant choice in %
Quality Mark stars	41	8
recommended by others	40	68
price list	38	33
own experience	29	78
external appearance	26	31
coincidence	22	24
advertisements	13	12
being arranged (e.g. work/ travel agency)	8	–
other information (including 3 other Q.M.)	8	3

The Customer Study

As previously discussed, this study focuses on two different Quality Marks: the Benelux hotel and the Michelin restaurant star classification. Table 3 shows what information and information sources are used in the decision process of buying hotel and restaurant services. Interesting here is that in buying hotel services, Quality Marks are the most frequently used indicators, followed by the recommendation of others. In selecting restaurants, Quality Marks are of minor importance. This can be explained by the vast experience customers have had in (local) restaurants and the availability of extrinsic cues such as external appearance and price lists. It is important to note that 68% of the customers claim that they use Quality Marks, among other information, in their decision processes when selecting appropriate hotels, restaurants and bars.

Quality Marks have a significant impact on customers in our selected area. Our study focuses on what they expect of Quality Marks and what is perceived to be controlled by the independent organizations and, therefore, guaranteed by the Quality Mark. Expectations based upon hotel and restaurant star classifications can be found in Table 4.

In particular, it is the hotel stars that are ambiguous: both "only input factors" and "input and output factors" are expected by a large proportion of customers. Benelux hotel stars are only concerned with some input quality factors, as can be verified in Table 2. People who are under the assumption that all quality factors are guaranteed at a given level may be disappointed in the Quality Mark but, more importantly, may also be disappointed in the service and its provider. The Michelin restaurant star classification seems to be better communicated.

Table 4. Expectations about controlled input and output factors of Quality Marks

expected quality factors	hotels in %	restaurants in %
only input factors	33	4
input and output factors	56	75
no clear expectation	11	21

Analysis of customer expectations concerning the eight quality factors in both Quality Marks are represented in Table 5. Both left columns give the percentage of customers that expected this quality factor for the two Quality Marks. The middle columns contain the actual quality factors included in the Quality Mark. The right columns show the misperceptions, including the difference between actual and expected quality factors. For both Quality Marks 3 out of 8 quality factors show a percentage of misperceptions above 50%, which means that the majority assessed wrong expectations concerning these quality factors. These factors are not the least important ones, as can be seen in Table 6.

Table 5. Quality factors attributed to hotel and restaurant stars Quality Marks

quality factors	Benelux hotel stars			Michelin restaurant stars		
	%	included	misperc	%	included	misperc
tangibles	78	yes	22%	67	yes	33%
security	68	in part	xxx	47	no	47%
responsiveness	55	no	55%	83	yes	17%
competence	50	yes	50%	93	yes	7%
access	46	yes	54%	36	no	36%
reliability	40	no	40%	41	yes	59%
courtesy	27	no	27%	45	yes	55%
communication	16	no	16%	19	yes	81%

In Table 6 the quality factors are given in order of importance as perceived by the customers.

Table 6. Expressed rank order importance of quality factors in hotels, restaurants and bars

order	quality dimension	input or output
1	responsiveness	output
2	competence	input
3	security	input
4	reliability	output
5	courtesy	output
6	tangibles	input
7	access	input
8	communication	output

Although responsiveness (as a representative of the interaction process) is the most important quality dimension in the selected service business sector, it is not included in the Benelux hotel stars or in most of the other service Quality Marks. Tangibles and courtesy are the service attributes most often tested but of minor importance to customers in this area.

When the respondents were asked whether Quality Marks should guarantee input and/or output factors, 76% preferred both while 17% had no explicit opinion on this matter.

Discussion

This chapter studies Quality Marks as a tool for managing service quality perceptions. Quality Marks offer excellent possibilities for guiding and forming quality expectations.

The unique characteristics of services result in quality perception problems for the service provider as well as the customer. Although inferential belief processing is perhaps the most commonly used method to form attribute perceptions, little research concerning this processing is available in the field of services. Besides this, controlling inferential perceptions is difficult because of individual relationships and associations. Informational beliefs circumvent this pitfall. In this perspective, neutral non-personal product information is interesting. From a theoretical point of view, Quality Marks provide suitable information on attribute levels. Research on the actual usage of Quality Marks in services could not be found. This study is an attempt bridging this gap in service literature. The results of our exploratory survey indicate that Quality Marks may be used in a variety of business sectors. There is, however, a lot of misperception and miscommunication. Especially Quality Marks that guarantee all relevant input and output quality factors are suitable for managing service quality.

Numerous implications for researchers interested in service Quality Marks have arisen as a result of the findings reported in this article. Some of the more intriguing research questions are:

- How can Quality Mark test criteria, especially the more intangible output factors, be quantified to make control feasible and payable? It is obvious that input factors are far more easy to control and test. This is perhaps the reason why most Quality Marks institutions concentrate on input factors. However, panel information or mystery shopper research information, for example, would help to form an impression of the output factors. These impressions can be compared with those from other service organizations to derive quality norms.
- What are the attribute expectation levels consumers hope or want to receive? Although the amount of Quality Marks will have to be reduced, more specific quality level information in Quality Marks seems to be advisable.

This research implicates that the independent Quality Mark institutions must carefully consider whether their Quality Mark must be (perceived to be) an overall (input and output) or a partial (input or output) 'guarantee' stimulus. The gap between what is guaranteed and what is perceived to be guaranteed must be closed. This can be achieved either by including the missing quality factors or by strictly communicating what is excluded. The importance attached to Quality Marks by customers in forming quality judgments justify the improvements to be made.

References

Bettman, J.R., *An Informational Processing Theory of Consumer Choice*, Addison-Wesley Publishing Company, Reading,1979.

Box, J.F., *Konsument en Informatie: De Rol van Vergelijkend Warenonderzoek*, Delftse Universitaire Pers, Delft, 1979.

Brown, S.W. and T.A. Swartz, A Gap Analysis of Professional Service Quality, *Journal of Marketing*, 53, April, 1989, pp. 92-98.

Cadotte, E.R., R.B. Woodruff and R.L. Jenkins, Expectations and Norms in Models of Consumer Satisfaction, *Journal of Marketing Reseach*, XXIV, August, 1987, pp. 305-314.

Carman, J.M., Consumer Perceptions of Service Quality: An Assessment of the Servqual Dimensions, *Journal of Retailing*, 66, Spring, 1990, pp. 33-55.

Crane, F.G. and S.M. DeYoung, Cue Management and Services Marketing, in H. Muhlbacher and C. Jochum (eds.), *Proceedings of the 19th Annual Conference of the European Marketing Academy*, Innsbruck, 1990, pp. 1587-1596.

Fishbein, M. and I. Ajzen, *Belief, Attitude, Intention and Behavior: An Introduction to Theory and Research*, Addison-Wesley Publishing Company, Reading, 1975.

Furse, D.H., G.N. Punj and D.W. Stewart, A Typology of Individual Search Strategies, Amon Purchasers of New Automobiles, *Journal of Consumer Research*, 10, 1984, pp. 417-431.

Garvin, D.A., Competing on the Eight Dimensions of Quality, *Harvard Business Review*, November/December 1987. pp. 101-109.

Grönroos, C., *Service Management and Marketing*, Lexington Books, Lexington, 1990.

Holbrook, M.B. and K.P. Corfman, Quality and Value in the Consumer Experience: Phaedrus Rides Again, in: J. Jacoby and J.C. Olson (eds.), *Perceived Quality*, Lexington Books, Lexington, 1985, pp. 31-57.

Jacobs, L. (1987), Kwaliteit, *Tijdschrift voor Inkoop & Logistiek*, 3, 1987, pp. 39-42.

Juran, J.M., *Quality Control Handbook*, McGraw-Hill Book Company, New York, 1984.

Kasper, H. and J. Lemmink, After Sales Service: Views Between Industrial Customers and Service Managers, *Industrial Marketing Management*, 18, 1989, pp. 199-208.

Kotler, P., *Marketing Management: Analyses, Planning, and Control*, Prentice Hall, Englewood Cliffs, 5th edition, 1984.

Levitt, Th., The Industrialisation of Service, *Harvard Business Review*, September/October 1976.

Levitt, Th., Marketing Intangible Products and Product Intangibles, *Harvard Business Review*, May/June, 1981, pp. 94-102.

Lovelock, C.H., Classifying Services to Gain Strategic Marketing Insight, *Journal of Marketing*, 47, 1983, pp. 9-20.

Miller, G.A., The Magical Number Seven, Plus or Minus Two: Some Limits in Our Capacity for Processing Information, *Psychological Review*, 18, 1956, pp. 81-91.

Monroe K.B. and R. Krishnan, The Effect of Price on Subjective Product Evaluations, in: J.Jacoby and J.C. Olson (eds.), *Perceived Quality*, Lexington Books, Lexington, 1985, pp. 209-232.

Morgan, L.A., The Importance of Quality, in: J. Jacoby and J.C. Olson (eds.), *Perceived Quality*, Lexington, Lexington Books, 1985, pp. 61-64.

Neijzen J.A. and M. Trompetter, *Kwaliteitszorg in dienstverlenende organisaties: De klant is Koning, Maar wie maakt er de dienst uit?*, Kluwer Bedrijfswetenschappen, Deventer, 1989.

Olson, J.C. and J. Jacoby, Cue Utilization in the Quality Perception Process, in: M. Venkatesan (ed.), *Proceedings 3rd Annual Conference of the Association for Consumer Research*, Association for Consumer Research, Iowa City, 1972, pp. 167-179.

Olson, J.C., Inferential Belief Formation in the Cue Utilisation Process, in: H.K. Hunt (ed.), *Advances in Consumer Research*, V, Association for Consumer Research, Ann Harbor, 1978, pp. 724-729.

Parasuraman, A., V.A. Zeithaml and L.L. Berry, A Conceptual Model of Service Quality and Its Implications for Future Research, *Journal of Marketing*, 49, Fall, 1985, pp. 41-50.

Parasuraman, A., L.L. Berry and V.A. Zeithaml, Understanding Customer Expectations of Service, *Sloan Management Review*, Spring, 1991, pp. 39-48.

Parasuraman, A., V.A. Zeithaml and L.L. Berry, Servqual: A Multiple-item scale for measuring consumer perceptions of Service Quality, *Journal of Retailing*, 64, Spring, 1988, pp. 12-40.

Porter, M.E., *Competitive Strategy: Techniques for Analyzing Industries and Competitors*, Free Press, New York, 1980.

Punj, G.N. and D.W. Stewart, An Interaction Framework of Consumer Decision Making, *Journal of Consumer Research*, 10, 1983, pp. 181-196.

Roest, H.C.A. and R.T. Frambach, Industrialisatie van dienstverlening als kwaliteitsbeheersingsinstrument, *Mark-it*, 1992. Also published as Service industrialization and its use in service quality management, 3rd. Workshop on quality management in services 1993, EIASM, Helsinki.

Roest, H.C.A. and F.L. Tijssen, Beheersing van het kwaliteitsperceptieproces bij diensten door middel van keurmerken, Research Memorandum FEW 499, Tilburg University, 1991.

Roest, H.C.A. and Th.M.M. Verhallen, Managing Service Quality Expectations by Quality Marks, Work in Progress, 21th Annual Conference of the European Marketing Academy, Aarhus, 192.

Schiffman, L.G. and L.L. Kanuk, *Consumer Behavior*, Prentice Hall, Englewood Cliffs, 3rd. edition, 1987.

Steenkamp, J.B.E.M., *Product Quality*, Van Gorcum, Assen/Maastricht, 1989.

Tettero, J. and J. Viehoff, Marketing voor dienstverlenende bedrijven, Kluwer Bedrijfswetenschappen, Deventer, 1987.

Thorelli, H.B. and S.V. Thorelli, *Consumer Information Systems and Consumer Policy*, Ballinger Publishing Company,Cambridge, 1977.

Uhl, K.P. and G.D. Upah, The Marketing of Services: Why and How is it Different?, *Research in Marketing*, 6, 1983, pp. 231-257.

Van Raaij, W.F., *Consumer Choice Behavior: An Information-Processing Approach*, Doctoral Dissertation, Tilburg University, 1977.

Van Raaij, W.F., Information Processing and Decision Making Cognitive Aspects of Economic Behavior, in: W.F. van Raaij, G.M. van Veldhoven and K.E. Warneryd (eds.), *Handbook of Economic Psychology*, Kluwer Academic Publishers, Dordrecht, 1988, pp. 74-106.

Verhallen, Th.M.M. and W.F. Van Raaij, How Consumers Trade Off Behavioral Costs and Benefits, *European Journal of Marketing*, 20, 3/4, 1986, pp. 19-33.

Weser, A., *Informative Warenkennzeichnungen, Eine Hilfe für die Kaufentscheidungen des Verbrauchers*. Verlag Eugen Ulmer, Stuttgart, 1980.

Wheatly, J.J and J.S.Y. Chiu, The Effects of Price, Store Image, and Product and Respondent Characteristics on Perceptions of Quality, *Journal of Marketing Research*, 14, 1977, pp. 181-186.

Wilkie, W.L., *Consumer Behavior*, John Wiley and Sons, New York, 2nd edition, 1990.

Willenborg, G.B.W., *Consumenten en Produktinformatie*, Research Report 29, SWOKA, Den Haag, 1985.

Zeithaml, V.A., Consumer Perceptions of Price, Quality and Value: A Means-End Model and Synthesis of Evidence, *Journal of Marketing*, 52, 1988, pp. 2-22.

Zeithaml, V.A., L.L. Berry and A. Parasuraman, Communication and Control Processes in the Delivery of Service Quality, *Journal of Marketing*, 52, April, 1988, pp. 35-48.

Zeithaml, V.A., L.L. Berry and A. Parasuraman, The Nature and Determinants of Customer Expectations of Service, Working Paper, Marketing Science Institute, Cambridge, 1991.

Zeithaml, V.A., A. Parasuraman and L.L. Berry, Problems and Strategies in Services Marketing, *Journal of Marketing*, 49, Spring, 1985, pp. 33-46.

Zeithaml, V.A., A. Parasuraman and L.L. Berry, *Delivering Quality Service: Balancing Consumer Perceptions and Expectations*, Free Press, New York, 1990.

6

The Impact of Cross-Cultural Dimensions on the Management of Service Quality

Audrey Gilmore and David Carson

Introduction

Recently, many ferry companies have been making considerable efforts to improve their services, and have adopted a more professional approach to catering for a variety of different customer segments. Until about ten years ago the essence of the service product on board ferries had been to provide a variety of extensive menus and silver-served meals. A variety of factors have contributed to a change in customers' expectations. Newer, faster ships, especially on relatively short routes, led to a need for 'faster' food if the majority of people on board were to be fed in transit. In addition, customer preferences were changing to favour lighter meals rather than the traditional three-course lunches or dinners.

Many ferries provide special services for different customer segments. For the business traveller, there are conference facilities and business class lounges providing fax and photocopying facilities, together with complimentary newspapers, tea, coffee and snacks. Other special services provided include motorist lounges with reserved seats in a relaxed atmosphere and snack meals and beverages, conveniently situated nearby for motorists and their passengers. Freight drivers are also specially catered for with their own separate lounges, waiter-served meals and a video lounge in which to relax during the journey. Many of the larger ferries have more spacious cabins, room service and minibar facilities. There are a variety of ways to 'while away' travelling time, including discos, casinos, gaming machines, duty-free shopping and a choice of sports facilities, gyms and saunas.

In the main, all or most of the entertainment and catering services described above are available on all northern European routes. Whilst these services may be generally similar the following question arises: are consumer expectations the same? Northern European countries are probably the most diverse group of countries within such a relatively small geographical area. In general, Scandinavians are perceived to be different from the French, Belgians and Dutch different from the Germans, and the English different from the Irish.

This paper addresses the issue of whether cultural differences affect customer responses to marketing activity on board by using a comparative study. United Kingdom-based car ferry companies are compared with Scandinavian-based car ferry companies in order to examine and compare British and Scandinavian passengers response to the variety of products and services offered on board these ferry operations.

Cultural Differences

Do cultural differences matter when marketing services such as catering and entertainment in ferry travel? Indeed, how does marketing cope with this concept of 'culture'? Doesenberry (1949) observed over forty years ago that all activities in which people engage are culturally determined and nearly all purchases and economic exchanges are undertaken either to provide physical comfort or to implement the activities that make up the life of a culture.

Culture is generally accepted by marketing theorists as one of the underlying determinants of consumer behaviour (Henry, 1976) and indeed it is cited as such in most of the standard marketing texts (Kotler, 1991; Pride and Ferrell, 1991). During the past twenty years there has been some discussion over the extent to which culture determines consumer behaviour. Some of these studies compare consumer behaviour in specific countries in relation to particular products, but there has been little development in providing a generalizable framework through which multi-country cultural differences can be appreciated. Whilst the studies reviewed for this article used a variety of research methods and were carried out in relation to specific products and/or markets they do present some insight into the impact of culture.

One of the most extensive studies reported to date was carried out by Hofstede (1984). His results were based on data from 40 countries which confirmed that there are quite large cross-cultural differences in the world in terms of attitudes towards work. Earlier studies reported differences between consumers in different countries in relation to various aspects of marketing activity such as locational convenience, importance of specials and coupons, and willingness to try new products (Green and Languard, 1975; Douglas, 1976).

Other studies indicate that there are certain elements which are similar across different nations which contribute to a similar pattern of customer behaviour. Hollander's (1970) study highlighted that richer nations were becoming more and more homogeneous and he concluded that the concept of good retailing should be independent of the country of operation. Consequently, some aspects of marketing activity could be replicated in different cultural areas. For example, advertising and promotional activity can be standardised for some products across different countries.

Conversely, Boddewyn and Hanson (1977) cite that differences in consumer tastes, habits and income for consumer goods are some of the most important obstacles to the standardisation of marketing strategies. However, Martinson (1987) reports that a completely standardised marketing programme must be seen more as an exception than a rule today.

Generally speaking, it is more difficult to standardise service levels across borders because multinational companies will compete with different firms in different markets. For example, competitors in Scandinavia are quite different from the competitors in the UK market both in the level of competition and in the quality of service offered by competitors. In addition, the differences in VAT taxes between countries and standards of living make it difficult to standardise prices.

Clearly the inference from this discussion is that consumers are likely to be subjected to different levels of service and customer care depending on the culture of the country in which they find themselves. Whilst cultural differences exist and are easily recognised, it is possible to overcome different cultural expectations by providing a high basic level of service regardless of country or culture supported by country-specific dimensions.

When these issues are considered in the context of quality in services marketing management then further dimensions come into play. The characteristics and varied aspects of delivering service quality need to be addressed by managers in the ferry service companies. A brief discussion and description of the Dimensions of Service Quality is given below.

Dimensions of Service Quality

The multidimensional nature of the quality construct is found in much of services marketing literature. Various studies (Grönroos 1982, Parasuraman, Zeithaml and Berry 1988; Carson and Gilmore 1990) identify and describe some dimensions of service quality. It is generally accepted that quality is about consistent conformance to customer expectations (Crosby 1979) and "fitness for purpose" (Juran 1988). Principally, customers have both instrumental and psychological expectations about a product or service performance (Swan and Combs 1976), where expectations relate to both quantifiable, hard data and qualitative, soft data. Hard data have been described as relating to performance and reliability standards or any tangible dimensions whereas soft data are those concerned with descriptions of and knowledge about customer feelings, perceptions and requirements (Smith 1987). These are more difficult to measure because they are intangible.

The important elements of this issue are brought together in a conceptual model of the Dimensions of Service Quality by Gilmore and Carson (1992) which has been adapted here for the on-board aspects of service delivery. The scope of these dimensions range from the hard, tangible relatively easy to measure and evaluate aspects, such as physical facilities and product range to the soft, intangible, more difficult to measure and evaluate aspects such as the staff interactions with customers. A focus on both tangible and intangible dimensions of marketing offerings is necessary in order to achieve a balanced approach to the delivery of the services marketing mix (Gilmore and Carson 1992).

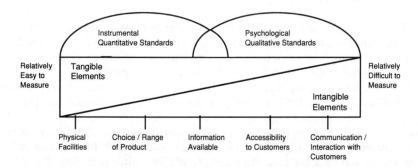

Figure 1. Dimensions of Service Quality

In order to provide a high basic level of service, ferry operators need to take account of both the tangible and intangible dimensions of service quality delivery. The ferry companies studied operate in market sectors which surround the whole of Northern Europe from Scandinavia, across Northern Europe countries to the UK and Ireland and these ferries offer a diverse range of services. With the harmonisation and standardisation philosophies arising out of the Single European Market the importance of service level and customer care is emphasised.

The experience of the researchers in this area suggests that a trans-European ferry traveller will be subjected to dramatic variances throughout different parts of Europe. The industry sector needs urgently to address the issues of assistance and advice to consumers across frontiers and to develop standard information and performance criteria to enable consumers to enjoy a common expectation of service.

The Comparative Study

This study was carried out in two stages. Stage one involved an in-depth study to identify the dimensions of service quality which had most significance to the car ferry service delivery. Stage two entailed a comparative study between UK and Scandinavian-operated ferries in relation to the dimensions of service quality delivery identified in the first stage. These two stages are described in more detail below.

Firstly, in order to develop an understanding of the quality in marketing dimensions involved in the delivery of a car ferry service a predominantly qualitative study was carried out. Qualitative methods were used to provide a rich portrait of the phenomena under study so that the researchers not only learn about the "inputs and outcomes but also gain an understanding of the texture, activities and processes" (Belk, Sherry and Wallendorf 1988) occurring in the day-to-day operations and activities.

Observations of the facilities on board and customer/staff interactions were carried out at the beginning of, during and at the end of each sailing. These were carried out by the two researchers at each location independently, and followed by extensive data recording. Additionally, focus group discussions with staff and customers were conducted initially to aid in the generation of constructs and eventually to analyse the company's quality in marketing activity.

Focus group discussions with customers and service staff were conducted in a non-directive and unstructured fashion (recommended by Calder 1977). For example, broad, open-ended questions were used and discussions centred around the experiences and expectations of customers, and the experiences and opinions of staff.

Extensive written transcripts of each focus group discussion was prepared by one researcher as the discussion was being conducted by the other. All focus groups were also recorded. The written transcripts supplemented by the audiotapes formed the basis for the development of the observation mechanism developed for further studies.

The data collection and analysis approach incorporated several recommended guidelines for theory construction through qualitative research (Belk *et al.* 1988, Thompson, Locander and Pollio 1989, Zeithaml, Berry and Parasuraman 1993). At the conclusion of each observation and focus group discussion the researchers informally discussed their impressions about the interview/observation to identify emerging themes for verification in subsequent groups for potential use. This practice is known as "memoing" and is well documented in Belk *et al.* 's study (1988).

The constructs and relationships identified in the ferry service delivery which were supported by consistent patterns of responses obtained from multiple focus group discussions and observations are embedded in the "Dimensions of Quality in Services Marketing" model.

The second stage of the research consisted of a comparative study of the quality and level of service on board together with observations of consumer responses and behaviour with regard to these services. This study was carried out on board a variety of UK and Scandinavian-operated ferries during May and June 1991.

The dimensions of service quality indicated on the model developed during stage 1 of this research were the focus of this comparative research study carried out in Stage 2. Consequently, observation studies were carried out in relation to:

1. Physical facilities and layout on board
   This included observations of the style of layout and spaciousness of ferry and how these contributed to the freedom or otherwise of passengers movement. The number of service outlets was also taken into account.

2. Choice and range of products/services available
   Observations focused on the range of food offered in the restaurants and cafeterias, the range of products in the on-board shops, the range of drinks in cafeterias and bars, and the range and scope of entertainment for each age group observed on board.

3. Information and advice available
   Visual and verbal communication and promotion to customers, tannoy announcements, guidance signs and information leaflets were all aspects of the information and advice observed on board.

4. Staff accessibility to customers
   This involved observing the presence of staff when they were required for delivering a service to customers in the various outlets on board such as the restaurants, cafeterias, bar and shops.

5. Staff communication and interaction with customers
   This included observing the courtesy and politeness shown, whether staff helped customers, and the competency of staff in carrying out their jobs.

6. Customer behaviour/response to the products/services offered
   Customer responses were observed in relation to all the on-board product and services offered such as their use of the restaurants, bars, entertainment facilities and the shops.

During each sailing observations were made in relation to these aspects of on board service delivery and recorded with descriptions and examples of occurrences. The monitoring of these observations was carried out at the beginning of, during and at the end of each sailing to take account of service consistency. The level of these offerings and activities were measured on a five-point schematic scale. A rating of 1 denoted the non-existence or a very low level of that element in evidence whereas a rating of 5 denoted a high level of such a circumstance. Figure 2 illustrates the average scores of the Scandinavian and the UK-operated sailings and the overall findings from this comparative study will be described briefly in relation to the aforementioned headings.

The Findings

The range of ratings scored by the Scandinavian and the UK-operated ferries are shown in Figure 2. These ratings are the sum averages of scores achieved in relation to all the aspects in the context of the key areas investigated. A brief description from this comparative study is given below.

Figure 2 illustrates two important aspects in relation to this comparative study. It shows that the variances between the levels of service quality on board the Scandinavian ferries are less than the variances on board the UK-operated ferries. This suggests that the quality of service delivery in Scandinavian ferries is more consistent and of a higher level than the UK ferry operators. Figure 2 highlights the levels of each aspect of service quality observed across both regions' ferry operations. The UK-operated ferries always indicate a lower level of service quality aspects than their Scandinavian counterparts.

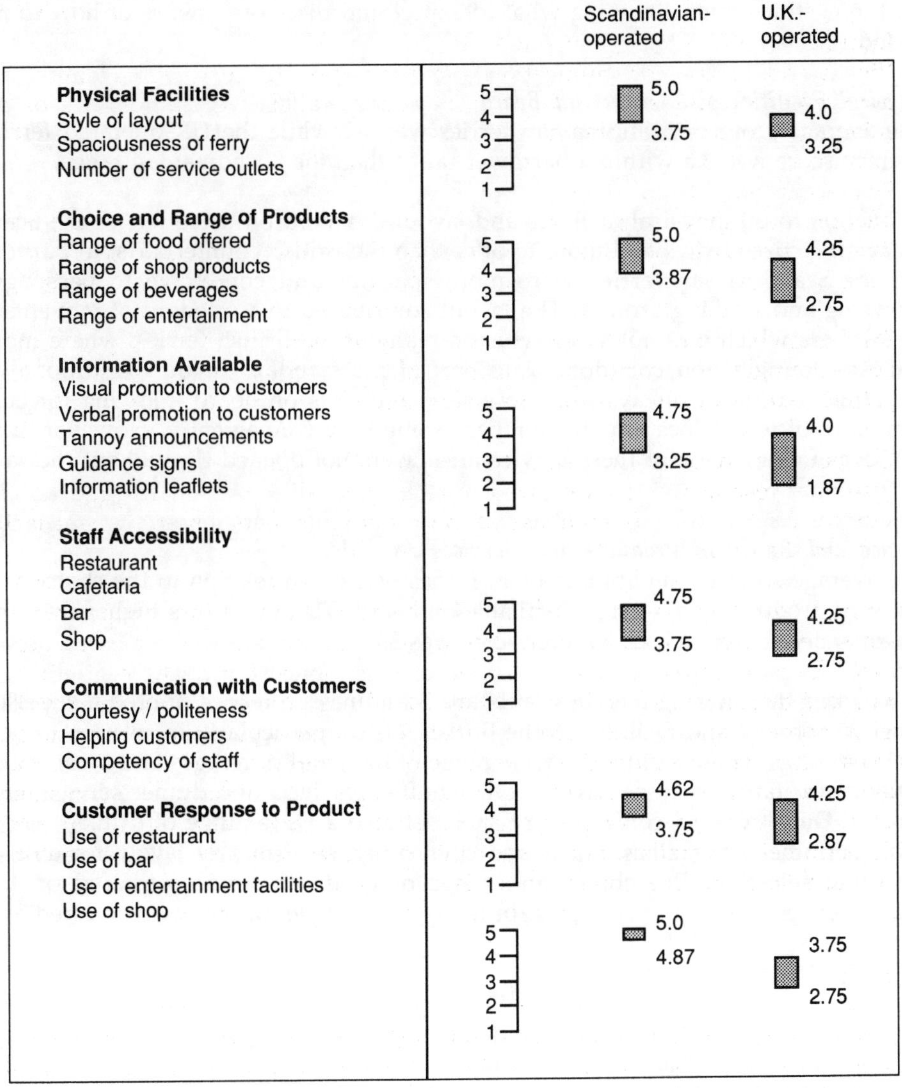

Figure 2. Comparison of average ratings between Scandinavian and UK-operated ferry services across dimensions of service quality

Taking account of both the variance and level of the average ratings illustrated in Figure 2 there is a considerable difference between the dimensions of service quality delivered on Scandinavian and UK-operated ferries. A smaller variance at the upper end of the scale observed on the Scandinavian ferries in relation to all service quality aspects, with the exception of information available, indicates a relatively high level of quality in service delivery. In contrast, a smaller variance at the bottom of the scale observed on the UK ferries in relation to the choice and range of products and customers response to these products indicates a poor level of quality in service delivery. Furthermore, a large variance in relation to any of the service quality aspects indicates an inconsistent service delivery, which may lead to customers not knowing what to expect and therefore unsure of how to respond.

Physical Facilities and Layout on Board
The average score of Scandinavian ferries was 4.2 while the UK-operated ferries average score was 3.5 within a narrower range than the Scandinavian range.

In relation to the physical facilities and layout observed on these ferries the Scandinavian ferries always had more to offer than the British counterparts. In particular, the Scandinavian ferries were more spacious and conducive to passenger browsing and walking around. The layout contributed to a freedom of movement atmosphere which was not so obvious on many of the British ferries, where more enclosed lounges and corridors were part of the standard layout. Additionally, Scandinavian ferries always had more service outlets on board allowing for customers in different locations to purchase something conveniently. However, in a number of cases some of these service areas were not opened throughout the sailing.

Choice and Range of Products and Services Available
The average score of the Scandinavian ferries was 4.3 in relation to the choice and range of products and services available on board. This score was higher than the UK-operated ferries, whose average score was 3.7.

In all cases the catering facilities on board Scandinavian ferries offered a superior range of services and facilities to the British ferries, particularly in relation to tangible offerings. These included a wide range of food and beverages and a variety of styles of operation such as silver service, buffet, cafeteria and dinner service with cabaret. Duty-free and confectionery shops offered a wide range of drinks, chocolates, perfumes, magazines, books and clothes in a supermarket layout for ease of customer selection. The choice and range of products/services offered on the British ferries were more restricted in terms of the style of operations offered and the range of goods in the shops.

Entertainment included cabaret, casino, gaming machines, discos and other leisure activities such as saunas and gyms on all Scandinavian routes. On the British routes entertainment offered less choice and usually consisted of gaming machines, a video film and sometimes a singing/musical group in the bar.

Information and guidance available
The average score for Scandinavian ferries was 4.0 while the UK ferries average score was 2.5.

Generally, Scandinavian ferry companies provided more formal information, which was given to the customer at the terminal. For example, leaflets, brochures, newsletters were given out at the terminal while customers waited to board, giving customers the opportunity to familiarise themselves with the ferry prior to boarding. In some cases large screens and pictures were used to highlight the main attractions of the ferry and stimulate customer interest.

On board, the visual displays, menus and promotional posters and literature were used throughout the ferry interior with each area using additional promotional material to highlight some selling opportunities for other areas and consequently stimulate customer interest in other service and products offered.

This contrasted strongly with the experience on UK-based ferries. Most ferries services did not provide any pre-boarding material to stimulate customer interest. Any on-board promotional material usually referred to the duty-free shop only - with little emphasis given to stimulating customers to use the restaurant or bar areas. Most menu displays were quite standard lists of dishes available with no pictures or displays of 'the eating concept' as experienced in the Scandinavian ferries.

Staff accessibility to customers
Scandinavian ferries average score was 4.1 for staff accessibility to customers while the UK-operated ferries average score was 3.8.

Although the degree of accessibility to staff was relatively similar across all sailings there were two UK-operated sailings which were particularly poor at maintaining accessibility to staff throughout the entire sailing.

In addition, the degree of customer accessibility to the services and staff experienced varied considerably throughout the sailing time on both Scandinavian and British routes. On some sailings there were no sales points open before leaving port at all and in some cases these did not open until 15 minutes after sailing had commenced. On other sailings there was some difficulty getting access or attention from staff even when facilities were officially open. All routes observed had this problem to some degree.

Staff Interaction with Customers
The Scandinavian-operated sailings average score was 4.2. Again, this was higher than the UK average score of 3.7.

There was a notable difference between the Scandinavian crews and British crews in the level of professionalism shown. The Scandinavian crews were obviously professional and well trained in relation to the functional aspects of their jobs. However, this professional efficiency sometimes generated an aloofness to customers.

In most cases customer announcements made using the tannoy system were neither friendly or stimulating. Most tannoy announcements were short, 'curt', and not particularly informative. All were delivered in the third person. In some cases when announcements were given in two languages, one language was spoken very badly resulting in customers not understanding what was said. Additionally, many tannoy systems used delivered a very poor sound production.

In general, most of the Scandinavian and British crews were courteous and polite to their customers and appeared to be relatively competent and knowledgeable about their jobs. Although most staff were helpful when customers approached them with a problem they were predominantly reactive rather than proactive in their customer interactions. On most occasions customers had to make the initial approach to staff before there was any staff communication. One of the British routes scored the lowest rating in the staff/customer interactions. On this route staff did not show any willingness to help customers, ignored customers as much as possible and did not try to resolve customers queries or problems to their satisfaction. Staff on these sailings chose the easiest option open to them when customers came to them with a query.

Customer Behaviour and Response to the Services Offered
There was a considerable difference in the average scores of the Scandinavian and UK-operated ferries in relation to customer behaviour and response to services offered on board. The average score was 4.6 for the Scandinavian routes while the UK-operated routes average score was 3.1.

There was a very obvious difference between British and Scandinavian customer behaviour and expectations in relation to ferry travel. The Scandinavian passengers appeared to perceive ferry travel as a leisurely way to travel. Most passengers were familiar with the ferry service and arrived punctually at the terminal for boarding. Cars arrived to join the queue for boarding at least half an hour before the sailing time, as requested by the company. All passengers appeared to come on board with preconceived expectations as they knew where to go and where everything was positioned on the ferry. This was apparent in the way most passengers queued for the à la carte restaurant and cabaret as soon as they boarded. The general pattern of behaviour was that the majority of people used all or most of the facilities and services on board. Consequently, they proactively sought leisure and entertainment and the only requirement from staff was that they were available to give the customer the products and services they needed. There was little need for customer stimulation by proactive behaviour of staff.

In contrast, there was less evidence of the same sense of enjoyment with British ferry passengers. On most routes cars did not arrive so punctually for boarding. Some did not arrive until twenty minutes before sailing although requested to turn up one hour beforehand. The majority of passengers arrived on board, had a look around and quickly established a territory by finding a seat and spreading their baggage around them. They usually did not leave their seat except for short periods, leaving something there to reserve that seat for their return. Some passengers brought packed meals and drinks on board with them, others bought from the shop or the duty-free and consumed these products on board. There was almost an unwillingness to spend money on board in many cases, with the exception of tax-free purchases. Unlike the Scandinavian passengers, who came on board obviously wanting to enjoy themselves, the general behaviour on board was one of passivity, with no desire to be disturbed.

Variances in Customer Responses and Behaviour

This would imply that in the UK ferry travel has a low market perception and is thought to be just a 'means to an end'. This may be seen to be the case particularly for motorists who want to take the car or a lot of baggage with them when they travel.

In contrast, ferry travel appears to be a way of life in Scandinavia. The geography of the country with its promontories and islands inspired a long tradition and culture in the use of ferries to visit friends and relatives on a regular basis. This means of travel is obviously enjoyed by Scandinavians, who participate in all the activity and facilities available on board. This appreciation and demand for ferry travel has encouraged many Scandinavian ferry companies to develop the 'cruise ferry' concept where people purchase non-landing tickets just to wine and dine and be entertained on board. As such, the cruise ferry is a stand-alone product.

Most ferry operators monitor the 'average passenger spend' (APS) on each ferry route by dividing the total amount spent on each sailing by the number of passengers on board. During this study the Scandinavian APS was always considerably higher than the UK-based company's APS. Sales in the Scandinavian duty-free shops in particular far exceeded UK sales, and sales in other areas such as the restaurants and bars also exceeded UK sales.

The Implications for Quality Management

There are clearly some problems in transferring a product which is acceptable in Scandinavia to the UK because of the different traditions and culture. However, this is not a new problem in international marketing as discussed earlier in this paper. Many companies have discovered that some aspects of marketing activity need to be tailored to suit specific markets.

Ferry companies clearly need to educate and stimulate potential customers to experience their new products/services through marketing activity aimed at these specific markets. In addition to proactive and stimulating advertising and promotional activity it will be vital to encourage and develop all the employees who operate this service to be more customer-oriented.

Any marketing programme and activity will need to take account of the traditional and cultural differences. The importance of customer/staff interactions should not be overlooked. This is a predominantly services operation where the entire company/customer interface is controlled and managed by individual staff who have an important role to play in proactively communicating and tailoring the service product to suit the customer. This will mean adopting a very proactive approach to the delivery of all their marketing activity where all staff communicate and initiate customer involvement and participation in the service. Clearly, all crews will need to be more proactive in their customer interactions in order to stimulate sales and encourage customers to use and enjoy all the facilities on board. More participation and involvement by staff in the delivery of the service through proactive communication with customers will provide them with a natural feedback on customer perceptions and requirements.

Together with attention to detail in all of the merchandising and point of sale activity, this should have a positive impact on the demand for products and services on board. Scandinavian ferry companies already offer a wide choice and range of products/services on Scandinavian routes. These could be adopted and tailored to suit the UK markets.

This adaptation must take account first and foremost of the cultural situation specific of a travel route. Thus, whilst basic services such as restaurant style, cinema, entertainment may be the same in the tangible sense, the intangible aspects of these services must be adapted to suit the route. Therefore, on the Scandinavian routes smorgasbords and saunas will be expected, on UK/Northern Europe routes duty-free and fast food will be required, and on the Irish/Welsh/Scottish routes there will be a preference for traditional fare, music and entertainment. That is to say, each route should have a clear element of autonomy within a broad corporate philosophy of customer service. By adopting this approach traditional ferry companies can introduce a 'cruise' concept without having to change the culture of the local traveller.

References

Belk, R.W., J.F. Sherry and M. Wallendorf, A Naturalistic Inquiry into Buyer and Seller Behaviour at a Swap Meet, *Journal of Consumer Research*, 14, March, 1988, pp. 449-470.

Boddewyn, J.J. and D.M. Hanson, American Marketing in the European Common Market 1963-1977. *European Journal of Marketing* (March), 11, 7, 1977.

Calder, B.J., Focus Groups and the Nature of Qualitative Marketing Research. *Journal of Marketing Research*, 14, August, 1977, pp. 353-364.

Carson, D. and A. Gilmore, Customer Care: The Neglected Domain, *Irish Marketing Review*, 4, 3, 1989/90, pp. 49- 61.

Crosby, P., *Quality is free. The Art of Making Quality*. McGraw-Hill Books, 1979.

Doesenberry, J.S., Income Saving and the Theory of Consumer Behaviour, *Harvard University Press*, Cambridge, MA, 1949.

Douglas, S.P., Cross-National Comparisons of Consumer Stereotypes: A Case Study of Working and Non-Working Wives in the U.S. and France, *Journal of Consumer Research*, June, 1976.

Gilmore, A and D. Carson, A Model of Quality Improvement in Services Marketing, European Institute for Advanced Studies in Management Workshop on Quality Management in Services 2, Maastricht, May, 1992.

Green, R.T. and E. Languard, A Cross-National Comparison of Consumer Habits and Innovator Characteristics, *Journal of Marketing*, July, 1975.

Gronroos, C., A Service Quality Model and its Marketing Implications, *European Journal of Marketing*, 18, 4, 1982, pp. 36-44.

Henry, W.A.,Cultural Values do Correlate with Consumer Behaviour, *Journal of Marketing Research*, 13, May, 1976, pp. 121-7.

Hofstede, G., *Culture's Consequences*. Sage Publications, Beverly Hills, 1984.

Hollander, S.C., Multinational Retailing, *MSU International Business and Economic Studies*, Michigan State University, East Lansing, 1970.

Juran, J.M.,*Juran on Planning for Quality*. The Free Press, New York, 1988.

Kotler, P., *Marketing Management. Analysis, Planning, Implementation and Control*, Prentice Hall. 7th Ed., 1991

Martinson, R., Is Standardisation of Marketing Feasible in Culture-bound Industries? A European Case Study, *International Marketing Review*, Autumn, 1987.

Parasuraman, A., V. Zeithaml and L. Berry, Serv-Qual: A Multiple-Item Scale for Measuring Consumer Perceptions of Service Quality, *Journal of Retailing*, 64, Spring, 1988, pp. 12-40.

Pride, W.M. and O.C. Ferrel, *Marketing. Concepts and Strategies*, Houghton Mifflin Company. 7th Ed., 1991.

Smith, S., How to Quantify Quality, *Management Today*, October, 1987, pp. 86-88.

Swan, J.E and Combs, L.J., Product Performance and Customer Satisfaction, *Journal of Marketing*, 40, April, 1976, pp. 25-33.

Thompson, C.J., W.B. Locander and H.R. Pollio, Putting Customer Experience back into Customer Research: The Philosophy and Method of Existential Phenemonology, *Journal of Consumer Research*, Vol. 16, September, 1989, pp. 133-146.

Zeithaml, V.A., L.L. Berry and A. Parasuraman, The Nature and Determinants of Customer Expectations of Service, *Journal of the Academy of Marketing Science*, 21, 1, 1993, pp. 1-12.

7

Managing Service Recovery

Colin G. Armistead, Graham Clark and Paula Stanley

Introduction

In service organisations the link has been made between customer retention over a period of time and profitability based on the assumption that the costs of maintaining customers are lower than the costs of recruiting new customers, and that there are further opportunities to sell additional services to the retained customer base and gain from their word-of-mouth advertising (Heskett, Sasser and Hart 1990). Heskett (1992) has developed a proposition from the findings of customer retention that customer retention links to customer satisfaction. This assertion is supported by the work of Technical Assistance Research Programme Inc. TARP (Lash 1989) who have demonstrated for a range of service organisations that the propensity to re-purchase (i.e., to be retained) is linked to customer satisfaction.

The question arises as to what leads to customer satisfaction. The common-sense supposition that a positive outcome of service is linked to the matching of expectation and experience of the service provision has been demonstrated quantitatively in the use of the SERVQUAL approach of Parasuraman, Zeithaml and Berry (1988). However, the expression of satisfaction is linked not only to the provision of fault-free service, but also to what happens when things go wrong. Hart, Heskett and Sasser (1990), Zemke (1991) and Zemke and Bell (1990) argue that service recovery (i.e., the ability to put things right for the customer in a meaningful way when they go wrong) is an important element in customer satisfaction. Again, the work of TARP would lend support to the argument; they demonstrate that customer satisfaction and willingness of customers to stay with the service provider are strongly associated with the way in which complaints are dealt with. Poor resolution of complaints or a perception on the part of the customer of being mollified leads to greater ill feeling towards the service provider than if no complaint had been made.

In the literature there is no consideration of differences which might arise in business to business and business to consumer service provision, in both the need for service recovery and the way in which service recovery is triggered and carried out.

Another strand to the argument of what makes for customer satisfaction comes from a consideration of service guarantees and services pledges. Hart (1988) and Hart, Schlesinger and Maher (1992) argue the case for unconditional guarantees as a powerful way of gaining customer satisfaction by in effect saying "we will meet all of your expectations". It is acknowledged by these authors that while the benefits to customers of unconditional guarantees which are meaningful may be self-evident, there are clearly risks associated with the cost of delivering on the promise.

The Service Profit Chain

The picture emerges of a chain of activities which are linked. Heskett (1992) refers to this as the chain of profitability. Customer retention results from customer satisfaction which is itself a consequence of unconditional guarantees (if offered) and the ability to recover when things go wrong. It is perhaps a reasonable proposition that if a service organisation is able to offer meaningful service guarantees without 'giving away the shop', it should be capable of delivering consistent service for 80 - 90% of service encounters and only have to put things right either through recovery or delivering the guarantee in the remaining 10%. It has been argued elsewhere (Armistead and Clark 1992) that the ability to recover is linked in part to the adoption of 'coping' strategies in managing capacity. Consistency of service delivery will arise from designing delivery systems with capable structures, processes, people, and systems and having effective operational control in the areas of quality management, capacity management, and resource productivity management. The resulting chain to customer retention is shown in Figure 1.

The Role of Empowerment

The writers (Hart *et al.* 1990) on service recovery suggest that the empowerment of front-line staff is an important element in the ability to recover. The case for empowerment has been discussed by Bowen and Lawler (1992). These authors consider that employees are empowered "if they:

- get information about organisational performance;
- are rewarded for contributing to organisational performance;
- have the knowledge and skills to understand and contribute to organisational performance;
- have the power to make decisions that influence organisational direction and performance."

journal

Other authors (Thomas and Velthouse 1990) have discussed in detail the relationship of empowerment to what they describe as the "intrinsic task motivation" linking empowerment with motivation to successfully complete a task. The task for service providers is associated with four elements:

- *impact*, i.e., the degree to which what the individual does is seen as making a difference;
- *competence*, i.e., the extent to which an individual can perform a task with confidence that the result will be satisfactory;
- *meaningfulness*, i.e., the extent to which the task of the individual leads to commitment and involvement rather than apathy and feelings of detachment;
- *choice*, i.e., the extent to which the individual can determine what is done and when it is done.

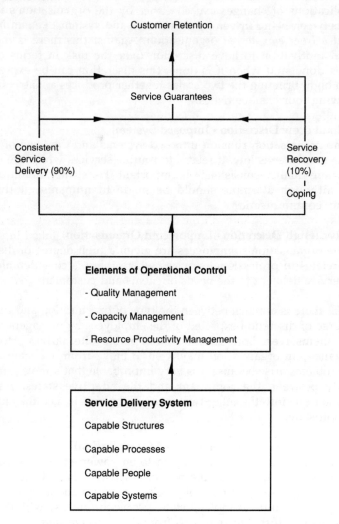

Figure 1. The Chain to Customer Retention

In the context of service delivery and service recovery the task is managing the service encounter and effecting service recovery.

Alpander (1991) has suggested that empowerment is concerned with meeting the needs of individuals in five areas that are relevant to the work situation. These are economic security, a sense of belonging, recognition, control and self-worth. Alpander's research indicated that *need to control* was the highest need.

These expressions of empowerment around the task of the individual suggest the importance of the individual's perception of empowerment rather than any intent on the part of an organisation to be an empowered organisation. Recognition of this potential inconsistency between the organisation's intent and the individual's needs and motivation has led us to propose the following model for considering the implications of changes caused either by the organisation's movement along a scale between being driven by procedures and systems, i.e., an *imposed* organisation and a freer *empowered* organisation. Against this there is the individual's need and motivation to have discretion over the task in terms of what is done, how it is done, and when it is done; this discretion can be expressed on a scale of low to high. Bringing the two scales together produces a matrix in Figure 2 with the following four characteristics:

Case 1: Compliant (Low Discretion - Imposed System)
In this case, the organisation runs on imposed systems and the level of discretion expected of the employee is low. It relates to routine services which are often cost-sensitive or where quality consistency is important. Here, the system drives service delivery although attempts should be made to humanise it through involvement and communication.

Case 2: Adaptive (High Discretion - Empowered Organisation)
In this case, the organisation's employees are given a high degree of discretion in their roles. It relates to professional services where there is considerable freedom to shape the service delivery to the needs of clients and customers.

In cases 1 and 2 there is a match between the type of organisation and the expectation of the degree of discretion expected of the employees by managers and by the employees of themselves. Both cases are acceptable alternatives. However, in some circumstances an organisation may wish to move from one state to another and here the problems arise because it is very improbable that a move can be made instantaneously between the compliant and the adaptive states. Instead any movement tends to be into the other two boxes in the matrix, i.e., the anxiety state or the frustration state.

Case 3: Anxiety (Low Discretion - Empowered Organisation)
In this case, the organisation may be seeking to empower employees but the perception, either real or imagined, on the part of employees is that they have a low level of discretion. This leads to people feeling anxious about their role. If the movement has been from the compliant state, people are uneasy with the lack of a strong guiding system. If the movement is from the adaptive state, people are confused by the loss of discretion.

Case 4: Frustration (High Discretion - Imposed Systems)
In this case, employees are frustrated by the constraints imposed by the systems when there is the expectation of a high degree of discretion. This is especially true when there is movement from the *adaptive* box into the *frustration* box or when employees are told and trained to have greater discretion but find that formal systems still constrain and dictate what happens.

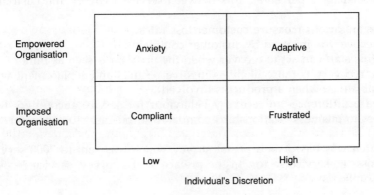

Figure 2. Empowerment matrix

A proposition is that any movement from either empowered to imposed by an organisation will lead to frustration or anxiety in some or all of its employees.

The model has implications for service recovery performed by front-line service staff and would lead to the propositions that:

Proposition 1: In the *compliant* state service recovery could only be delivered successfully within clear guidelines on what employees could do and when.

Proposition 2: In the *adaptive* state service recovery relies on individuals responding to the needs of customers with the assurance that the organisation will support their actions.

Proposition 3: In the *anxiety* or *frustration* states it is unlikely that service recovery could be successfully achieved.

Research Questions and Methodology

The present study investigated service recovery across a range of organisations in the service sector. The aims of the study were to find out:

- The perception of managers of the importance of service recovery to maintaining customer satisfaction;
- The actions being taken to build recovery into the service delivery system;
- How recovery is triggered, either by formal measurement systems or by informal means.

Research Propositions

In association with the research questions a number of propositions were established on the basis of the literature and anecdotal dealings with service organisations.

1. Service managers perceive a link between service recovery and customer retention.
2. Few organisations measure customer loss rates.
3. Most recovery is initiated by customer complaint.
4. Front-line staff can act to recover when the problem is seen as minor.
5. Service recovery is more likely to involve refunds and replacement where this is possible (i.e., when a product is involved).
6. There are differences in recovery behaviour for service encounters which are business-to-business relationships compared to business-to-consumer.

The research was based on a postal survey which was sent to 2000 service managers across the service sector. In the preface to the survey, service recovery was defined as follows:

> "It is said that one of the marks of a good service organisation is the ability to recover effectively from problems and mistakes.
>
> We define 'recovery' as specific actions required to ensure that the customer receives a reasonable level of service after problems have occurred to disrupt 'normal' service. These problems may be a direct result of problems or errors in the service organisation itself, or may be to some extent outside its control. These may be customer-induced or the result of the actions of other associated organisations. The three groups of situations requiring recovery are illustrated below, using the example of an airline:
>
> Service Provider Error: The airline fails to have aircraft ready on time or loses luggage in transit.
>
> Customer Error: A customer forgets his or her passport or fails to meet the check-in time.
>
> Associated Organisation Error: Immigration is overloaded, or air-traffic controllers are on strike.
>
> Many service organisations are able to tell stories about specific occasions when employees have worked exceptionally hard, beyond the call of duty to keep customers happy. The problem is that these examples of exceptional service may not be the norm, customers experiencing on average rather more indifferent service.
>
> We are interested in your organisation's experience of the following:
>
> a. Avoiding the need for recovery by "doing it right first time".
>
> b. Developing techniques and procedures for dealing with problems.
>
> c. Changing attitudes throughout the organisation to increase the degree of responsiveness of employees to customer needs.
>
> d. Establishing the importance of recovery to the customers' perception of the service you provide."

The survey instrument contained a mix of open-ended and specific questions.

Results

Replies were received from 157 managers with a distribution across the service sector as shown in Table 1. The category Customer Service includes service activities associated with manufacturing organisations. One of the reasons for a relatively low response rate might be that some manufacturing organisations do not recognise the Service aspects of their task.

Table 1. Spread of respondents

Sector	Percentage
Professional Services	17.5
Banking and Finance	9.5
Retail and Hotels	8.0
Customer Service	48.9
Distribution	9.5
Public Sector	6.6

Respondents were asked to indicate the importance of service recovery to their business on a scale of not important (1) to vital (5). The weighted result of 4.5 indicates the strength of the perceived importance.

Respondents were asked the extent to which they linked service recovery and customer retention. The responses were not quantified but fell into the following categories:

- "We perceive that there is a strong link"
- "It is difficult to prove the link"
- "We are trying to measure the link"
- "There was no link!"

An attempt was made to explore the extent to which the respondents measured either the cost of a lost customer or make measurements of customer retention. The cost of a lost customer was claimed to be measured by 40% of respondents. However, the way in which measurement occurs was in most cases on the basis of the perception of lost business rather than detailed measurement. There was only one respondent who has a system for tracking customer satisfaction.

Only 43% of respondents measure customer retention with repeat business or renewal of service contracts or market research information being the indicators of retention. There was no clear evidence of service organisations tracking the retention of specific customers over a period of years.

Respondents were asked to identify the need for recovery in a typical operating unit. The replies are shown in Table 2.

Table 2.   Frequency of the need for recovery in a typical operating unit

Timing	% of Sample
Continuously	25.6
Daily	19.5
Weekly	13.4
Fortnightly	7.3
Monthly	6.1
Quarterly	6.1
Every two years	1.2
Not known	20.7

Respondents were asked to state the factor which caused the need for service recovery on a scale between "it never occurs" (1) and "very frequently" (5). The results are shown in Table 3.

Table 3.   Most common causes of problems

Cause	Weighting 1-5
Customers	3.2
Other service organisations	3.0
Front-line staff	3.3
Information system faults	3.0
Equipment faults	2.9
Back-room support	3.0
Communication	3.5

The means by which a judgement of the causes was made was either on the basis of the perception of managers (64% of replies) or measurement (44% of replies). There was no attempt to reconcile which factors were assessed by measurement and which by perception.

Respondents were asked the extent to which service recovery was initiated by staff or management monitoring, formal measuring systems, customer complaints, or on the initiative of front-line staff. The extent of the responses was on a scale of "it never occurs" (1) to "very frequently" (5). The results are shown in Table 4. Perhaps not surprisingly, customer complaint was the most frequent trigger for recovery.

Table 4.   How service recovery is triggered

Action	Weighting 1-5
Staff/management monitoring	3.5
Formal measurement systems	3.0
Customer complaint	4.1
Front-line initiative	3.5

Respondents were asked how quickly they needed to initiate service recovery. The results were within minutes for 30% of respondents, within hours for 46% of respondents, and within days for 24% of respondents. Associated with time to initiate recovery is the time to complete service recovery. Respondents reported times within minutes (13% of replies), within hours (35% of replies), within days (44% of replies). Only 47% of respondents reported having escalation procedures for service recovery (for when front-line staff need assistance).

Respondents were asked the extent to which front-line staff take extraordinary action to resolve problems when there is a minor problem, a major problem, and when the problem is clearly caused by the customer on a scale between never (1) and always (5). The results are shown in Table 5. There is a greater tendency for front-line staff to deal with minor problems and to seek additional advice or support for major problems.

Table 5.   The extent to which front-line staff take action to solve problems

Problem type	Weighting
When there is a minor problem	4.4
When there is a major problem	3.5
When the customer has caused the problem	3.9

Respondents were asked to identify if they were empowering staff; 75% claimed to be doing so. Critical factors in the process of empowerment included: training, support, communication and information availability, delegation and partnership.

As recovery is often associated with a spend on resources the authority given to front-line staff to spend up to a given amount may be important. Respondents were asked the extent of this authority given to front-line staff and the results are shown in Table 6.

Table 6.   Extent of authority of front-line staff

Extent	% of Sample
Nil	27.4
Less than £50	12.4
Less than £100	6.2
Over £100	49.6
No Limit	4.4

The value of the spend allowed to front-line staff as a percentage of the average customer spend is shown in Table 7.

Table 7.   Value of average customer spend front-line staff can use for recovery

Value	% of Sample
Less than 25%	61
25% to 50%	6
50% to 75%	4
More than 75%	29

The actions taken to recover can be grouped in the categories of replacement (particularly if a product is involved), financial reparation or other gifts, refunds, or reparation and refunds. It was not possible from the survey data to establish the extent to which each was viewed as the most important. However, there are some indications that replacement was the more likely mode of recovery when a product is part of the service package; if not some reparation and partial refund was preferred. Full refunds or financial reparation are the less likely actions.

When recovery is clearly initiated by customer complaints the following comments summarise the statements given by respondents:

- there is little evidence of statements which indicate finding out exactly what customers want;

- there were few statements of offering apologies to customers;

- there is recognition of the need to respond honestly and with a personal contact which may involve more senior staff if the problem is perceived to be major;

- refunds and doing work free of charge where appropriate are common approaches;

- relating to recovery more generally, some respondents made the point of the need to balance recompense and resolution of problems.

Finally, respondents were asked to reflect on the future importance of service recovery. Some saw it becoming more important especially with respect to increasing the speed of response. Others talked of quality programmes removing the need for service recovery through a right-first-time approach.

Discussion and Analysis

The results from the survey go some way to providing answers to the questions raised earlier. Service managers do perceive that service recovery is important to their business and many feel there is a link with customer retention. However, others would maintain that there is no link or that it is difficult to measure. The issue of measurement corresponds with the lack of evidence of many service organisations having formal methods of measuring customer retention, and no stated cases from the sample of measuring customer perceptions of service recovery as an indicator of customer retention.

The need to recover can be caused by many different factors associated with service delivery by front-line staff and no one factor emerged as significantly more prone to cause things to go wrong. The ability of managers to give a view of causes on the basis of measurement rather than perception was encouragingly high, suggesting that many have formal measurement of when things go wrong. This is substantiated by the responses to the question on their need to recover: 80% of the respondents were able to identify the frequency. The 20% who claimed not to know how often recovery occurs may be delivering highly consistent service or more likely, may be in a constant state of recovery.

The ways in which service recovery is initiated tends to be a result of customers complaining rather than by the action of staff and management. If service firms were to be more proactive in anticipating when recovery is necessary, future surveys of this type would perhaps see a greater emphasis on front-line initiative or formal measuring systems.

What happens when service recovery occurs depends on whether it is perceived by the front-line staff to be a minor or a major problem. This is not surprising, although it would be interesting to know more about how front-line staff make a decision to deal with the matter themselves or to call for assistance. What would have been expected would be that in all cases front-line staff start the process of recovery, if only by acknowledging the fact either to colleagues or supervisors or customers. The fact that only 30% of respondents said that recovery is started within minutes is disturbing, if this is a true reflection of what happens.

The extent of the authority given to front-line staff to make reparation, give refunds of replacements, or financial gifts, and the value related to the cost of the service shows two zones. Over 50% of the sample reported that front-line staff have the authority to spend over £100 and about 30% say that this amounts to more than 75% of the value of the service. This suggests that for 30% front-line staff are providing a straight replacement or refund for a product and or service as the means of recovery.

Some of the responses appear to blame front-line staff for lack of responsiveness. It would be interesting to repeat this research from the perspective of the employee rather than that of the manager.

For the 25% of respondents who give no authority to front-line staff to spend to recover, it suggests either that they must refer all cases to managers or other groups, or that the respondents were only considering the authority to spend money rather than to consume resources in the service recovery process.

Business-to-Business versus Business-to-Consumer

The business-to-business relationship is likely to be different to the business-to-consumer. In business-to-business relationships the buyer and user are often different individuals or groups and the overall value of services bought are greater. The consequence is that the expectations of service delivery and the need for recovery may be different.

The sample was split into two categories, business-to-business and business-to-consumer, using data on the nature of their business. Separate analyses for each group were undertaken.

The results showed significant differences in some areas for the sample. The business-to-consumer firms are more likely to be part of a network rather than single site and consequently employ more staff. They are more likely to need to recover on a continuous or daily basis or not know how frequently. In consequence, they are more likely to initiate service recovery within minutes rather than waiting the hours that business-to-business service firms do. Also, business-to-consumer firms are more likely to authorise front-line staff to spend more than 50% of the value of the average customer spend on service recovery. In other respects there are no significant differences.

These results correspond with the business-to-consumer service organisation which has a high number of service encounters, and hence, the need to recover continuously. The service package is more likely to be fairly standard; hence the authority given to staff to spend a high proportion of the average customer spend on service recovery, as the costs of what is being given is known and the risks of giving away too much can be assessed.

Implications for Empowerment

The present study was focused on service recovery and not on empowerment of service workers. However, 75% of the respondents claimed to be empowering staff through training, delegation with authority, involvement in procedures, communication of policy. There was also considerable mention of formal measurement systems including the quality standard BS5750.

These findings would suggest that the service organisations represented in the sample perceive themselves to be moving upwards on the imposed empowered scale of the empowerment matrix. What is not known is the perceptions of staff of these changes. Talk of formal procedures would suggest that in reality the modus operandi is more *imposed*. Hence, it is likely that staff are often frustrated unless the extent of the empowerment for service recovery is clearly defined.

There are indications of a realisation of the dangers of moving staff into the *anxiety* quadrant of the matrix as instanced by one comment:

"Empowerment must mean something to the staff themselves. I believe front-line staff do not necessarily want to be empowered at all times. It needs to be handled with care and gradually implemented so it becomes part of the culture of the organisation."

Conclusions

Service managers perceived service recovery to be important to their business and likely to increase in the future with the need to meet service pledges associated with Service Charters. They also generally perceive a link between service recovery and customer retention.

Less than half the service organisations currently measure the cost of a lost or dissatisfied customer and customer retention.

Service recovery is still most likely to be triggered by customer complaint and if it is a business to consumer service, it will be initiated within minutes and be resolved by front-line staff having the authority to use over 50% of the average customer spend to put things right, mainly by replacement or refund. Business-to-business services take longer to activate service recovery (hours or longer) and the front-line staff have less authority to use a high proportion of the average spend, although there may be no difference in the actual amounts involved between the classes of services.

Overall, the service organisations in the sample are taking steps to bring about service recovery. However, the indications are that it could be improved by better measurement and triggering and by a consideration of the most appropriate strategies for recovery (for instance, a wider use of escalation procedures). Whether a true reflection or not, the impression given by respondents is of a lack of checking with the customers of what is needed.

Over 75% of the service organisations claim to be empowering service staff. However, there still remains doubts as to the overall effectiveness of the changes. In some cases the front-line staff do not wish for the change or are not adequately prepared and, consequently, fail to fulfil their new expected roles. In other cases the intention to empower is blocked by inappropriate systems and frustrated staff.

References

Alpander, G.G., Developing Managers' Ability to Empower Employees, *Journal of Management*, 10, 3, 1991, pp. 13-24.

Armistead, C.G. and G. Clark, The 'Coping' Capacity Management: Strategy in Service and the Influence on Quality Performance, *The International Journal of Service Industry Management*, 4, 4, 1993.

Bowen, D.E., and E.E. Lawler, The Empowerment of Service Workers: What, Why, How, and When, *Sloan Management Review*, Spring, 1992, pp. 31-39.

Hart, C.W.L, The Power of Unconditional Guarantees, *Harvard Business Review*, July/August, 1988, pp. 54-62.

Hart, C., J.L. Heskett and W.E. Sasser, The Profitable Art of Service Recovery, *Harvard Business Review*, 8, 4, July/August, 1990, pp. 148-156.

Hart, C.W.L, L.A. Schlesinger and D. Maher, Guarantees Come to Professional Service Firms, *Sloan Management Review*, Spring, 1992, pp. 19-29.

Heskett, J.L., A Service Sector Paradigm for Management: The Service Profit Chain, in C.G. Armistead (ed.),*Service Sector Management Research at Cranfield*, 1992.

Heskett, J.L., W.E. Sasser and C.W.L. Hart, *Service Breakthroughs: Changing the Rules of the Game*, Free Press, New York, 1990.

Lash, L.M., *The Complete Guide to Customer Service*, John Wiley, 1989.

Parasuraman, A, V.A. Zeithaml and L.L. Berry, SERVQUAL: A Multiple Item Scale for Measuring Consumer Perceptions of Service Quality, *Journal of Retailing*, 64, Spring, 1988, pp. 12-40.

Thomas, K.W., B.A. Velthouse, Cognitive Elements of Empowerment: An Interpretive Model of Intrinsic Task Motivation, *Academy of Management Review*, 15, 4, 1990, pp. 666-681.

Zemke, R., and C. Bell, Service Recovery: Doing It Right the Second Time, *Training*, 27, 6, 1990, pp. 42-48.

Zemke, R., Service Recovery: A Key to Customer Retention, *Franchising World*, 23, 3, May/June, 1991, pp. 32-34.

8

Service Performances as Drama: Quality Implications and Measurement

Raymond P. Fisk and Stephen J. Grove

Introduction

The phenomenon of service quality has generated much attention in the marketing literature. In the attempt to understand the phenomenon better, various models of service quality have been posited during the period (cf. Grönroos 1990; LeBlanc and Nguyen 1988; Lindqvist 1987; Parasuraman, Zeithaml and Berry 1985). A critical principle that is implicitly or explicitly specified among most of these models is that service quality is an assessment of the service one receives compared to his/her expectations regarding it. Hence, service quality is essentially defined from the customer's point of view. For example, in their widely recognized Gap Analysis Model, Parasuraman *et al.* (1985, 1988) note that service quality is a function of the magnitude and direction of a gap between a customer's expected and perceived service performance. Similarly, in his model of service quality, Grönroos (1990) stresses that a comparison of expected service to perceived service is the cornerstone of the service quality concept. Overall, consumer expectations set the benchmarks against which service performance is judged and quality is determined (Zeithaml, Berry and Parasuraman 1993).

Recently, however, questions have been raised regarding the efficacy of including customers' expectations as an integral component of the service quality puzzle (Cronin and Taylor 1992; Grönroos 1993; Liljander and Strandvik 1992). Beyond the fact that customer expectations are complex and may take many forms (Boulding, Kalra, Staelin and Zeithaml 1993; Tse and Wilton 1988, Zeithaml *et al.* 1993), difficulties emerge when attempting to obtain independent measures of expectations and perceptions of service performance (Grönroos 1993). Further, empirical evidence suggests that "a performance-based measure of service quality may be an improved means of measuring the service quality construct" (Cronin and Taylor 1992, p. 55). Rather than specify expectations *a priori*, such measures indirectly tap customers' expectations as the comparison points against which one determines the excellence of his/her service experience. Although unarticulated, service expectations are nevertheless present in performance-based measures of service quality. However, it is the performance of the service and its impact upon customers' experiences that takes the foreground in this approach to service quality.

A focus upon service performance as the key to service quality raises several issues for those who seek to grasp the phenomenon accurately. A significant part of this stems from the processual nature of service performance. Services occur over time and their excellence is manifested in both process and outcome terms (Boulding *et al.* 1993, Grönroos 1982, Parasuraman *et al.* 1985). It is the dynamic characteristic of services performance that makes service quality a difficult and elusive phenomenon. Most service models are essentially static, relying on before and after comparisons (i.e., expectations and perceptions, respectively) and remiss in attending to the processual dimension of services (Grönroos 1993). Over the duration of a service performance, many different elements may affect customers' experiences and, hence, define service quality. These elements often emerge in the service performance itself and their character may not be known as *a priori* expectations (Fisk 1981). Further, customer expectations and quality perceptions change continuously during the service encounter (Grönroos 1993). To accommodate these circumstances, models which reflect the characteristics of service performance as processes are needed.

The purpose of this article is to present a model of service performances as drama as a means to capture the processual character of services. This effort will (1) provide arguments to support the proposition that services are dramatic performances, (2) develop implications for service quality that emerge from such an approach, and (3) posit what a theatrical framework for services means for quality measurement.

Service Performance as Drama

The fact that services are delivered in real time, i.e., production and consumption of services occurs simultaneously (Bateson 1989; Berry 1980; Parasuraman *et al.* 1985), forces marketers to attend to this feature in any discussion of service quality. A depiction of services as theatrical performances accomplishes this task. Born from the metaphor of behavior as drama that is the foundation of the dramaturgy literature in sociology and social psychology (Burke 1945, 1950, 1968; Goffman 1959, 1967, 1974; Perinbanayagam 1974, 1982, 1985), conceiving of services in theatrical terms offers many insights to quality issues.

The Drama Metaphor and Services Marketing

As with any metaphor, approaching services as theater moves beyond the literal to evoke 'chunks' of information and the transfer of qualities of a familiar phenomenon, theater, to one that is unknown, services (Ortony 1975). Metaphors can generate analysis and hypotheses regarding complex phenomena (Morgan 1980) and, in some cases, they may represent the basis for entire schools of thought (Arndt 1985; Morgan 1980). While the utility of metaphors for marketing has received some attention over the years (Arndt 1985; Stern 1988; Zikmund 1982), specific application of the behavior as drama metaphor to marketing phenomena has been somewhat limited (e.g., Deighton 1992; Grove and Fisk 1983; Grove, Fisk and Kenny 1990). In addition, despite its seemingly apparent appropriateness for describing marketplace phenomena that involve social interaction, such as service encounters, articulation of the drama metaphor for services can be found in only a few writings (Grove and Fisk 1983, 1989, 1992b; Grove, Fisk and Bitner 1992).

The drama metaphor suggests that human social behaviors are essentially theatrical 'performances' involving 'actors' who present themselves and their actions in such a way as to foster a desired impression before an 'audience'. Actors continually adjust their expressions during social encounters to maintain a credible and/or sincere 'front-region' performance (i.e., discourse before an audience). To accomplish this requires a general coherence among various theatrical elements that necessitates planning and practice (i.e., rehearsal) in a 'back region' away from the audience's view. This is particularly true since performances are fragile processes that can be easily destroyed by even the slightest of mishaps (Goffman 1959). Further, through verbal and nonverbal responses during an interaction, an audience may provide inputs to guide actors in their quest to create a successful performance. Thus, the meanings and interpretations assigned by an audience to the elements of behavioral exchanges are a driving force behind a performance's nature.

The parallels between the drama metaphor and the character of services performances are fairly obvious. The strategies that people use to form and maintain desirable impressions before an audience are at the heart of both. In addition, for both drama and service performances, careful attention to an actor's expressive behavior and the physical setting in which it occurs are important to achieve a desirable definition of the situation. As with services, the central feature of the drama metaphor is processual in nature in that both involve people who actively seek to transform the impression-forming character of their behavior into impression management (Miller 1984). From these insights, we combine drama and service performance into a single framework that portrays service performances as drama. The following subsection briefly develops the theatrical nature of the service performance by describing and explaining its components in drama terms.

Theatrical Nature of Service Performances

Service performances are dramatic in nature. Various aspects of service performances, like human social interaction in general, have referents in the drama metaphor. While all marketing actions may be described as dramatic (Deighton

1992), services are particularly intense with dramatic character. Services may vary widely in terms of their specific dramatic make-up, but most reflect several key drama components. Among these are the actors, audience, and setting that comprises the service performed. In a sense, service performances and the quality that they engender are the result of the interplay of these elements over the duration of the service enactment.

Actors

As in dramatic productions where success is often tied to the acumen of those on stage, the quality of a service performance is affected by a service contact personnel. In fact, the actors who perform the service are often perceived by customers as the service itself (Grönroos 1985). Their manner and appearance to enact their service roles are all important contributions to quality perceptions (Parasuraman *et al.* 1985; Solomon 1985). In fact, organizations can distinguish themselves among their competition through the quality embodied by their service actors, a concept referred to as the "people factor" by Berry, Zeithaml and Parasuraman (1985).

Audience

The audience (or customers) receiving the service also plays a critical role in the determination of a service performance's quality. Clearly, an audience is required for many services to occur (e.g., physician, hotel visit, etc.) and they can affect the quality of the service's delivery and/or outcome (Booms and Bitner 1981; Parasuraman *et al.* 1988; Shostack 1977). Beyond influencing one another's service experience (Martin and Pranter 1989), audience members contribute to the quality of a service performance by articulating their needs/wants regarding the service, adhering to proper procedures, and understanding the service script (Bateson 1985; Bowen 1986; Mills and Morris 1986).

Setting

The physical setting or environment in which the service is delivered can affect perceptions of a performance's quality in much the same way that the staging of a dramatic production influences an audience's experience. A myriad of setting features exist that might influence the character of a service and, hence, its quality. One's impression of a service is clearly affected by the setting (Shostack 1977) whose features (e.g., lightning decor, temperature, props, etc.) help to define and facilitate the service enactment (Baker 1987; Booms and Bitner 1982; Bitner 1992). Further, by mixing or manipulating various elements of the service setting, marketers may change or rearrange the audience's perceptions of a service performance. Additionally, as in theater, it is important to note that what occurs 'back stage' in the effort to present a quality 'front-stage' performance cannot be ignored. Much of the planning, rehearsal, staging decisions, and coordination of effort that result in a quality service enactment 'front stage' in the service setting occurs in the service's back region. For that reason, to maintain perceptions of authenticity and the aura of quality, it is important to keep the two regions separate in terms of audience access.

Performance
As suggested, the service performance is the enactment of the service process that results from the combined efforts of the actors, audience, and setting. To create a quality performance requires coordination of these various components for the duration of a service's enactment. If any component or aspect of it fails to support the others, the quality of the performance is likely to be compromised. Thus, as in dramatic productions, service performance quality is a tenuous proposition that requires attention to detail from start to finish. One's perception of the quality of service performance occurs continually as it unfolds.

Two Drama Models of Service Experience as Drama
Grove *et al.* (1992) proposed two conceptual models that portray the drama perspective on services. The first model, Figure 1, of the service experience as drama incorporates the key elements of actors, audience, setting and performance. In their model, the actors and audience are positioned at the center to emphasize that a service performance is largely a product of the interaction between actors and audience within the context of a particular setting.

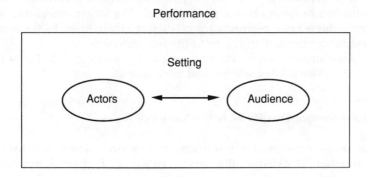

Figure 1. The service experience as drama (Adapted from Grove et al. 1992)

The second Grove, Fisk and Bitner (1992) model (Figure 2) attempts to portray the relative importance or significance of the three theatrical elements comprising a service performance using a three-dimensional plus-minus structure (a "+" indicates more importance while a "−" indicates less importance). Put simply, the 'service performance' is portrayed as a function of actors, audience, and setting. One aspect of the model is the idea that each of these three theatrical elements can be managed before the performance begins. Another aspect of the model is that a service organization may choose to 'position' itself in terms of its emphasis on actors, audience, or setting.

Each of the drama elements portrayed in the Grove, Fisk and Bitner (1992) models can be explored for its implications for service quality, which we turn to in the next section.

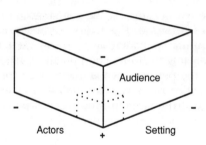

Figure 2. The service performance cube (Adapted from Grove et al. 1992)

Implications for Service Quality

The drama metaphor offers numerous implications for the improvement of service quality. Perhaps the key insight is that theatrical performance, like service quality, is a "Gestalt" experience that is not easily broken apart. Like theatrical performance, the impression of quality emerging from service performance can be affected by a myriad of factors both large and small. The larger overall factors are essential to give the service performance credibility. Inattention to the smaller factors, the details, can cause disruptions to the service system.

Drama's implications for improving service quality can be grouped into three categories: actor/audience roles, setting, and performance.

Improving the Service Quality of Actor/Audience Roles

Five drama-based strategies for improving the service quality of actor/audience roles are proposed: 1) Audition the Service Actors, 2) Employ Scripting, 3) Train and Rehearse, 4) Develop Performance Teams, and 5) Select and Train the Audience.

Audition the Service Actors
One of the truisms from the general quality literature is the idea that it is much less expensive to produce a product without defects than it is to fix a defective product. In services, the counterpart to this idea is that it is much less expensive to hire an excellent employee than it is to train a defective employee to be excellent. Drawing on drama, service organizations should go beyond the standard methods of employee selection of resumes and interviews to 'auditioning' their prospective employees. This method has the clear advantage of letting the potential employee demonstrate their job skills. An important insight from the 'auditioning' concept is the idea that some people fit a part better than others and some are not right for any part that puts them in front of an audience.

Employ Scripting
In a drama, the script is the vehicle through which all key details of the drama are conveyed (dialogue, staging, lighting, scene changes, etc.). In short, a script is a very detailed plan of action. For services, a script might consist of a detailed de-

scription of appropriate behavior(s) for a given situation, yet might not include the exact spoken words. Service scripts should contain all of the behaviors necessary to fashion a credible performance and should always be mindful of audience expectations (Smith and Houston 1983, 1985; Surprenant and Solomon 1987). Using scripts for routine service behaviors would be particularly effective at reducing the risk of inconsistent service quality. For example, a professional accounting firm could create scripts for day-to-day office procedures to reduce the risk of errors. Overall, service organizations could develop a repertoire of scripts for each service actor, as well as anticipated service encounters.

Train and Rehearse
An actor training for a part has the goal of giving a flawless performance. Actors engage in intensive rehearsals to reach this goal. Hence, the drama-based strategy for a service organization is to develop elaborate training and rehearsal procedures for its service actors. Some service organizations want employees to perform standardized behaviors for all customers, others empower their employees to adapt to the needs of the customer (Bowen and Lawler 1992). When service organizations choose to empower their workers, it requires greater training because they must improvise to meet the needs of customers. Jazz improvisation is a powerful analogy for this process. The best jazz improvisation is done by experienced musicians, not by novices. Hence, service organizations (especially those with empowerment strategies) should attempt to train and rehearse their employees to the level of jazz musicians who 'know their chops'.

Develop Performance Teams
Another strategy for improving service quality is to develop performance teams combining highly skilled service actors (mentors) with relatively unskilled novices (apprentices). A related approach that might be desirable for complex services would be using an 'understudy' arrangement where a new service worker was assigned to develop his/her skills 'at the feet' of one more experienced. Both approaches foster teamwork, encourage sharing of experiences, and minimize the risk of service failures caused by novices. Creating performance teams requires the service organization to invest time, money, and confidence in its employees.

Select and Train the Audience
The idea of selecting and training the audience may sound unusual, but every service organization desires an appreciative audience for its performances. This is clearly related to the traditional marketing idea of target marketing, which is used to attract customers. However, the drama perspective goes beyond selecting the audience to training the audience in order to enhance the show. An audience member that does not have an understanding of opera, melodrama, or mime will not enjoy the performance. In the same sense, service customers who do not understand an ATM machine or a self-service gas pump will not enjoy the service performance. In both kinds of examples, the perceived service quality would be lower because the audience had not been trained in how to experience the service. Nevertheless, few service organizations actually train their patients, clients, patrons, customers, etc.

An important approach to training the audience is to create a system for identifying new customers. When customers are new, efforts can be made to educate them as to the customer's role expectations during the service performance. Of course, enhancing the quality of the first service experience for a new customer is likely to increase the probability of repeat patronage. A wide variety of props, setting changes, and other drama devices are available to enhance the customers' orientation to the service (Wener 1985) and their role in its performance (Lovelock and Young 1979; Martin and Pranter 1989; Solomon, Surprenant, Czepiel and Gutman 1985).

Improving the Quality of Service Settings

Three drama strategies for improving the quality of services settings include: 1) Experimenting with the Service Setting; 2) Front-Stage vs. Back-Stage Decisions; and 3) Managing Tangible Evidence.

Experimenting with the Service Setting

Like a stage setting, the service setting can be controlled by managers. Hence, it is possible for service providers to experimentally test variations in settings just like manufacturers of physical goods might test product improvements (Farrell 1984). Some nationwide service organizations are able to field test new setting choices in one or two local markets before committing larger resources to it. This is analogous to a theater play that opens 'off-broadway' first while the cast and crew refine the performance. If 'real world' field tests are not possible, it may be possible to create computer models, drawings, slides, or photographic simulations that can be used to gather customer feedback prior to implementing the service setting. The value of any tests of service settings is that they enhance the chances of delivering the service quality desired by the customer.

Front-Stage vs. Back-Stage Decisions

Front-stage vs. back-stage decisions are a common aspect of the theater. A services manager must decide which service features should be performed on the front-stage (in the audience's full view) and which should be delivered back-stage (away from the audience's inspection). In service environments where it is difficult to meet customer expectations of a particular front-stage service delivery, service managers may find it prudent to move such aspects to the back region. On the other hand, moving the back-stage dimensions of a service performance to the front stage requires greater attention to other performance components, such as the actors' roles and scripts, the audience's participation, and the setting's physical cues.

Managing Tangible Evidence

Tangible evidence, as documented by Parasuraman *et al.* (1988), is a determinant of a consumer's perceived service quality. Hence, the goal of managing tangible evidence should be conveying consistent perceptions of service quality. Physical appearance of service employees is one important component of such tangible evidence. Many service organizations (airlines, hotels, restaurants, hospitals, law firms, etc.) use employee uniforms (costumes) to convey such perceptions (Solomon 1985). The use of props is a second influential component. Every service industry can be identified by unique props. Consider how easy it is to identify the service industry associated with the following props: stethoscope, chalkboard, bar tray, and scissors. Service organizations should be vigilant that the props seen by their customers convey desired service quality perceptions.

Improving the Quality of the Service Performance

Three drama strategies for improving the quality of the service performance are available: 1) Test New Performances, 2) Document Performances, and 3) Critique Performances.

Test New Performances
Testing new performance alternatives may be expensive, but it is less expensive than launching a new service performance without a 'dress rehearsal'. From a drama perspective, organizations need to develop a tradition of constantly testing 'new routines'. This approach is similar to the practice among comedians of regularly testing new jokes because the old jokes are becoming too familiar. The public may take longer to become bored with an old service performance than an old joke, but eventually it will happen. For many service customers, an old service performance is a poor quality service performance.

Document Performances
Documenting service performances improves the service organization's ability to raise the quality of employee performances. One of the simplest methods of doing this is the use of management observation similar to what Peters and Austin (1985) discuss as Management by Wandering Around and 'naive listening'. Another method is the use of customers' recollections of critical service performances to document and track the quality of service performance (Bitner, Booms and Tetreault 1990).

Critique Performances
The purpose of critiquing an employee's service performance is to maximize the performance. As a result, two practices are desirable: 1) Reward Excellent Performance, and 2) Correct Poor Performance. When excellent performance is rewarded it is not only a powerful motivator to the individual excellent performer but also a powerful motivator to other employees. The harder task is correcting poor performance. If the employee is reprimanded or fired in a very public way, it only serves to terrorize the remaining staff. It is usually wiser to privately show the employee the mistake and teach him/her how to avoid it. Schneider (1980) has shown that most employees want to perform well and give good service.

Observational Measurement of Service Quality

Grove and Fisk (1992a) presented a detailed exposition of the appropriateness of observational data-collection methods for services. With the notable exception of the Critical Incident Technique (Bitner *et al.* 1990), observational methods have received little attention in the services marketing literature. Observational methods are data-gathering techniques that focus on services experiences as they unfold (e.g., the speed with which service contact personnel process a transaction) or indirect evidence of a service's nature following its performance (e.g., tallying cash register receipts to identify the popularity of menu items at various times of the day). Observational methodologies seek 'real-world' information and the preservation of the authenticity of the service phenomena's natural state. In short, observational methodologies offer services researchers fundamentally different approaches than traditional data-gathering techniques and are particularly well suited to the dynamic, processual nature of services phenomena (Grove and Fisk 1992a).

Grove and Fisk (1992a) presented numerous specific applications of observational data collection, including services quality. The best-known research techniques for studying services quality are from the research team of Parasuraman, Zeithaml and Berry (Parasuraman *et al.* 1985, 1988; Zeithaml, Berry and Parasuraman 1988, 1990, 1993). Parasuraman *et al.* (1985) created a model of services in which five potential gaps can affect the quality of service. Parasuraman *et al.* (1988) discussed survey-based methods for researching the gaps (e.g., their SERVQUAL scale). Observational research can be used as a qualitative supplement to surveys or as a means of gleaning preliminary insights to be used in developing later survey efforts. As presented in Grove and Fisk (1992a), each of the service quality gaps can be researched via observational data-collection methods.

We contend that observational methods may also be used to investigate service quality from a drama perspective. Each of the major drama dimensions may be investigated with observational methods: actors/audience, setting, and performance. Actors/audience issues may be explored with variations of participant observation techniques or mechanical observation techniques. For example, mystery shoppers can be used to document aspects of the service quality provided by service actors. Audio or videotaping of actor/audience interactions can be done with their permission and this can be a rich source of data. Human and mechanical observation can also be combined. Such a use is akin to the way most focus groups are performed. Observation of service settings can be done via a range of both human observation and mechanical observation techniques. Participant observation of service settings can be employed and mystery shoppers would again be one way of doing this. A mechanical method would be videotaping service settings for subsequent analysis. The advantage of such a videotape is that it would allow a more leisurely analysis, though it forgoes some of the experiential aesthetics of service settings. Another observational approach for service settings is the use of physical trace analysis to determine the degree of wear occurring on service features. For example, the thickness of floor tiles could be used to help decide where to replace floor tiles before they become unsightly. Observation of service performances can also be done with a range of human and mechanical observation techniques. For example, as mentioned earlier, manager's may be trained to observe and document the quality of service performances. However, one hazard of this approach is that the manager's observation may disrupt the service performance. A mechanical observational technique for accomplishing the same purpose would be the use of audio and/or videotaping to document the service performance. Such taping has the advantage of providing a relatively permanent and unbiased record of the service performance.

The use of observational techniques beyond those mentioned here are certainly possible. The value of observational methods in assessing service quality may be greatly enhanced if employed in conjunction with survey research such as SERVQUAL (Parasuraman *et al.* 1988). Nevertheless, observational techniques offer the services researcher an attractive alternative and/or supplementary method for examining service quality dimensions.

Conclusion

Service performances were presented from a drama perspective. This perspective was used to develop drama- based strategies for improving service quality. In addition, observational techniques were offered as an alternative method for measuring service quality. The major strength of the service performances as drama perspective is its ability to organize the dynamic aspects of service quality into a cohesive Gestalt. A second strength is that the drama perspective is easily understood and communicated to service employees, which facilitates better training.

References

Arndt, J., On Making Marketing Science More Scientific: Role of Orientations, Paradigms, Metaphors and Puzzle Solving, *Journal of Marketing*, 49 (Summer), 1985, pp. 11-23.

Baker, J., The Role of the Environment in Marketing Services: The Consumer Perspective, in: J.A. Czepiel, C.A. Congram and J. Shanahan (eds.), *The Services Challenge: Integrating for Competitive Advantage*, Chicago: American Marketing Association, 1987, pp. 79-84.

Bateson, J.E.G., Perceived Control and the Service Encounter, in: J.A. Czepiel, M.R. Solomon and C.F. Surprenant (eds.),*The Service Encounter: Managing Employee/Customer Interaction in Service Businesses*, Lexington, MA: Lexington Books, 1985, pp. 67-82.

Bateson, J.E.G., *Managing Services Marketing: Text and Readings*. Hinsdale, IL: Dryden Press, 1989.

Berry, L.L., Services Marketing is Different, *Business*, 30 (May-June), 1980, pp. 24-29.

Berry, L.L., V.A. Zeithaml and A. Parasuraman, Quality Counts in Services, Too, *Business Horizons*, 28 (May-June), 1985, pp. 44-52.

Bitner, M.J., Servicescapes: The Impact of Physical Surroundings on Customers and Employees, *Journal of Marketing*, 56 (April), 1992, pp. 57-71.

Bitner, M.J., B.H. Booms and M. Stanfield Tetreault, The Service Encounter: Diagnosing Favorable and Unfavorable Incidents, *Journal of Marketing*, 54 (January), 1990, pp. 71-84.

Booms, B.H. and M.J. Bitner, Marketing Strategies and Organizational Structures for Service Firms, in: J.H. Donnelly and W.R. George (eds.), *Marketing of Services*, Chicago: American Marketing Association, 1981, pp. 47-51.

Booms, B.H. and M.J. Bitner, Marketing Services by Managing the Environment, *The Cornell Hotel and Restaurant Administration Quarterly*, 23 (May), 1982, pp. 35-39.

Boulding, W., A. Kalra, R. Staelin and V.A. Zeithaml, A Dynamic Process Model of Service Quality: From Expectations to Behavioral Intentions, *Journal of Marketing Research*, 30 (February), 1993, pp. 7-27.

Bowen, D.E., Managing Customers as Human Resources in Service Organizations, in: R. Zemke and C.R. Bell, *Service Wisdom*, Minneapolis: Lakewood Books, 1989; reprinted from Human Resources Management, John Wiley and Sons, 1986.

Bowen, D.E. and E.E. Lawler III, The Empowerment of Service Workers: What, Why, How, and When, *Sloan Management Review*, 33 (Spring), 1992, pp. 31-39.

Burke, K., *A Grammar of Motives*. New York: Prentice-Hall, Inc., 1945.

Burke, K., *A Rhetoric of Motives*. New York: Prentice-Hall, Inc., 1950.

Burke, K., Dramatism, in *International Encyclopedia of the Social Sciences*, VII. New York: Macmillan, 1968, pp. 445-452.

Cronin, J.J. and S. Taylor, Measuring Service Quality: A Reexamination and Extension, *Journal of Marketing*, 56 (July), 1992, pp. 55-68.

Deighton, J., The Consumption of Performance, *Journal of Consumer Research*, 19 (December), 1992, pp. 362-372.

Farrell, K., Franchise Prototypes, Venture, (January), 1984, pp.108-113.

Fisk, R.P., Toward a Consumption/Evaluation Process Model for Services, in: J.H. Donnelly and W.R. George (eds.), *Marketing of Services*, Chicago: American Marketing Association, 1981, pp. 191-195.

Goffman, E., *The Presentation of Self in Everyday Life*. New York: Doubleday and Co, 1959.

Goffman, E., *Interactional Ritual*. Garden City, NJ: Doubleday and Co, 1967.

Goffman, E., *Frame Analysis: An Essay on the Organization of Experience*. New York: Harper and Row, 1974.

Grönroos, C., An Applied Service Marketing Theory, *European Journal of Marketing*, 16 (7), 1982, pp. 30-41.

Grönroos, C., Internal Marketing - Theory and Practice, in: T. Bloch, G. Upah and V. Zeithaml (eds.), *Services Marketing in a Changing Environment*, Chicago: American Marketing Association, 1985, pp. 41-47.

Grönroos, C., *Service Management and Marketing: Managing the Moments of Truth in Service Competition*. Lexington, MA: Lexington Books, 1990.

Grönroos, C., Towards A Third Phase in Service Quality Research: Challenges and Future Directions, in: T. Swartz, D. Bowen and S. Brown (eds.), *Advances in Services Marketing and Management*, Vol. 2, Greenwich, CT: JAI Press, 1993.

Grove, S.J. and R.P. Fisk, The Dramaturgy of Services Exchanges: An Analytical Framework for Services Marketing, in: L.L. Berry, G.L.Shostack, and G.D. Upah (eds.), *Emerging Perspectives on Services Marketing*, Chicago: American Marketing Association, 1983, pp. 45-49.

Grove, S.J. and R.P. Fisk, Impression Management in Services Marketing: A Dramaturgical Perspective, in: R.A. Giacalone and P. Rosenfeld (eds.), *Impression Management in the Organization*, Hillsdale, NJ: Lawrence Erlbaum Associates, 1989, pp. 427-438.

Grove, S.J. and R.P. Fisk, Observational Data Collection Methods for Services Marketing: An Overview, *Journal of the Academy of Marketing Science*, 20 (Summer), 1992a, pp. 217-224.

Grove, S.J. and R.P. Fisk, The Service Experience as Theater, in: J.E. Sherry, Jr. and B. Sternthal (eds.), *Advances in Consumer Research*, Provo, Utah: Association for Consumer Research, 1992b, pp. 455-461.

Grove, S.J., R.P. Fisk and M.J. Bitner, Dramatizing the Service Experience: A Managerial Approach, in: T.A. Swartz, S.W. Brown, and D.E. Bowen (eds.), *Advances in Services Marketing and Management: Research and Practice*, Greenwich, CT: JAI Press, 1992, pp. 91-121.

Grove, S.J., R.P. Fisk and J.T. Kenny, Personal Selling as Drama: A Metaphorical Assessment of Buyer-Seller Interaction, in: D. Lichtenthal *et al.* (eds.), *1990 AMA Winter Educators' Conference: Marketing Theory and Applications*, Chicago: American Marketing Association, 1990, pp. 75-81.

LeBlanc, G. and N. Nguyen, Customers' Perceptions of Service Quality in Financial Institutions, *International Journal of Bank Marketing*, 6 (4), 1988, pp. 7-18.

Liljander, V. and T. Strandvik, The Relation Between Service Quality, Satisfaction, and Intentions, Working Paper. Helsingfors, Finland: Swedish School of Economics and Business Administration, 1992.

Lindqvist, L.A., Quality and Service Value in the Consumption of Services, in: C. Surprenant (ed.), *Add Value To Your Service*, Chicago: American Marketing Association, 1987, pp. 17-20.

Lovelock, C.H. and R.F. Young, Look to Consumers to Increase Productivity, *Harvard Business Review*, 57 (May-June), 1979, pp. 168-178.

Martin, C.L. and C.A. Pranter, Compatibility Management: Customer-to-Customer Relationships in Service Environments, *Journal of Services Marketing*, 3 (Summer), 1989, pp. 6-15.

Miller, T.G., Goffman, Social Acting, and Moral Behavior, *Journal for the Theory of Social Behavior*, 14 (2), 1984, pp. 141-163.

Mills, P.K. and J.H. Morris, Clients as Partial Employees of Service Organizations: Role Development in Client Participation, *Academy of Management Review*, 11 (4), 1986, pp. 726-735.

Morgan, G., Paradigm, Metaphors, and Puzzle Solving in Organizational Theory, *Administrative Science Quarterly*, 25 (December), 1980, pp. 605-622.

Ortony, A., Why Metaphors are Necessary and Not Just Nice, *Educational Theory*, 25 (Winter), 1975, pp. 45-53.

Parasuraman, A., V.A. Zeithaml and L.L. Berry, A Conceptual Model of Service Quality and Its Implications for Future Research, *Journal of Marketing*, 49 (Fall), 1985, pp. 41-50.

Parasuraman, A., V.A. Zeithaml and L.L. Berry, SERVQUAL: A Multiple-Item Scale for Measuring Consumer Perceptions of Service Quality, *Journal of Retailing*, 64 (Spring), 1988, pp. 12-40.

Perinbanayagam, R.S., The Definition of the Situation: An Analysis of the Ethnomethodological and Dramaturgical View, *The Sociological Quarterly*, 15 (Autumn), 1974, p. 521-541.

Perinbanayagam, R.S., Dramas, Metaphors, and Structures, *Symbolic Interaction*, 5 (2), 1982, pp. 259-276.

Perinbanayagam, R.S., *Signifying Acts*, Carbondale, IL: Southern Illinois University Press, 1985.

Peters, T. and N. Austin, *A Passion for Excellence*. New York: Warner Books, 1985.

Schneider, B., The Service Organization: Climate is Crucial, *Organizational Dynamics*, 9 (Autumn), 1980, pp. 52-65.

Shostack, G.L., Breaking Free From Product Marketing, Journal of Marketing, 41 (April), 1977, pp. 73-80.

Smith, R.A. and M.J. Houston, Script-Based Evaluations of Satisfaction With Services, in: L.L. Berry, G.L. Shostack and GD. Upah (eds.), *Emerging Perspectives on Services Marketing*, Chicago: American Marketing Association, 1983, pp. 59-62.

Smith, R.A. and M.J. Houston, A Psychometric Assessment of Measures of Scripts in Consumer Memory, *Journal of Consumer Research*, 12 (September), 1985, pp. 214-224.

Solomon, M.R., Packaging the Service Provider, *Service Industries Journal*, 5 (March), 1985, pp. 64-72.

Solomon, M.R., Ca.F. Surprenant, J.A. Czepiel and E.G. Gutman, A Role Theory Perspective on Dyadic Interactions: The Service Encounter, *Journal of Marketing*, 49 (Winter), 1985, pp. 99-111.

Stern, B., Medieval Allegory: Roots of Advertising Strategy for the Mass Market, *Journal of Marketing*, 52 (July), 1988, pp. 84-94.

Surprenant, C.F. and M.R. Solomon, Predictability and Personalization in the Service Encounter, *Journal of Marketing*, 51 (April), 1987, pp. 86-96.

Tse, D.K. and P.C. Wilton, Models of Consumer Satisfaction Formation: An Extension, *Journal of Marketing Research*, 25 (May), 1988, pp. 204-212.

Wener, R.E., The Environmental Psychology of Service Encounters, in: J.A. Czepiel, M.R. Solomon and C.F. Surprenant (eds.), *The Service Encounter: Managing Employee/Customer Interaction in Service Businesses*, Lexington, MA: Lexington Books, 1985, pp. 101-112.

Zeithaml, V.A., L.L. Berry and A. Parasuraman, Communication and Control Processes in the Delivery of Service Quality, *Journal of Marketing*, 52 (April), 1988, pp. 35-48.

Zeithaml, V.A., L.L. Berry and A. Parasuraman, *Delivering Quality Service: Balancing Customer Perceptions and Expectations*. New York, NY: Free Press, 1990.

Zeithaml, V.A., L.L. Berry and A. Parasuraman, The Nature and Determinants of Customer Expectations of Service, *Journal of the Academy of Marketing Science*, 21 (1), 1993, pp. 1-12.

Zikmund, W.G., Metaphors as methodology, in R.F. Bush and S.D. Hunt (eds.), *Marketing Theory: Philosophy of Science Perspectives*, Chicago: American Marketing Association, 1982, pp. 75-77.

9

The Limits of Internal Marketing

Mohammed Rafiq and Pervaiz K. Ahmed

Introduction

Since the seminal papers by Berry (1981) and Grönroos (1981) there has been a rapid growth in the internal marketing literature. And, although the internal marketing concept emerged from the services marketing area, its use is no longer confined to services. In services marketing the impetus behind the emergence of internal marketing was the need to manage the interaction between contact staff and customers as these interactions have a major impact on customers' perception of quality of the service product and, hence, its demand. A further reason for its emergence was the recognition of the importance of effective co-ordination between contact staff and support staff to ensure the delivery of a quality product at the point of service. Parallel to this development has been the emergence of the total quality management (TQM) concept in the manufacturing sector, which also emphasises the need for an integrated company-wide effort and hence the need for internal marketing.

Whilst the need for internal marketing is well understood, there does not exist at present a single unified notion of what is meant by internal marketing. This is further compounded by the fact that some formalisations of internal marketing appear to suggest that activities traditionally associated with the personnel function (such as recruitment, development and motivation of staff) should be subordinated to the marketing function. This has prevented the widespread adoption of internal marketing in business practice. This chapter, therefore, attempts to clarify and explore the limits of the concept of internal marketing. We begin with a discussion of the various concepts of internal marketing.

The Concepts of Internal Marketing

Initially the impetus behind the development of the internal marketing concept was the concern that because contact employees involved in services become involved in what is referred to as interactive marketing, it is essential that they are responsive to customers' needs. This is reflected in Grönroos' statement that the *"... objective of internal marketing is to get motivated and customer-conscious personnel"* (Grönroos 1981, p. 237). However, for effective service delivery it is not sufficient to have customer-conscious employees, it is also necessary to have effective co-ordination between contact staff and background support staff. Hence, the internal marketing concept is also seen as a means of integrating the different functions which are vital to customer relations of service companies (Grönroos 1981).

Another strand of thought emerging from the services marketing literature is reflected in Berry's (1984) definition of internal marketing as *"viewing employees as internal customers, viewing jobs as internal products that satisfy the needs and wants of these internal customers while addressing the objectives of the organisation"* (p. 272). What this view implies is that *"... to have satisfied customers, the firm must also have satisfied employees"* (George 1977, p. 91). Sasser and Arbeit go even further and contend that internal marketing holds that personnel is the first market of a service company (Sasser and Arbeit 1976, p. 61).

Moreover, in the quest for satisfied employees Berry and Parasuraman (1991) extend the limits of internal marketing even further to include activities which are traditionally carried out by the personnel function:

"Internal marketing is attracting, developing, motivating and retaining qualified employees through job-products that satisfy their needs. Internal marketing is the philosophy of treating employees as customers ... and it is the strategy of shaping job-products to fit human needs." (Berry and Parasuraman 1991, p. 151).

This tendency of extending the sphere of marketing is part of a wider movement within marketing led by Kotler (1972, Kotler and Levy 1969) to broaden the activities and concept of marketing, for according to Kotler *"... marketing is a relevant subject for all organisations in their relations with all their publics, not only customers"* (Kotler 1972, p. 47). Kotler includes employees in his definition of publics and even talks about "employee-directed marketing" (Kotler 1972, p. 51).

Grönroos (1985) also succumbs to this tendency by extending his original definition of internal marketing as a method of motivating personnel towards customer consciousness to include the use of marketing-like activities in this pursuit:

"... holding that an organisation's internal market of employees can be influenced most effectively and hence motivated to customer-consciousness, market orientation and sales-mindedness by a marketing-like internal approach and by applying marketing-like activities internally" (Grönroos 1985, p. 42).

Piercy and Morgan (1991) are even more forthright in their call for the use of marketing techniques in the internal market place as they view internal marketing as the *"... development of a marketing programme aimed at the internal market place in the company ... by using the same basic structures used for external marketing"* (p. 84).

In contrast, in the total quality management approach the focus is not on the relationship between the organisation and the employee but on relationships between employees themselves. The idea of the internal customer means that every person is both a supplier and a customer, and the workings of an organisation can be thought of as a series of transactions between customers and suppliers. This series of transaction is referred to as 'quality chains' (Oakland 1991, p. 4, see Figure 1 below). The TQM approach requires that employees be motivated to view each other as customers/suppliers and to get employees to perform to measurable standards, either set internally or externally as for instance in the case of BS5750 in the UK or the international standard ISO 9000.

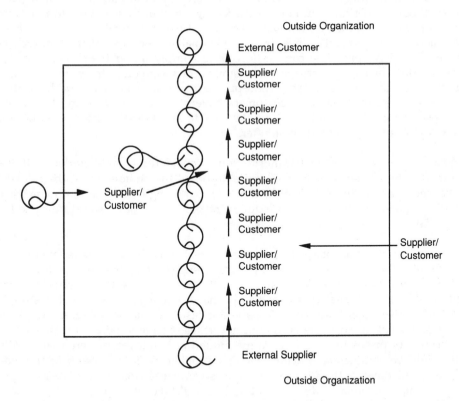

Figure 1. Quality Chains (Source: Oakland 1991, p. 4)

The discussion above highlights the fact that the concept of internal marketing is based on the idea of employee as customer. However, this concept is used differently in the TQM and services marketing approaches. In addition, the services marketing approach to internal marketing claims that the best way to motivate employees is to use marketing techniques in the internal marketplace. Below we examine these aspects of internal marketing in turn but begin with a look at the concept of customer and its implications for internal marketing.

Problems with the Concept of 'Employee as Customer'

Underlying the notion of employee as customer is the idea of exchange namely that customers receive products they desire in exchange for some kind of payment (that is, a price). Products are bought in order to derive some form of utility. When applied to employees, the concept of customers encounters several problems.

One of the key problems is that the 'products' that employees are being sold may be unwanted or may in fact have negative utility; that is, employees may incur extra costs without adequate returns and they may, therefore, not want them (e.g., new methods of working). In normal marketing situations customers do not have to buy products that they do not want. This is not true for employees as they must either accept the 'product' (since, in the final analysis, because of the contractual nature of employment, they can be 'forced' to comply under the threat of disciplinary action) or face the prospect of dismissal or resignation. In normal marketing situations the consequences of non-purchase are not so drastic. Additionally, in normal marketing situations customers have a range of (competing) products to choose from; this is unlikely to be the case in an internal marketing situation where a particular policy will be on offer.

In general, the use of force or authority is not considered to be a marketing solution to a problem. Hence, Kotler when he proposed the broadening of the marketing concept was careful to define the limits of marketing by stating that marketing consists of non-coercive actions to induce a response in another social unit (Kotler 1972, p. 50).

Moreover, the idea put forward by Sasser and Arbeit (1976) that "personnel is the first market of a service company" appears to suggest that the employee market has primacy. This stands on its head one of the basic axioms of marketing theory, namely, that the external customer has primacy. For it is the external customer that is the raison d'être of any company. For instance, many restaurant workers would prefer not to work late hours but nevertheless have to because that is when the customers prefer to dine out. Accommodating employee preferences in this case would be commercial suicide. Another problem with the notion of the employee as customer is the idea of customer sovereignty (that is, the idea of customer is king, customer is always right and so forth). For if employees did behave as if they are customers they could potentially make impossible demands upon the organisation and its resources. It is for this reason that in this approach employees do not explicitly know they are customers even though they may be treated as such!

Furthermore, the assertion that satisfied employees lead to satisfied customers is largely an untested assertion. In fact, it is quite conceivable that an unsatisfied employee may outperform a satisfied employee. For instance, a school teacher in mid-career may be satisfied with his job but his students may be unhappy because his material tends to be out-of-date and it may be difficult to arrange appointments with him to explain things after lesson time. Whereas, a younger teacher teaching the same subject but at lower salary level may be unhappy about her position but nevertheless may have up-to-date material and try harder to meet her students needs out of professional pride.

These problems are largely avoided in the TQM approach as the emphasis is on relationships between employees themselves. In other words, employees place demands upon each other rather than their organisation. Furthermore, the types of demands that they can make upon each other are limited to making sure that they as suppliers ensure that their 'products' meet their customer requirements and vice versa. If these requirements are met then quality of the final product will be assured.

The simplicity of the TQM idea of customer has meant that it has gained widespread acceptance. In contrast, the services marketing concept of 'employee as customer' has not been very widely adopted at all (Grönroos 1985). This is not surprising in view of the problems highlighted above in operationalising such a concept.

Application of Marketing Techniques in the Internal Context

The services marketing approach to internal marketing suggests, as mentioned above, that marketing or marketing-like techniques should be used to motivate internal customers. However, how useful are marketing techniques such as segmentation, market research, and the concept of the marketing mix (that is, product, price, place, and promotion) in creating customer-conscious employees? This section suggests ways of operationalising these concepts and techniques, dealing firstly with four traditional elements of the marketing mix and then moving on to segmentation and market research techniques.

Product
At the strategic level, the product can refer to marketing strategies; what is sold is those values and attitudes needed to make a plan work. At the tactical level the product could include new performance measures, new ways of handling customers. Products can also be used to refer to services and training courses provided by HRM (Collins and Payne 1991). At a more fundamental level, the product is the job (Flipo 1986; Berry and Parasuraman 1991). The product concept implies the need to ensure that the job product meets the needs of the employee while bearing in mind the requirements of the job and organisational resources.

Price
Price can refer to the psychological cost of adapting to new methods of working, projects that have to be foregone in order to carry out new policies (i.e., the oppor-

tunity cost); or to transfer pricing and expense allocation between departments. As opportunity costs are difficult to measure precisely (unlike the monetary price of goods and services) employees may tend to over-estimate the costs of undertaking new practices. This may be one major explanation of employee inertia and resistance to change. This also suggests that unlike normal marketing situations the price variable is not under the control of the management, as the 'price' paid by an individual is largely subjectively determined according to individual perceptions and circumstances. This emphasises the need to stress the benefits of new 'products'.

Place

Place refers to the channels of distribution (or third parties) that are used to get products to the final customers. In the internal context, place could mean meetings, conferences, etc. where policies are announced. Channels could also be used to refer to third parties (for example consultants, training agencies, or other departments within the organisation) used for delivery training programmes.

Promotion

The use of the correct communication strategies is of paramount importance in motivating employees and influencing their attitudes towards becoming more customer-oriented. Human resource managers already use a wide variety of techniques and media to communicate with employees, ranging from oral briefings and company newspapers to corporate videos. However, effective communication requires a co-ordinated use of these various media. Interest in new policies and training courses, for instance, can be generated by publicising them in company newspapers and on company notice boards. This needs to be followed up with the setting up of contact points and leaflets and brochures giving further information.

Ordinarily, marketers use a number of communication (or promotional) strategies including advertising, publicity, personal selling (face-to-face presentations) and promotions (incentives to purchase) in order to inform and to influence potential customers' attitudes favourably toward a firm and its products. The application of these strategies in the internal context is discussed briefly below, beginning with personal selling.

Personal selling

Face-to-face communication is regarded as having far greater impact than other communications methods in the area of management communications to employees (Townley 1989). Hence, face-to-face presentations to individuals and groups can be even more effective than in external marketing situations because the presenter (manager, supervisor) has implicit (if not explicit) authority behind what he or she is saying.

Incentives

It is clear from the concept of 'employee as customer', that employees must be offered some benefits in order to change their behaviour. The use of incentives in personnel management, such as cash bonuses, awards, recognition programmes, prize draws, or competition directed at contact personnel in the services industry, is very common. These can be used to overcome short-term resistance or to motivate employees toward consistent behaviour or to increase productivity.

Advertising
The use of mass media (i.e., newspapers and television) to communicate with employees (in order to motivate them) is rare. It is only used in special circumstances such as strikes, where normal workplace methods of communications would be ineffective. This is because of the vast expense of this media and the fact that it is not narrowly targeted at any particular organisation's employees. However, organisations need to take care of what image they are projecting of themselves and their workforce in their advertising aimed at external customers as they are likely to be seen by their employees as well.

However, with the emergence of narrow-casting technology, organisations can now use live television to communicate with large numbers of employees simultaneously in diverse locations in a more targeted and cost-effective way. Traditionally, large multi-sited organisations have communicated with their disparate workforce through newsletters, corporate videos and annual conferences. These are very costly methods, particularly conferences which in addition to hotel bills and travel time, take employees away from their workplace. This is why recently, instead of holding its biannual review meeting for officers and directors in Memphis, Federal Express which has the largest corporate television network in the world with 1,200 sites able to receive transmissions, transmitted a live three-hour broadcast simultaneously to locations in the UK, Paris, Brussels, as well as the USA. All employees were able to watch the broadcast with officers and directors participating in a 'phone-in session'. The advantages of using such a medium for internal marketing are obvious.

Despite its potential, only a handful of companies in the UK use business television and the market is currently worth only £3 million. In comparison, in the USA the market for business television is currently estimated to be worth $350 million and estimated to be worth $1 billion by 1995. Business television is therefore likely to be a growth area of employee communications because of the speed and reach of the medium (Button 1991).

Market segmentation
Segmentation in marketing is the process of grouping customers with similar characteristics and needs and wants. In services, for instance, employees may be grouped on the basis of whether they are contact employees or not. Other bases for segmentation might include the type of benefits that employees want, and the roles and functions that they perform. The existence of complex grading systems, departmental, functional and other organisational structures suggests that the use of segmentation is already widespread in the HRM area. It is suggested, however, that employees need to be segmented along motivational and behaviouristic lines rather than departmental, or other lines traditionally associated with HRM.

Marketing research
Marketing research involves identifying the needs and wants of customers and monitoring the impact of marketing policies on their behaviour. This type of research has a long history in the HRM area in the form of employee attitude surveys. In the UK, for instance, employee attitude surveys date back to the 1930s, when the National Institute of Industrial Psychology started using them to study labour turnover; but nowadays they are used for a wide array of issues including

attitudes held on supervision, remuneration, working conditions, specific personnel practices, incentive schemes, etc. The number of companies that use these types of surveys are relatively small and estimated to be around eight per cent (Millward and Stevens 1986, p. 153); nevertheless, some companies attach a great deal of importance to them. IBM, for instance, has been using them since 1962. It has now computerised the process to make it even more effective. Obviously, the use of market survey type techniques are much more likely to be used by larger firms for reasons of cost effectiveness.

Employee surveys need to be handled with care, even more so than consumer surveys because of employee fears of repercussions. These fears may be justified as attitude surveys have been used to weaken and deter unions (Jacoby 1988). Hence, it may be necessary to guarantee absolute confidentiality and may even require the use of an external research agency in order to ensure a good response. This also implies the need to interpret data with care even where the response rates are high. Another important difference between employee and consumer surveys is that employee participation is not likely to be high if employees are not given feedback on the survey results. More importantly, management needs to show that action is taken over issues of concern uncovered by the surveys.

The foregoing analysis highlights the fact that it is possible to apply marketing techniques and concepts to the internal context. The most useful contribution that marketing can make in this area are the ideas of customer (or employee) orientation, the idea of using a co-ordinated set of promotional or communications techniques, and marketing research. However, great care needs to be taken as to how these concepts are applied.

Internal Marketing and HRM

There is an implicit assumption in discussions of internal marketing that effective implementation of internal marketing can solve all employee-related quality problems and, consequently, the personnel function is relegated to the background. It is contended here, however, that there are limits to what internal marketing can achieve by itself and that it is of crucial importance to involve the HRM and other relevant functions. This is illustrated by a case study reported by Richardson and Robinson (1986).

Richardson and Robinson (1986) report a study on the implementation of internal marketing within a retail bank in which the effectiveness of the internal marketing programme is assessed by using groups of 'shoppers' to evaluate the service provided over a period of three months. Although the programme was generally considered to be a success, it is interesting to note how some of the problems that arose during the programme were solved. For instance, in one branch three tellers were found to have performed particularly badly. After their weaknesses were pointed out to them, the performance of only one of them improved. Further investigation revealed that the other two individuals did not enjoy the customer contact aspect of the job. That is, they were typical of task-oriented people doing people-oriented jobs (Blake and Mouton 1964). They were therefore moved to back office positions and replaced with more suitable staff resulting in improved performance for the department.

What this example illustrates is that in certain circumstances, administrative action by the personnel function is much more likely to be effective than internal marketing. The example also illustrates the importance of careful recruitment and selection for the motivation and effectiveness of staff.

In another instance, a branch suffered a loss in performance during a period when some members were on training courses or on leave and the replacement staff were from administrative (that is, task-oriented) jobs and hence less skilled in dealing with people. Another branch, whilst showing a small improvement in performance, was well below the overall improvement levels achieved. On investigation it was discovered that shortage of staff was leading to careless mistakes in this department and consequently to lack of satisfaction on the part of customers. The employment of an extra member of staff led to an increase in morale and a dramatic improvement in performance. These two examples illustrate the need for training and adequate staffing levels. Internal marketing cannot compensate for lack of training and inappropriate staffing levels.

This case study has been dealt with at length to illustrate the differing roles of internal marketing and the HRM function and the need for marketing and HRM to work together to set service levels. Another purpose has been to show that the HRM function already has a wide array of techniques to improve performance and motivation which include, for instance, job rotation, self-managing groups, career planning. Internal marketing techniques merely add to that array.

Another illustration of the limitations of internal marketing is provided by the UK retail industry where many large food retailers began to trade on Sunday. The problem here is that the majority of the employees prefer not to work on Sunday. The internal marketing solution to this problem would involve an attempt to change the attitudes of employees towards Sunday working by a well-executed communications campaign and by offering proper incentives to those who work on Sunday. In fact, this has been tried but the response from employees has been relatively poor and incentives programmes have proved to be too expensive or at least difficult to sustain in the long run. The solution that the retailers have hit upon is to recruit employees who are specifically required to work on Sundays in their employment contract. These employees are paid slightly higher than normal weekday rates but less than the special rates that existing employees were paid to work on Sunday. Hence, once again, the solution in this case was not internal marketing but external recruitment.

Who Should be Responsible for Internal Marketing?

Marketing management has for a long time viewed itself as the integrative function responsible for co-ordinating other company functions to ensure that the company is customer-oriented (Kotler 1980). The basis for this claim rests on the marketing function's direct contact with external customers. It is, therefore, not surprising to find that it is generally assumed, particularly in the services marketing literature, that internal marketing ought to be undertaken by marketers. In fact, George (1977) goes much further than this, as according to him the internal marketing approach suggests that:

"it is time to replace the personnel department in service firms with product managers who can implement a marketing approach to service employment management." (George 1977, p. 92)

Similar ideas are present in Berry and Parasuraman's (1991) work as is evident from their wide definition of internal marketing (cited above).

If such a policy were to be adopted by an organisation then it is bound to lead to conflict between marketing and HRM and operations management departments. Indeed, conflict would arise irrespective of which department led the implementation of internal marketing. This is because it may be seen by others as an attempt by that department to increase its influence within the organisation. It is, therefore, suggested that internal marketing needs to be the responsibility of senior management at the strategic management level and that internal marketing policies should be implemented through the HRM, marketing, and operations management departments. Such an approach avoids interdepartmental conflict and gives internal marketing the high level of managerial commitment necessary for its effective implementation and the achievement of high product and service quality.

Conclusions

The internal marketing concept has a major role to play in making employees customer-conscious. The value of the concept lies in the fact that it directs attention to employees and emphasises the key role of employees in the service process, service quality management, and quality management in general. However, the major thrust of the internal marketing concept of treating employees as customers has serious theoretical and practical drawbacks. This is evident in the relatively low adoption of this aspect of internal marketing. In contrast, the TQM concept of treating 'everyone as customer and supplier' has seen widespread adoption because of its relative simplicity and demonstrated effectiveness.

Another major concern of internal marketing is the use of marketing techniques to motivate employees. Although it has been shown that marketing techniques and concepts can be applied to create motivated employees, great care needs to be taken as to how these concepts and techniques are applied in practice. From the evidence presented above the most useful contributions that marketing can make in this area is the idea of customer (or employee) orientation, the idea of using a co-ordinated set of promotional (or communications) techniques, and marketing research. However, marketing concepts and techniques are unlikely to be sufficient by themselves to achieve customer consciousness amongst employees. Moreover, HRM already has a wide array of effective techniques to motivate employees; marketing techniques only add to that array.

The assumption of internal marketers that marketing should be the lead department in implementing internal marketing also needs to be challenged since this is a potential source of inter-functional conflict. Indeed, this would be the case whichever department led the implementation of internal marketing whether it is marketing, HRM, or operations. It is for this reason that we suggest that strategic management needs to be responsible for implementing internal marketing. This would also indicate to employees the high level of organisational commitment to internal marketing.

In view of the problems highlighted above there are very few existing models of how internal marketing should be implemented. Moreover, the simple and ad hoc transfer of marketing concepts is unlikely to produce results until precise specification is provided of how these concepts can be operationalised in the internal context. It is suggested that future research needs to develop models which specifically address the issues of the level(s) at which internal marketing is relevant and the inter-functional linkages and actions necessary for effective implementation of the internal marketing concept in services and non-service organisations. Only then will there be a more widespread use of internal marketing.

References

Berry, L.L., The Employee as Customer, *Journal of Retail Banking*, 3, March, 1981, pp. 25-28.

Berry, L.L., The Employee as Customer, in: C. Lovelock (ed.), *Services Marketing*, Kent Publishing Co., Boston, Massachusetts, 1984, pp. 271-278.

Berry, L.L. and A. Parasuraman, *Marketing Services: Competing Through Quality*, The Free Press, New York, 1991.

Blake, R. and J. Mouton, *The Management Grid*, Gulf Publishing Co, Houston, Texas, 1964.

Button, K., Business Television: Management From Outer Space, *Management Week*, 20th November, 1991, pp. 46-49.

Collins, B. and A. Payne, Internal Marketing: A New Perspective for HRM, *European Management Journal*, 9, 3, 1991, pp. 261-270.

Flipo, J.P., Service Firms: Interdependence of External and Internal Marketing Strategies, *Journal of European Marketing*, 20, 8, 1986, pp. 5-14.

George, W.R., The Retailing of Services - A Challenging Future, *Journal of Retailing*, Fall, 1977, pp. 85-98.

Grönroos, C., Internal Marketing - An Integral Part of Marketing Theory, In: J. H. Donnelly and W. E. George (eds.), *Marketing of Services*, American Marketing Association, 1981, Chicago, pp. 236-238.

Grönroos, C., *Internal Marketing - Theory and Practice*, American Marketing Association's Service Conference Proceedings, 1985, pp. 41-7.

Jacoby, S.M., Employee Attitude Surveys in Historical Surveys, *Industrial Relations*, 27, 1, 1988, pp. 74-93.

Kotler, P., A Generic Concept of Marketing, *Journal of Marketing*, 36, April, 1972, pp. 46-54.

Kotler, P. *Marketing Management: Analysis Planning and Control*, 4th edition, Prentice Hall, Englewood Cliffs NJ, 1980, pp. 9-10.

Kotler, P. and S.J. Levy, Broadening the Concept of Marketing, *Journal of Marketing*, 33, January 1969, pp. 10-15.

Millward, N. and M. Stevens, *The Second Workplace Industrial Relations Survey 1980-1984*, Gower, Aldershot, 1986.

Oakland, J.S, *Total Quality Management*, Butterworth - Heineman, London, 1991.

Piercy, N. and N. Morgan, Internal Marketing the Missing Half of the Marketing Programme, *Long Range Planning*, 24, 2, 1991, pp. 82-93.

Richardson, B.A. and G.C. Robinson, The Impact of Internal Marketing on Customer Service in A Retail Bank, *International Journal of Bank Marketing*, 4, 5, 1986, pp. 3-30.

Sasser, W.E. and S.F. Arbeit, Selling Jobs in the Service Sector, *Business Horizons*, June 1976, pp. 61-62.

Townley, B., Employee Communications Programmes, in: K. Sisson (ed.), *Personnel Management in Britain*, Basil Blackwell, Oxford, 1989, pp. 329-355.

10

The Service Encounter as a Learning Process

Hans Chr Garmann Johnsen and Harald Knudsen

Introduction

"If we can agree that the economic problem of society is mainly one of rapid adaptation to changes in the particular circumstances of time and place, it would seem to follow that the ultimate decisions must be left to the people who are familiar with these circumstances, who know directly of the relevant changes and of the resources immediately available to meet them. (...) But the "man on the spot" cannot decide solely on the basis of his limited but intimate knowledge of the facts of his immediate surroundings. There still remains the problem of communicating to him such further information as he needs to fit his decisions into the whole pattern of changes of the larger economic system."

F.A. Hayek
The Use of Knowledge in Society (1945)

The Service Encounter as a Learning Process

The service encounter can be understood as the moment when the customer meets the organization. This meeting involves many different processes that can be analyzed in different ways: the customer reaction to the product, to the artifacts or to the behaviour of the employee; the different types of production processes that are activated by customer demands; and the reaction of the employee to customer behaviour, i.e., the interaction processes. The service encounter may also involve reflections by both members of the organization and its customers. Some of these can be analyzed and implemented by administrative procedures. We might call these the *analytical elements* of the encounter: analyzing customer expectations, improving technical quality or improving delivery systems (Zeithaml,

Parasuraman and Berry 1990, Normann 1991). Once an organization has found the best 'formula', it might be able to copy it and make a routine.

The service encounter also onsists of other elements, what we might refer to as intuitive *elements*. These situations cannot easily be copied because they do not follow any particular pattern. Such situations could be critical incidents, for example when the customer has a special need, when the delivery system does not function or when an employee behaves in an unforeseen manner (Bitner, Booms and Tetreault 1990). But they could also be everyday situations when the employees show interest in the customer. Or situations involving ethical dilemmas (Rynning 1992), or situations that we describe in this paper as involving "theory building in practice" (Knudsen 1993).

Both typical analytic situations and intuitive situations involve a learning process. By learning we mean the *ability to master new situations*. In situations where one has to respond to immediate requests that are not planned or expected, the person in charge faces a challenge. He or she will have to make an immediate appraisal of the situation. The sort of knowledge required to master such a situation is different from the sort of knowledge applied in a routine situation.

The distinction that Senge (1990) has made between reactive, responsive and generative patterns of behaviour is of great help. Reactive means that one automatically behaves in a certain way when a new situation occurs. Typical manners of reactive behaviour are anger, fear, and other emotional responses. In a service encounter this could mean responding towards customer complaints with anger. *Responsive* behaviour, on the other hand, means response to the information immediately available to oneself. In a service situation this might mean that if a customer complains about a product, one tries to change it. By *generative* knowledge, Senge refers to the type of knowledge that is not immediately available to oneself, but knowledge that might explain why people behave as they do. In a service encounter, this might mean that the customer's complaint has nothing to do with a product. It might be a consequence of the customer's own problems or it might be some sort of 'system failure'. A system failure might be due to distance in time and place (the customer's complaint refers to some earlier encounters).

Knowledge of system structure and the need for generative knowledge is important in complex situations. But generative knowledge might involve two kinds of knowledge related to two kinds of complexity: Complexity due to a large number of cues (which is a analytical problem) and complexity due to the fact that there is no 'logic' solution (what we call intuitive situations). In intuitive situations where there are no readily available solutions, judgement has to be made on the basis of generative knowledge. Learning means knowing both the special and the general structure of the situation. The challenge is to be able to combine the intimate knowledge of the service encounter with the more general knowledge of the larger economic system.

Service literature is more and more concerned with the processes that take place in the service encounter. In a 'state-of-the-art' survey by Olsen in his doctoral thesis on qualities in services, he concludes by expressing the need for more knowledge about the service process and its relation to analytical models of service quality (Olsen 1992, chapter 3). Our conclusion is that insight into the learning process will improve our knowledge of the service encounter.

The Learning Process

Service Management as an Intuitive Task

An important choice underlying our discussion, is to give priority to those aspects of service management that are not easily subjected to analytical problem solving or easily derived from textbook recipes. The learning model focuses on the generation of up-front knowledge and intuitive task challenges. Since the level of prior expectations are important determinants of the subjective evaluation of service among customers, service quality depends to a great extent on 'up-front' and creative solutions to service issues.

The various tasks encountered by the organization are divided into two main groups: intuitive tasks and analytical tasks. No one area of problem solving, decision making or policy change can be seen as separate areas. This is shown in Figure 1, where the total amount of knowledge needed in various areas and for various issues is ranked on a scale of greater or less emphasis on intuitive or analytical aspects.

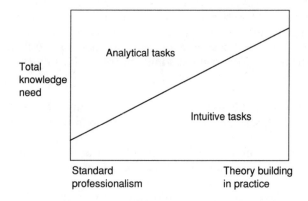

Figure 1.
Intuitive and analytical tasks in service management
(Source: Knudsen, 1993, Chapter 2)

Obviously, the total amount of knowledge needed to solve problems in different companies, at different times, and in different problem areas, vary considerably. Our concern here, however, is to illustrate how the total knowledge need may differ per case. In some cases we face mainly analytical tasks, for which professional education and standard professional competency provide solutions. In other cases we are facing mainly intuitive tasks, for which 'theory building in practice' is necessary —over and above the standard professional solutions. It seems that the development of service quality involves a great deal of the latter.

Hammond (1980, 1981) and Feldman (1986) suggest a cognitive continuum, with an intermediate category called "quasi-rational tasks". For purposes of illustration, however, we prefer the bipolar model. Typical analytical tasks in service management include such programmatic and routine tasks as staffing, scheduling, routine repair jobs, practising standards of politeness and customer assistance. Also included are advanced analysis concerning such issues as estimating returns on service expenditures and optimizing service packages. Whatever the level of sophistication, analytical tasks distinguish themselves by:

- The analytical steps needed to find a solution. These are generally known in advance. Analysis implies that the job may be broken down into constituent parts.

- Successful execution. This involves a limited number of cues and guidelines that may be defined in advance.

- The relationship between cues, which is marked by systematic order. The analytical task consists in varying the amounts and the composition of ingredients.

In order to utilize textbook solutions or apply scientific results to practical problems, some level of analysis will always be needed. Frequently, however, the number of contingencies and contingency combinations is so great, the level of uncertainty so high, and the need for additional insights so vast, that even tasks that can potentially be analyzed in a rational manner, turn out to be more intuitive than analytical. Intuitive tasks distinguish themselves by the following characteristics:

- The steps necessary for a solution are not known in advance. Often, not even *post hoc* rationalizations can be made about the cognitive process involved.

- The number of cues cannot easily be limited, and cannot be defined in advance. The relationship between cause and effect, between cues and result, is unclear.

- The cues are not easy to quantify, and cannot even always be defined. Rather than relying on data and systematic analysis, the decision maker engages in a learning process, where a wide variety of experiences and 'hunches' become part of innovative solutions.

Intuitive tasks in service management are characterized by great diversity. At the operational level, the encounter between service personnel and customers —the service encounter— involves a great number of incidents, challenges, and needs that cannot always be planned for in advance. Customers often feel that they see the 'true' picture of the company, when some critical incident occurs. Optimal behavior on the part of employees —when facing intuitive tasks— may take a great deal of creativity, cunning, discretion, courage, empathy, and stamina. In fact, developing such qualities in the work force is in itself an intuitive task. In spite of 'searches for excellence', no generalized recipe for developing a motivated, intelligent, service-oriented work force has been devised —so far!

Intuitive tasks are also seen at the top strategic and administrative levels of service management. Selecting a service 'slogan' is such a task. Coming up with inventive services and packages of service are intuitive tasks. Customer enthusiasm does not depend on having their expectations fulfilled —but rather surpassed. In order for this to occur, service strategies have to be 'up front'. Textbook solutions, based on empirical observations of the successful firms of yesterday, may form a lower level of customer acceptance. Bold, new solutions to familiar problems, and differentiated service designs, form the basis of customer enthusiasm and loyalty. Even where success-generating service schemes are to be copied from other firms, intuitive tasks are involved. No other firm has exactly the same environmental and organizational contingencies as the one they are copying from. Except where the analytical conditions are satisfied, the 'for copy' type of knowledge plays a minor role in service management.

Intuitive Tasks and Experimental Learning

If textbook solutions and contingency-battered empirical research cannot be the answer to intuitive tasks in service management, some other learning process must! If academic solutions and theories do not provide the answer, the practitioner must somehow construct his own theories. He becomes a 'theory builder' and engages in 'theory building in practice' (Knudsen 1990, 1991a, 1991b, 1993, Knudsen and Holbek 1988, 1990). And as much as we are accustomed to appreciating the qualities of an academic environment, we need to recognize the importance of environmental qualities surrounding the theory-building practitioner.

Theory building in practice is concerned with the development of new major concepts and solutions. But intuitive problem solving at all levels in the organization, as well as creative new behaviors, new ideas for customer assistance, and other additions to 'tacit knowledge', may be included. For purposes of simplicity all of these are called 'theory building in practice'. An overriding issue is under what **arena conditions** such theory building in practice is facilitated. Another overriding issue is what kind of **experiential processes** tend to enhance the development of personal qualities and "meta-cognitive" skills, that may assist the practitioner in his theory-building endeavors. A comprehensive extrapolation of the learning model is now being worked out (Knudsen 1993). The main concepts and elements of the learning model are described below.

The Theoros Theory Builder in Practice

Ever since antiquity, the word 'theory' has been associated with academics, and with the observation of some phenomenon by an independent student. The roots of the word are traditionally traced to the Greek word 'theorein', meaning to observe, behold, or gaze at. German linguistic-philosophical sources, notably Rausch (1982), has traced the original meaning derived from the Theoros figure in a Theoria legation. Based on his findings, Rausch has identified the Theoros as a theory built in practice. His own theory on *theory building in practice* is based on this observation. In ancient Greece, several centuries before antiquity, a Theoros was a representative of a village, participating in religious festivals in neighbouring villages (festivals that gradually grew to become the Olympic, Pythean, and other games). Thus, the Theoros role involved the crossing of borders into new realms and new varieties of experience; intimate communication with participants and the peer group, and a high level of involvement; exposure to audience acclaim and peer evaluation both during the 'festival' and upon return to the home environment; an element of identity —being chosen or appointed by a home audience, to which he is also responsible for whatever spiritual or material enrichment that might result from the festival; an element of discipline— operating in the tension between support and demands, security and challenges, sometimes partaking in competitive sports, always subject to festival norms and standards.

Theoria Arena Requirements of Theory Building

Personal faculties of emotion, motivation, and cognition are fostered in the intimate arenas of the home, the classroom, the playground —and the workplace, and society at large. But in order for theory building in practice to take place, certain additional requirements must be considered. In addition to the Theoros role elements of variety of experience and intimacy of communication, the elements of responsiveness, discipline and identity are involved. Furthermore, we may consider more broadly the Theoria elements most conducive to Theoros cognition during the festival encounter: the variety of experience represented by the participating Theoroi; communicability (language and cultural distance) between participants; freedom to cross borders and account for experiences; and an institutional/constitutional framework honoring basic Theoros roles.

While developmental and cognitive psychology tells us that prominent Theoros elements are conducive to human growth, and to emotional, motivational and cognitive development, historical reviews strongly indicate that societies marked by Theoria qualities have become arenas of economic and cultural progress (Knudsen 1993, chapter 3). Recent contributions in strategic management (Porter 1990), economic development (Jacobs 1984) and economic growth theory, essentially underscore that competitiveness, development and growth are the results of learning processes. Therefore, more than specifying rational behaviors, or models and ideals of excellence, improvement results when arena contingencies are obtained that stimulate experiential learning.

The various elements of theory building in practice can be examined and reinforced through five different learning cycles, or 'loops' —spanning from individual mastering and experiential learning, through modelling and systems dynamics, to the cultural and cognitive challenges of expanded variety of experiences. We call this the 'loop system' of theory building in practice.

Loop 1: The basic experiential learning model
The key to the Theoros role, then, is the expanded variety of experience subjected to intimacy of communication and feedback response. Interestingly, these are at the same time key variables in modern studies of personal mastery and meta-cognitive experience. By meta-cognitive experience we mean experiences that enhance our ability to learn, i.e., help us learn to learn through and from experience.

It is part of growing up, but it is also a process that may be improved through exposure of viewpoints, positions of responsibility, and through critical incidents - and particularly so when experiences that are neither completely unfamiliar or completely familiar are encountered (Flavell 1987).

A precondition for learning from such a variety of experience, is that the subject has a mastery orientation (motivation, willpower, achievement orientation, sense of project). The alternative is to incur helplessness in front of challenging varieties of experience. Again, it turns out that a mastery orientation is fostered through intimacy of communication, through dialogue between parents and child, between mentor and subject. By gradually being exposed to greater variety, to more demanding tasks and greater personal independence and responsibility, developmental psychologists tell us that 'immunity' against helplessness and a 'sense of project' and persistence is developed (Seligman 1975). The person grows in maturity to cross new borders and handle greater variety of experience —facing more and more challenging intuitive tasks without surrendering to helplessness.

Strikingly, faculties of emotion, motivation, and cognition —all of them basic ingredients for learning and mastery— are simultaneously developed in the psychological space of variety of experience and intimacy of communication! This is the essence of the basic loop of experimental learning shown in Figure 2.

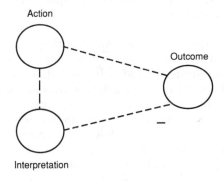

Figure 2.
The basic loop of experience learning
(Source: Knudsen, 1993, Chapter 4)

Experiential learning is superior to all other kinds of learning. This is a simple conclusion after a hundred years of pedagogical and psychological examination. However, as pointed out, among others by Senge (1990), the effectiveness of such learning is severely reduced when the time/space distance between action and outcome is increased.

Under ideal circumstances, outcomes of action are interpreted, and new actions are improved and corrected through feedback. Obviously, such ideal conditions do not always prevail in our organizations and societies. What is missing in the model is a number of distortions. The present learning model (Knudsen 1993) recognizes four main sources of distortions, some of which are due to arena deficiencies and some that are due to personal inadequacies. In order to correct for the distortions, new elements are added to the basic loop, gradually making it more complex, but also more conducive to theory building in practice and to finding sensible solutions to intuitive tasks.

Loop 2: The Cybernetic Loop - time, space, and complexity distortions
A basic problem of learning from experience is the distance between action and outcome. The distance causes time, space, and complexity distortions. The linkage between action and outcome becomes causally weak. What management can do, is primarily to introduce cybernetic elements. In service management - where the linkage between action and customer response is weak, the systematic use of detectors is introduced. Where communication between detector elements in the organization and decision-making elements is weak, systematic feedback is implemented. Goals and standards of performance are refined. Implementation control is overhauled. Beyond the basic control elements of cybernetics, however, the organization may engage in more advanced systems analysis and control mechanisms, such as archetypal identification (Senge 1990), soft modelling and the like. Another general recommendation is to reduce organizational complexity, through the reduction of organizational interdependence, through the simplification of strategies (fewer product areas, markets) and through relying on simpler signal systems in the organization, such as price-quantity-quality signals and normative standards of decision making.

Loop 3: The disciplinary loop - intersystemic distortions
Even when an organization is internally 'cybernetically sound', things may go wrong. A company may be profitable only as long as it enjoys such preferred treatment as: government subsidies, tax haven benefits, protection by the local 'mafia' or a local 'oligarchy' of powerful banks and business firms, or —in the case of public organizations— monopoly power and the steady income of tax money. It may have access to an abundance of public infrastructure, or it may for various reasons be deprived of such production factors. A company may be 'cybernetically sound', yet fails if competition is unfair, government regulations 'skewed' or practised in an arbitrary manner, or if markets plunge in a completely unpredictable manner. To fix the disciplinary loop is primarily the responsibility of society. However, business firms and public organizations need to be aware of intersystemic distortions, or else their theory building in practice will be in vain or at least subject to the erosion of time and change. The crucial question to ask is to what extent competition is fair, whether it is a good platform from where to build the company's theory in practice.

Loop 4: The democratic loop - overcoming interpersonal experiential distortions by creating identity
A basic problem in all hierarchical or bureaucratic organizations is that first-hand experiences are gained at the bottom of the organization, at the level of salesmen, stewards, reception desk officials, bartenders, cashiers ... and that these people are not involved in decision making. The fundamental links of Loop 1, the basic experiential learning model, are broken, because the people acting and registering the outcome are not the people responsible for interpretation and decision. The

democratic ideal tells us that people who are affected by decisions should take part in those decisions. Thus, democracy is a key ingredient in experiential learning.

An organization may be under-democratized or over-democratized. By under-democratized we mean the kind of "not being heard" problem of the hierarchy and the bureaucracy. By over-democratized we think of organizations where everybody is represented in all decisions, and where the people really affected and really concerned 'are drowned' in meetings and in their quest for 'representation'.

The key to the democratic loop is to make the connection between critical incidents and a critical development in the organization on the one hand, and a personally felt "sense of crisis" on the other. This is called the principle of identity. Unless some person identifies with the problem, nothing will result - no learning takes place. Company goals need to be aligned with personal values, personal objectives and imagination. Company feedback systems need to involve a personal sense of crisis and stimulate a personal sense of project. Company decision-making needs at some point to be equal to the personal interpretation of Loop 1.

Loop 5: The expanded variety of experience loop - overcoming cognitive and cultural distortions
An organization may have built-in cybernetic mechanisms of every kind, it may be subjected to fair competition and a balance of taxation and infrastructural support, it may have high standards of democratic participation —yet the people in command simply do not respond rationally to key signals. A number of —personal or cultural— problems may account for this. Cognitive distortions include lack of cognitive ability, psychologically determined distortions such as cognitive dissonance, personal helplessness, depression or 'burn-out'. Cultural distortions take the form of 'in-house blindness', making strategies become final values, being a slave of success. Counter-distortive measures include the crossing of experiential borders, amplification of chaos, and the implementation of processes of defreezing and refreezing (Knudsen and Holbek 1988, Nonaka 1988, Lewin 1947). Where the personal psyche of the actor is marked by helplessness, a process of rehabilitation and immunization is called for. Where the problems are of the dissonance and in-house blindness type, confrontation through the exposure to variety of experience is called for.

The Total Model of Learning to Learn

The model builds upon meta-cognitive experience as the basis of learning to learn —not on meta-cognitive instruction or technical drills. A great number of learning techniques, superlearning or accelerated learning techniques are presently available through books, tapes and videos. The individual can learn methods for more effective recall, better cognitive organization and mapping, etc. Clearly, particularly in the field of cybernetics and systems improvement, some techniques can be of great value. The archetype techniques used by the Center for Organizational Learning at MIT is a case in point.

In the present model we do not exclude the application of technical tools. The main concept, however, is to facilitate meta-cognitive experiences and theory building in practice, to make the workday an act of discovery, and to facilitate innovative thinking —not by copying textbook and research solutions or by imitating companies of excellence— but by merging the experience of the excellent with that of one's own company to formulate new concepts, new theories in practice.

The Learning Arena and the Market Process

The Learning Arena

In our search for qualities that characterise a good learning environment in organizations, we have been able to identify three important phenomena. One is what we have called *intimacy of communication*: the possibility of communicating and learning from each other. Intimacy means to be sensitive, even to customers. Intimacy is also a precondition for trust and sympathy, which is an important quality for encouraging employees. A hotel manager told us that if his front desk personnel did not know him, his way of thinking, and if he did not show them his trust, they could not handle complicated situations to the satisfaction of the customer. Without the trust, support and sympathy of the manager, the employee would behave in a bureaucratic, uneasy and insecure manner in critical situations.

On the learning arena one can bring together individual qualities like variety of experience and imagination. *Variety of experience* means that we have the ability to take knowledge from one arena and use it on another, or better, to combine experiences from different arenas anew to develop new theories. We noticed during our work that a department of the municipality had much to learn from the way the local hotel treated its customers. But still, it is the level of *imagination* that will decide whether the employee has the ability to explore alternatives. Imagination is also a quality that might be encouraged in a learning environment.

Division of Knowledge

Intimacy of communication, variety of experience and imagination are elements that explains **why** learning takes place. It does not explain **how** learning takes place *in the market*.

The situation described by Hayek at the beginning of this discussion introduces the perspective of division of knowledge in society. We take the liberty here to apply the same approach to organizations by focusing on the division of knowledge in organizations. To utilize the knowledge in the organization is one of the biggest challenges of organization theory. To accept the idea of division of knowledge, and to explore methods to utilize different types of knowledge on different levels, is relevant to the service encounter. Kirzner has called this the Knowledge Problem A (Kirzner 1992, p. 169). The central aspect of Knowledge Problem A is *coordination* of knowledge (it corresponds roughly to *analytical tasks* in Figure 1).

But there is also a Knowledge Problem B. Knowledge Problem B is related to developing new knowledge, inventing new ideas or building new theories. Knowledge Problem B cannot be solved through coordination, it cannot even be comprehended as a coordination problem. Knowledge Problem B is related to how genuine creation or learning, take place (it corresponds roughly to intuitive tasks in Figure 1).

The service literature has often focused on *'the moment of truth'* —when the organization meets its customers (Normann 1991). But this moment of truth might sometimes be a process, a dialogue, or an exchange of values. The intuitive elements of this process are related to the dialogue with the customer both because his demands might change during the process and because the environment in which the business operates is constantly undergoing change. The question we address is: How does the organization learn to conduct better service under these circumstances?

We think it is important to accept that learning takes place on different levels in the organization. These levels have different time-spans, they are related to customer encounters in different ways. There is a division of knowledge and learning in the organization, but it is kept together by a common constitution, a common set of administrative routines, or a common set of norms and codes. Hayek has addressed the question of how it is possible to act in a complicated world when it is impossible for each individual to know every piece of information that might be relevant to his decision? The Hayekian answer to this coordination problem (Knowledge Problem A) is that people relate their actions to common **norms** (Kirzner 1992, p. 173). The constitution of society with its general structures and norms is a common point of reference for the social process.

The Structure of Our Argument

The idea of the organization presented here is one similar to the type of systems and sub-systems we have in society: There is a constitutional system and sub-systems of administrative behaviour (Gibson, Ivancevich and Donnelly 1973, p. 84, Silverman 1974, p. 55, Burgleman and Sayles 1986, p. 107).

When the customer meets the organization in a service encounter, he steps into the arena of the organisation and, to some extent, takes part in the production process. But in this process, a *new* arena is established, one that exists in the *border* between the market and the organization. The reason for this is that the organization can only to *a certain extent* direct the customer. The customer is not part of the organisation arena. On the other hand, the service encounter is to *a certain extent* directed by the organisation, so it is not the same as the market arena.

The *service arena* has a structure, and within this structure there are processes. Who will direct these processes is a matter of the relative strength of the organisation compared to the market. Based on our research, we have been able to identify five elements in this structure and five processes that exist between them:

First, there is an *constitutional element*. The constitution of the arena lays down rules for how the service encounter will proceed. Some organisations are very open to the influence of their customers, while others are more closed. Some have very strict rules as to how to interact with customers, while others leave this to the employee. The constitution will, in general, be an unwritten code that legitimises the interactions between customer and organisation.

A constitution will be interpreted differently and have different meaning for different functions in the organisation. There is a process of diversity related to the division of knowledge in the organisation. Division of knowledge is one element that encourages variety of experience. This variety will decide what amount of complexity exists in the organisation, and on the other hand, the process of complexity brings us to the discourse. The element of discourse will be a function both of the constitutional element and of the division of knowledge.

There will always be an element of discourse related to the organisation. In the discourse, a lot of opinions will be expressed. Like in a democratic society, the challenge is to utilise this discourse in order to make better decisions. Therefore a process of simplicity follows from the element of discourse. This process leads to the formation of norms. Norms are the basis for exchange, but between the norm level and the exchange level, there is a process of choice.

This is the outline of the structure of our argument. The question is: How does the learning process operate within this model? The answer that we discuss here, is that it operates on different levels and on different processes. Managers can influence the constitutional level, they can bring in variety of experience and they can influence norms and make choices. On the other hand, they have limited influence on the complexity of the discourse activity and on the division of knowledge.

The quality of learning in the market will be a function of all these processes, and one of the main challenges for a learning organisation is to be able to establish the right interplay between these elements and processes.

A Liberal Constitution of the Learning Arena

A learning arena is a place where the dialogue both internally in the organization and externally with the customer can take place. The learning arena might also be a place both for reflection and distance to problems and for a discourse.

A liberal discourse process depends on three principles:

- that individuals are equal partners in the discourse;
- that the discourse in itself is useful; and
- that each individual regards the discourse as useful (Johnsen 1992).

If these principles are recognized, then there is the possibility that the discourse will continue. The alternative to discourse could be exit, conflict or some sort of use of authority.

The organization's purpose and strategy are an important basis for the discourse. When a customer makes demands, is faced with alternatives, or expresses his opinions, he steps into the discourse arena. Over time, some patterns of reactions will emerge which might lead to the changing of the company strategy: this is the process of learning.

The learning process will be a function of variety of experience, intimacy of communication and imagination. In order for people to use their knowledge qualities to the advantage of the organization, they have to be committed to the task and to identify with the needs of the organization. People can bring in new experience in the organization, or stimulate the development of experience by learning from other organizations. They will have responsibility for establishing intimacy of communication. Our hypothesis is that the sort of sensitivity and intimacy that exists within the organization, will affect to what extent the organization will be sensitive to its customers. Commitment will be a function of trust and dialogue and will be encouraged by the same process. If customers feel that they are taken seriously, they will be more loyal to the organization.

But still there might be unexpected, critical incidents where the employee must rely on his own judgement. How does he act and how does he learn from such a situation? In an Hayekian theory, individuals will search for very simple structures to which they can relate their actions. This might be norms (I do that but not that!) or prices (I chose the cheapest alternative!) or rules (I do that because that seems to be right!). Our hypothesis is that in order to act, one must simplify the decision problem (Miller 1993) (see loop 2 in part 1).

According to Hayek, it is possible to observe, over a period of time, that liberal societies with general structures (as opposed to those with detailed state planning) to which the individual can relate their actions, are those societies that are the most prosperous (Hayek 1988). The same might apply to organizations. Although we have not gone into details about the normative aspect of this theory and we know very little about how decisions are actually made (Rynning 1992), we will base our argument on this 'Hayekian' approach. This means that we will have to show how our learning model will help organizations to improve their service performance.

Our assumption is that the service encounter encourages learning. The organisation might even learn more through its service encounter thanthrough its internal processes. The reason for this, we think, is that the service arena in general has a more liberal constitution and its discourse represents more variety of experience than that within organisations.

We would like to draw attention to one aspect of the liberal constitution that might explain why it encourages growth and prosperity: The discourse operates on the basis of voluntary exchange of ideas. In a voluntary exchange, both parties will increase their value by the exchange. This fundamentally creative process of exchange forms the basis of the liberal constitution.

However, this is an ideal situation based on the principles that those who are effected by the exchange participate in the process (see loop 4 in part 1). It is also based on the discourse process operating in a sound way (see loop 3 in part 1). In addition to this, it is important that the exchange relates to the formation of norms in a way that improves the quality of society. Let us now turn to this last condition.

The Organization and the Market Process

The idea of the market process presented here is that of the neo-Austrian school of economics. In Kirzner's words: *"For us the existence of systematic market forces means the existence of a spontaneous process of learning."* (Kirzner 1992, p. 201). This means that the organization is a learning arena within a market that is a learning process.

What are the driving forces behind the learning process in the market? According to Kirzner: " ... they are driven by alertness of individuals intent on achieving their purposes" (Kirzner 1992, p. 204). Alertness and purposes cause individuals to explore possibilities, learn from mistakes or try new alternatives. Having a specific purpose in mind means that one constantly looks for something, that is, looks in a specific direction. In the service encounter, for instance, only certain customer demands are relevant to the organization. Purposes, which for an organization means strategy, explains which.

According to Kirzner, purposes and alertness are sufficient elements to explain how the spontaneous coordination of the market process emerges. It is sufficient to explain how Knowledge Problem A is solved: It is solved because unless the seller is able to agree with the buyer on a price, there will be no exchange. As long as both seller and buyer has a purpose, and therefore become involved in exchange, they must generate enough knowledge about each other to agree on a price. In a service encounter, this might also be a norm, or a quality standard.

Knowledge Problem B, however, is not solved in this way. Knowledge Problem B is not a coordination problem, it is the problem of how genuinely new knowledge is created. Knowledge Problem B is related to genuine creation and discoveries. One might ask: why do some people go on expeditions of discovery and what are the qualities of the discoverer? (see loop 5 in part 1). Take the story (metaphor) of Columbus: what was it that led him to travel, and what were the qualities needed for him to complete the project? Note that these might have been two different sorts of qualities. It is also important to acknowledge the distinction between production, discovery and luck (Kirzner, 1992, p. 221): When Columbus invested resources in his travels, he did not know the outcome, so it was not a production process. However, the eventual outcome was not a result of blind luck. Columbus did have a plan, he did search in a particular direction, so he was a discoverer.

This phenomenon cannot be explained by the market process (Kirzner 1992, p. 178). It is the personal qualities of the individual, such as courage, sense of mission, or sense of crisis, which makes him a discoverer. But there are some qualities of the learning environment that might encourage discoveries.

The Service Encounter and the Market Process

The service encounter is the organization's encounter with the market. This encounter forms the basis for the organization's learning and decision making. The market process is in itself a learning process. Learning in the market process is related to knowledge problems A and B. Problem A is a coordination problem. Learning means to gain insight into the customer's preferences and needs in order to establish exchange. Norms play an important role in this coordination. Knowledge Problem B, however, is **not** a coordination problem and requires a different kind of learning.

Since learning is going on in the market process constantly, the organization must constantly adapt to new realities. The ability to learn, or to learn how to learn, is important when one is working in a changing environment (Agyris 1982). Organizations that are very dependent on the market, have to be alert to market changes. One important way in which the organization learns is through the service encounter, since that is when the customer steps on to the discourse arena of the organization. The service encounter is a voice situation, i.e., a situation where the customer expresses his opinion. Note that the activation of voice by the customer is a function of loyalty, i.e., that the customer is entering the discourse arena (Hirschman 1970, p. 77). The alternative situation is exit, when customers leave, or do not enter the arena of the organization at all. In both situations, it is important for the organization to acquire knowledge about the market. This knowledge is not about each individual customer, but about the norms that customers refer to (Feldman 1984, Cadotte, Woodruff and Jenkins 1987). In order to understand the market, it is important to understand the process of emergence of norms.

When we introduce norms in the exchange process, we are able to understand how the gap between customer expectations and management perceptions is bridged (Zeithaml *et al.* 1990, p. 37). One way of bridging this gap is to obtain enough information about the customer in order to meet his expectations. Analytical tools might help us in this process. However, we think it is often impossible to collect all the relevant information. The function of norms is to establish a common point of reference between the organization and the customer.

Norms are created in different ways, and the development of service in society is one example of a new norm. What we will address here is the question of how norms are maintained and why they exist. A classification of norms has been made by Ullmann-Margalit (1977). She has identified three groups of norms: PD norms, Coordination norms, and norms of partiality.

PD norms (derived from game theory: prisoner's dilemma type of norm) are based on convention. There might therefore be individuals that are rent-seeking and calculate that others will be loyal to the convention while they are not (the free-rider problem). For the service encounter, in the case that service performance is based on a convention between the organization and its customers, it is important to build loyalty. However, as long as service is based on a norm of the PD type, there will be a possibility for one part to violate the covenant (Ullmann-Margalit 1977, p. 67). An example of service as a PD norm might be illustrated by the case of a Norwegian retailer in stoves: In a small village, there were two retailers who sold stoves. One of them invested in a large showroom for his stoves. His competitor had no showroom. What happened was that customers went to the retailer with the showroom, where they could see the stoves and get information. But this retailer did not sell any stoves, while his competitor, the one with no showroom, increased his sales considerably. Customers in the village had improved their level of service because they had a showroom where they could see stoves, while they could buy it at a considerable discount from the other retailer, whose overhead was lower since he did not have a showroom. When service performance is of this PD type, it is important to build up loyalty with the customer (which, however, is difficult in a competitive environment).

Service as *coordination norm* avoids this dilemma. If we have a coordination effect, everybody will be 'better off' and no-one would have anything to gain from violating the norm. New concepts, like the supermarket in retailing, could be examples of this type of norm. In the old type of grocery store, one had to wait to be served at the front desk. In supermarkets, people are allowed to walk around, to select goods by themselves, and enjoy low prices. Many people regard this as an improvement in service and there is no free-rider problem since they can only enjoy the service by using it. The supermarket is an invention that has improved service performance and set new norms for service in retailing.

Norms of partiality are norms where one part 'gets more' than the other. It is a type of norm that legitimates inequality. Norms of partiality are therefore not a result of 'rational' exchange. For a service situation, this would mean the same as if some customers received more than they paid for. There could be very good reasons for that, for instance when disabled people get the best seats in a theatre, or children receive some free services. Sometimes, partiality will be accepted and will promote loyalty. In other situations, for example. when politicians enjoy too many privileges (on behalf of the citizens), norms can be with disapproval. Norms of partiality very often refer to special traditions or culture.

These three groups of norms are distinct, and it is important to be aware of what type of norm one refers to in the service encounter. Improving service might be a coordinating task, solving Knowledge Problem A. But that does not hold for all forms of service. And often it is the case that solving Knowledge Problem A by introducing an new coordination norm involves Knowledge Problem B (in inventing the new norm). This indicates that there are two separate learning processes related to the market process. In Kirzner's words, the problem can be formulated as follows: *"To be sure, the spontaneous emergence of any institution indeed relies on the very same process through which Knowledge Problem A is solved in markets. (.....) On the other hand, however, it has been our aim to point out (...) that these earlier economic insights into the spontaneously co-operative properties of markets do not, in themselves, provide any reassurance concerning the benign quality of the long run tendencies of institutional development. (.....) The explanation for such benign tendencies, if indeed they exist, must be sought elsewhere."* (Kirzner 1992, p.179)

This is exactly what we have tried to do by presenting the learning model. It is our main argument that the quality of the service development, its benign tendencies, which in our context means the same as improvement in service performance, depends on the quality of the learning process and of the learning arena.

Conclusions

The Service Encounter as a Learning Process

We have tried to discuss the service encounter in relation to the learning process. We think it is important to understand and identify the main elements of the learning process. Our model looks at both the elements that constitute learning on the individual level, and the learning arena that operates inside the organization and in the market.

We have identified two types of learning: Coordinated learning and creative learning. We have identified some crucial elements in the individual learning process as well as qualities of the learning arena that stimulate learning. We have discussed the function of alertness and purposes, and we have discussed the function of norms.

Our idea of the service encounter is that it involves exchange and learning. We have looked at three aspects of learning: The individual qualities of learning, the qualities of the learning arena, and the learning process in the market. The challenge in the learning process is to be able to combine the intimate individual knowledge with that of the greater economic system.

When people meet in a service encounter, they try to learn enough about one another to make an exchange. This involves learning and a medium of exchange, what we have called norms. The service encounter might result in an improvement of norms; this is what we have called service development (and which will have normative implications). But since norms are of different types, it is important to understand the nature of norms in order to understand what service development implies. We referred to this earlier as generative knowledge.

In order to reach a level of exchange in the service encounter, the three following elements have to be present: the utility of the process, purpose and alertness. If these three elements are present at both parties in an exchange, it should be possible to find a solution to the pure coordination problem (Knowledge Problem A). However, in order to be able to improve service, to invent new and better norms, Knowledge Problem B must be solved. In order to solve this problem, we have introduced what we have called the Theoros qualities as well as the qualities of the liberal constitution of the service arena. These qualities stimulate creative learning, which in our view is an important precondition for improving service performance.

References

Agyris, C., *Reasoning, Learning and Action*, Jossey-Bass Publishers, London, 1982.

Bitner, M.J., B.H. Booms and M.S. Tetreault, The Service Encounter: Diagnosing Favourable and Unfavourable Incidents, *Journal of Marketing*, 54, 1990.

Burgleman, R., and L. Sayles, *Inside Corporate Innovation. Strategy, Structure, and Managerial Skills*, McMillan, London, 1986.

Cadotte, E., R. Woodruff and R.L. Jenkins, Expectations and Norms in Models of Consumer Satisfaction, *Journal of Marketing Research*, August, 1987.

Feldman, D., The development and enforcement of group norms, *Academy of Management Review*, 9, 1984.

Feldman, J., On the Difficulty of Learning from Experience, in: H.P. Sims Jr. and D.A. Gioia, *The Thinking Organization: Dynamics of Organizational Social Cognition*, Jossey-Bass, San Francisco, 1986.

Flavell, J.H., Speculations about the Nature and Development of Metacognition, in: F.E. Weinert and R.H. Kluwe, *Metacognition, Motivation and Understanding*, Lawrence Erlbaum Ass. Publishers, Hillsdale, N.J., 1987.

Gibson, J.L., J. Ivancevich, J.M. Donnelly jr, *Organizations: Structure, Process, Behaviour*, Business Publications, Texas, 1973.

Hammond, K.R., Principles of Organization in Intuitive and Analytical Cognition, Report no. 231, Center for Research on Judgment and Policy, University of Colorado, 1981.

Hammond, K.R., The Integration of Research in Judgment and Decision Theory, Report no. 226, Center for Research on Judgment and Policy, University of Colorado, 1980.

Hayek, F. A., *The Fatal Conceit*, Routledge, London 1988.

Hirschman, A., *Exit, Voice, and Loyalty*, Harward, 1970.

Jacobs, J., *Cities and the Wealth of Nations*, London, 1985.

Johnsen, H. Chr Garmann, Mot en liberal Argumentasjonsteori; *Norsk Filosofisk Tidsskrift*, 1991.

Kirzner, I., *The Meaning of the Market Process*, Routledge, London, 1992.

Knudsen, H. and J. Holbek, Bordercrossing Strategies and the Concept of Theory - Prescripts for Teaching Business Strategy, Paper presented to the 1988 International Symposium on Pacific Asian Business in Honolulu, Hawaii, January 6-9, 1988.

Knudsen, H. and J. Holbek, Bridging the Gap between Theory and Practice, Paper presented to the 10th Annual International Conference of the Strategic Management Society, Stockholm, Sept. 24-27, 1990, Kristiansand, Agder College/Trondheim, University of Trondheim, 1990.

Knudsen, H., Background notes: Building Bridges Eastward, Paper presented to the Nordic Conference on Social Ethics, Sigtuna, November 8-11, 1990, Kristiansand: Agder College, 1990.

Knudsen, H., Democratic Ideals and Economic Viability - An Interactive Business Simulation Approach. Paper presented to the Kristiansand Workshop on Economic Turnarounds, Kristiansand, Agder College, 1991a.

Knudsen, H., Teoribygging i Praksis. Draft. Kristiansand: Agder College, 1993. Ch. 1-4.

Knudsen, H., Why Theoros Managers are Scarce in the Soviet Union - The case of frustrated learning structures, Paper presented to the 11th Annual International Conference of the Strategic Management Society, Toronto, October 23-26, 1991, Kristiansand, Agder College, 1991b.

Lewin, K., Group Decisions and Social Change, in T.M. Newcombe and E.L. Hartley (eds.), *Readings in Social Psychology*, Holt, Reinhart & Winston, 1947.

Miller, D., The Architecture of Simplicity, *Academy of Management Review*, 18, 1, 1993, pp. 116-138.

Nonaka, I., Creating Organizational Order out of Chaos: Self-Renewal in Japanese Firms, *California Management Review*, Spring, 1988.

Normann, R., *Service Management*, Oslo, 1991.

Olsen, M., Kvalitaet i Banktjaenester, Hoegskolan i Karlstad, Forskningsrapport 92:2, 1992.

Porter, M.E., *The Competitive Advantage of Nations*, London, 1990.

Rausch, H., *Theoria: von Ihrer sakralen zur philosophischen Bedeutung*, München, 1982.

Rynning, H., *Commitment and Ethical Decision-Making in the R&D Process in Pharmaceutical Industry*, Åbo Academy University, June, 1992.

Seligman, M.E.P., *Helplessness: On Depression, Development, and Death*. Freeman Press, San Fransisco, 1975.

Senge, P., *The Fifth Discipline - The Art and Practice of the Learning Organization*, New York, 1990.

Senge, P., The Leader's New World: Building Learning Organizations, *Sloan Management Review*, Fall, 1990.

Silverman, D., *The Theory of Organisations*, Heinemann, London, 1974.

Ullmann-Margalit, E., *The Emergence of Norms*, Clarendon Press, Oxford, 1977.

Zeithaml, V.A., A. Parasuraman and L.L. Berry, *Delivering Quality Service. Balancing Consumer Perceptions and Expectations*, New York, Free Press, 1990.

11

Government Service Centres:
Three Models in Practice

Robbert Masselink, Jan Post
and Rob Schouten

Introduction

For a number of years now the Dutch government, specifically the Ministry of Home Affairs, has tried to stimulate initiatives in order to improve the quality of services offered to its citizens. Much research has been carried out and at this moment experiments are conducted in order to test models of service concepts. The results of the research and the experiments provide valuable information for the 650 municipalities in The Netherlands, many of which have launched initiatives to improve the provision of services to the public.

We think that the cycle of studies on governmental service quality in The Netherlands conducted in the past two years provides interesting insights for managers active in the field of governmental services who are coping with similar developments. We have the feeling, and some of the research performed confirms this, that the Dutch situation is unique with respect to the field of Government Service Centres, where many different governmental services are offered to the public at one counter or one location.

This paper is divided into four parts. The first part describes the basic research, which led to the development of three models of a Government Service Centre (GSC). We will discuss an analysis framework on the service-rendering process, a description of requirements for a GSC and, finally, the three models.

The second part describes the experiments that have been set up in four municipalities. Firstly, the Dutch situation with regard to their offering of services is briefly discussed. Next, the set-up and goal of each experiment are described, followed by the accompanying research method and the quality audit on the experiments.

In the third part, the "Quality Audit on Government Services" is explained with regard to two aspects: quality service and the efficiency of the service-rendering process.

The experiments with the Government Service Centre models are still in progress. The results, as well as the knowledge and experience gathered and the instruments developed in order to conduct the experiments, are shared with other municipalities in The Netherlands. As a result, many municipalities develop service centres based on the newly developed insights with a higher level of service quality and more efficient work processes both behind the counter and in the back office.

The Government Service Centre

The research which laid solid foundations for the development of the three models is split up into five phases. The first phase gives a general outline on the development of the relation between the government and society. In the second phase a framework for analysis on the processes of service provision is developed. This framework is based on literature research and on quantitative research among the Dutch population. On the basis of this analysis a programme for requirements for the GSC has been developed (phase 3). This programme brings us to the fourth phase, in which three models of GSCs are developed. Finally, in the fifth phase, the three models are worked out in more detail on the basis of the outcome of a workshop on this topic.

The Roots and the Use of the Framework

One of the basic assumptions in the GSC research is that the service provision process can be divided into several steps or phases. This assumption is for a major part inspired by the 'system movement' (for example, Robbins 1976, Rosenthal, Van Schendelen and Ringeling 1987). Several authors have independently performed research into the provision process of governmental services. Post (1991) studied the major barriers in the service provision process, and Masselink and Sprecher (1991) split up the provision process into six phases: attention, orientation, reaction, interaction, settlement and distribution.

The process model was very helpful in analysing problems in government service provision. Schouten (1992) performed further research and ultimately came up with a framework that consisted of four phases which seemed appropriate for the general governmental service provision process. This framework served three purposes:

- to make an inventory of bottlenecks in the service provision from the *citizens' perspective*;
- to describe any deficiencies in the organization with regard to the service provision process from the *viewpoint of the organization*;
- to provide *recommendations* on how to improve the service provision.

In view of the inventory of bottlenecks in the service provision two steps were taken: first, the existing literature concerning bottlenecks in the service process was examined (content analysis). Second, a representative telephone survey was held among 1,200 people who had been in contact with a government organization over the preceding period of six months. Combined with interviews and workshops with employees of service organizations, this research led to an overview of the major 'gaps' in the organization of the service provision process. From this overview, prescriptions, or so-called 'programme requirements', could be derived as to how to improve service provision. This ultimately led to the formulation of three models of Government Service Centres.

The Four Phases of Service Provision

The process of service provision starts, in our framework, even before the actual contact between the government and members of the public, or rather: its clients. Before clients contact the government they must first know that they may obtain something from the government and, secondly, to whom they can address their question. Once they know where to go, their actual interaction with the government takes place. Finally, the service will be provided (or not, as the case may be). This means there are four phases that can be distinguished within the process of service provision: awareness, formulation of demand, actual interaction and service provision. These four phases are discussed in detail below.

Bottlenecks in Service Provision: The Citizen's Perspective and the Organizational Perspective

The Awareness Phase

First of all, the members of the public must be aware of specific rights and duties before they can formulate a demand.

The Citizen's Perspective
While citizens often lack sufficient knowledge of governmental services, we discovered an inadequate use of services (non-use of facilities). For example, a study into the lack of applications for Social Security in Tilburg revealed that an average of 30% of respondents, all of them recipients of benefit in Tilburg, were not aware of specific social security regulations (for example, income thresholds) with which they had to comply to qualify for a specific service. The weaker members of society lack the skills that are needed to make effective use of the services being offered (In 't Groen and Konings, 1984).

The Organizational Perspective
This means, from an organizational perspective, that the government lacks a proactive attitude and the governmental service organization lacks the structures that are needed to overcome this problem.

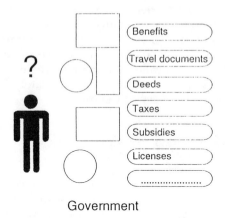

Government

Figure 1. The awareness phase

In the awareness-raising phase, each service provider has a promotional role to play with regard to his products and services. An important consideration for the government is that social groups —for example, the elderly, handicapped or unemployed people— are reached with a large number of products and services (merit goods). The public must know what they can ask from the government. From the government's perspective this means that it must have sufficient knowledge about its target groups to achieve optimum coverage. Making people aware of a need will urge them to search for information and to formulate questions. It is at this point that the second phase of the process starts: the formulation of demand.

Formulation of Demand

Members of the public must be able to operationalize their need in one or more demands that tie in closely with the government's provisions. What is more, they must know whom to address with these demands.

The Citizen's Perspective
The telephone survey has shown that the formulation of demand causes difficulties in seven per cent of all cases where people had been in contact with a government organization over the preceding period of six months, ranging from minor to major difficulties. Other studies, focusing on, for example, applications for individual rent subsidies, recompense for Municipal Land Tax, dog tax and waste levies, revealed that non-users of government facilities hardly knew where to apply for these services. This is all the more serious when we come to think that these people are clients of the government, i.e., of the social welfare departments, anyhow. They are unable to translate their problems into a bureaucratic question. One might say that they are not bureaucratically competent. They need money and

thus ask for social welfare payments and do not think of or, consequently, ask about other possible and important facilities.

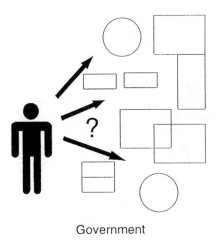

Government

Figure 2. Formulation of Demand

The Organizational Perspective
On the other hand, social welfare departments also seem unable to find an overall solution for citizens' questions. In other words, social welfare departments deal with social welfare payments, rather than, for example, social rent subsidies. Difficulties in formulating the demand arise when the question is not put to the proper (part of the) organization, or when the question has to be translated before it can be expressed in terms of the government's products and services. This problem will particularly occur in the case of more complex services: services that involve several providers or whose required level of expertise is high, or both.

Interaction Phase

After the client has formulated his demand, the interaction phase starts. This phase is concerned with the actual interaction: the service process.

The Citizen's Perspective
During the phase of actual interaction, approximately 30% of those who had been in contact with a government organization over the preceding period of six months were dissatisfied with the process.

The Organizational Perspective
When analysing this dissatisfaction, a distinction can be made between problems connected with contact between the public and a civil servant and problems connected with the organization and structure of the government's service provision.

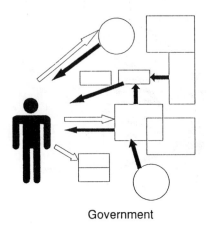

Government

Figure 3. Interaction

We will first address the latter problem. The government recognizes the need for a more organized service provision, especially with regard to its own information supply: Many civil servants dealing with the public are dissatisfied with the level of internal information they are able to supply to clients as to where to go with their question within the organization.

The second problem, which is related to the contact between civil servant and citizen, deals with the above-mentioned bureaucratically differentiated government organization. The public demand, particularly the demand of members of the public with less bureaucratic competence, does not correspond with the government's logical structure. Therefore, several bodies or departments have to be addressed in order to find an appropriate solution for one of the clients' problems.

A third kind of problem was discovered: the civil servant's attitude. In the survey, a lot of people complained about the unfriendly way in which they were treated.

The Service Provision Phase

Depending upon the problem, one or several government organization(s) supplies the public with one or more products and/or services in response to the latter's demand.

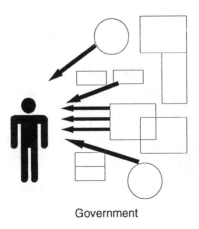

Government

Figure 4. Provision of service

The Citizens' Perspective
A significant proportion of dissatisfaction is caused by the respondents that do not receive what they had asked for. Of course, the question remains whether or not the decision taken by the civil servant is a legitimate one. If so, and if the explanation for the decision is not accepted by the client, a certain level of dissatisfaction has to be taken for granted.

The Organizational Perspective
If decisions that lead to non-provision are illegitimate organizational bottlenecks have to be analyzed. One of the problems is the bureaucratically differentiated government organization. The products offered do not solve the problem of the client completely but only part of it. Or they receive the wrong products. For example, when people are given an unemployment benefit rather than a job.

Programme Requirements

The main problem in the contact between the government and the public in providing services lies in the adjustment of the public's demands to fit the services provided by the government. In fact, this is a problem of translation. The problems concerned with the 'bureaucratic operationalisation' of the public's demand and the handling of this demand by the government in the form of providing products or services to the client are summarized in Table 1.

The overview presented below clusters the programme requirements in each phase of the process of service provision. The key issues and its consequences are described from the perspective of both government and public. They are connected with the personal interaction between the public and the civil servants with whom they are in contact on the one hand, and with the way in which the service is structured and organized on the other. Where possible, we indicate the relative importance of the key issues as revealed by the telephone survey.

Table 1. Problems concerning the Dutch governmental service provision

	Citizen	Organization
Awareness raising	° Incomplete/inadequeate use of facilities ° Lack of bureaucratic knowledge ° Lack of initiatives from public ° Latent dissatisfaction	° Insufficient knowledge of target groups ° Little pro-active group approach ° Inadequate/incorrect coverage of target groups
Demand	° Incomplete use of facilities ° Searching difficult ° Problem or production-oriented ° Referrals	° Wrong questions ° Questions to wrong place ° Lack of questions ° Inadequate/incorrect coverage of target groups ° Loss of efficiency within organization
Interaction	° Dissatisfaction with course of events: · unfriendly staff · use of language · opening hours · waiting times · referrals · fragmented provision	° Lack of clarity ° Lack of information ° Link between back-office and front-office ° Loss of efficiency
Result	° Dissatisfaction with provision of service ° Failure to obtain product requested ° Long waiting times ° Failure to keep promises ° Unfriendly reception ° Referrals	° Compartmentalisation ° Bureaucracy ° Lack of definition of product quality ° Deficiency in coordination of product provision

The programme requirements constitutes, so to speak, a reversal of these issues. It indicates what requirements a GSC must satisfy in order to resolve the existing bottlenecks. The programme requirements are summarized on the vertical axis. The horizontal axis shows the phase(s) in the process of service provision to which the programme requirement is (are) particulary relevant.

First, there are programme requirements whose main purpose is to inform and educate the target group. Such programme requirements can be satisfied by better guiding the organization, i.e., by a front-office approach. Other programme requirements are more strongly aimed at the structural and organizational set-up of the service: here, the emphasis is on the back-office approach.

Although more professional client contact and the front-office approach display a high degree of similarity, they are not the same things. The same applies to modifications to the production structure and the back-office approach. The first pair of concepts, making client contact more professional and modifying the production structure, can be described as directions into which a solution can be found. The second pair of concepts, the front-office and back-office approaches, refer to the development of the GSC concept into three models: the information point, account management, and clustering by client groups. We will discuss these three GSC concepts in the next section.

Table 2. Twelve programme requirements for a GSC

PROGRAMME OF REQUIREMENTS FOR GSC	PHASES			
	Awareness raising	Formulation of demand	Interaction	Service provision
Increase knowledge of target groups	•	•	•	•
Formulate objective at (sub)target group level	•	•	•	•
Pro-active approach to target groups	•	•		
Lower thresholds to facilities so as to encourage initiative by public	•	•		
Effective signposting	.		•	
Limit referrals			•	•
Effective supply of information on what is going on and where within the organisation		•	•	
Higher service quality (personal contact)		•	•	•
Improved coordination function (with complex services)			•	•
Effective progress control (keeping appointments)			•	•
Clear description of product quality			•	
Reduce compartmentalisation			•	•

Three GSC Models

The Information Point Model

The major characteristic of an information point is that the public has a single, central point of contact, where it can make its initial contact with the government (see Figure 5). From an analytical angle, it is important to make a sharp distinction between the various models. For this reason, we assume that the sole task of an information point is to transfer information, without providing other services.

The Account Management Model

Characteristic of the account management GSC models is the principle that services to the public are processed by a single contact (the account manager). The aim is that the service is provided by the account manager himself within the GSC. The starting point here is that as wide a package as possible is offered, spanning one or more policy areas. If this principle were to be introduced, the result would be an expansion of responsibilities that can be compared with the traditional front-desk official. Another principle involved may be that the client is not referred any further. If background departments have to be brought into play, the acccount manager deals with them. He processes the replies from the organizations and ensures an appropriate reaction. In other words, a client does not have any contact with the production departments (see Figure 6) and is protected from internal bureaucracy.

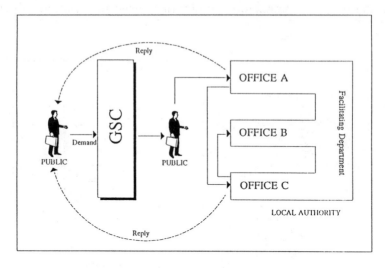

Figure 5. Variant 1: Information point

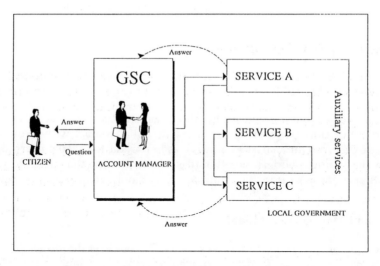

Figure 6. Variant 2: Account management

Clustering by Client Groups

This GSC model goes furthest in tackling the government organization and, thus, the problems of coordination between supply and demand according to our central concept. The central idea is that activities of the existing government machinery and the GSC are regrouped and clustered on the basis of the pattern of demand from certain client groups.

Clustering by client groups leads to various GSCs. Each client group has its own GSC and the original organization continues to exist in a slimmed-down form (see Figure 7).

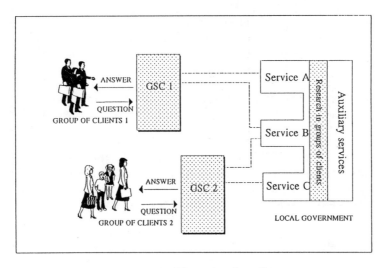

Figure 7. Variant 3: Clustering by client groups

Experiments in Real-Life Situations

The three models described in the previous section are all theoretical models, which have to be tested in real-life situations. In order to test the efficiency of these models, experiments have been set up in four municipalities. These experiments are subsidized by the Ministry of Home Affairs.

The models will seldom be found in their purest forms: In a real-life situation elements of the different models are combined into new forms. Which model offers most opportunities depends on the specific situation and on the nature of the services offered through the GSC. The experimental phase is used to gather insight into the situational factors that determine the choice for a certain model or a combination of elements.

Before we discuss the experiments it might be useful to give a brief description of the Dutch situation (SGBO 1992) with regard to the services offered by the government.

First of all, the municipal counter offers most of the governmental services (60%). The remaining services are divided among different organizations: national government departments (5%), Employment Exchange (4%), public service corporations (4%), etc. It must be emphasized that many of these organizations are supervised by the national government.

The goal of the Ministry of Home Affairs in respect of GSCs is to improve cooperation between organizations with regard to public services as to limit the amount of contact points between government and the public to the greatest extent possible. This kind of cooperation will not only be advantageous for the public, but for the government as well. There are indications that the quality service can be more user-friendly *and* more efficient at the same time. However, there is another important advantage. For example, with the organizational division between the Employment Exchange and the Social Services, unemployed people can keep their social security benefits for years, without being urged to find a new job. They are a customer of the Social Services and not of the Employment Exchange. When the two organizations cooperate, unemployed people are forced to find a job much more quickly and as a result the government can save a considerable amount of money.

In order to test the three models in real-life situations, the Ministry of the Interior initiated experiments in four municipalities: Beesel (30,000 inhabitants), Bussum (30,000 inhabitants), Alphen aan den Rijn (65,000 inhabitants) and Groningen (170,000 inhabitants). These experiments will be described briefly below.

Municipality of Beesel

In Beesel the information point model will be tested. Before the experiment is started, a thorough analysis will be made of the nature of questions for information with which the local and other governmental service providers are confronted. The goal of this analysis is to find out which questions will be dealt with by the information point. The analysis will also focus on the way the information can best be made accessible.

Municipality of Bussum

The municipality of Bussum will experiment with the 'account management' model. More specifically, cooperation between the municipality and the public service corporations will be the focal point of investigation. Thus, a connection will be made with an experiment where the governmental Employment Exchange, a commercial employment firm, the municipal Social Service and industrial insurance boards cooperate in a so-called 'job centre'. At the start of the experiment, the way in which the cooperation will take place will be investigated. This will be followed by a study into the effects of the cooperations.

Municipality of Alphen aan den Rijn

This municipality will pay attention to the concept of 'clustering by client groups'. This GSC will concentrate on the segment of elderly and handicapped people. The preliminary investigation has focused specifically on the accomplishment of the necessary support from the different organizations that offer facilities to these people (approximately 50 in Alphen aan den Rijn). The result of the preliminary research is an investigation plan which describes the way in which such a centre must be set up.

Municipality of Groningen

The city of Groningen has already had a public service centre in use for a number of years, and a second one has been recently opened. These centres are organized on the basis of the model of "clustering by client groups" and they focus specifically on people in multiple disadvantageous situations, such as unemployment and societal problems. In order to provide as many services as possible, experiments are conducted with expert systems that are able to calculate social payments. In this experiment, the effects of the use of these expert systems on the clients and the personnel will be studied. Also, the side-effects in respect of efficiency gains will be looked at, as well as the correctness of the decisions made.

Before a GSC can actually go ahead —and this also holds for the experiments— a considerable number of barriers have to be removed. These barriers have an organizational, a personnel, a managerial or a technical nature. Additionally, in The Netherlands the privacy of citizens is a barrier as well. In the GSC, the counter clerks need access to many different files. However, the Dutch law often prohibits electronic connections between these files.

When setting up an experiment, many negotiations are necessary in order to remove these barriers. Although the ultimate goal of the experiments is to see how a GSC functions in actual practice, the process of setting up the experiments in itself produces valuable information. There is no such thing as a laboratory situation: the municipalities are real. With the exception of Groningen (where the experiment started three years ago), the other three municipalities will conduct feasibility studies in order to list the consequences for the organizations involved. And not only for the organizations themselves —the departments under which the organizations operate are also involved. For example, the job centre in Bussum is hindered by legal restrictions. For reasons of privacy, the organizations are not allowed to link their information systems. Negotiations and feasibility studies are being continued.

This does not alter the surprising conclusion that the organizations show a considerable amount of willingness to cooperate for the benefit of the public or, more appropriately, the customer. Furthermore, it is striking that the organizations that do not participate in the experiments show considerable interest in the initiatives taken by the Ministry of Home Affairs. It seems that in the past decade a significant cultural change, has taken place, resulting in more client-oriented behaviour. Of course, the future will show whether or not this behaviour will become structural, particularly when it requires financial investment from the organizations, which cannot be recovered in the short run.

As mentioned previously, the goal of the experiments can be stated very simply: "Do the models function?" In this context, 'Function' is defined both as:

- quality service; and
- efficiency in the service process.

Whether or not the experiments will function is determined by the "Quality Audit on Government Services".

The Measurement of Effects

In the previous sections, the theoretical models and the set-up of the experiments were described. In this section we will discuss the use of a measurement instrument. This instrument is a monitoring system aimed at measuring the effects of actions that are taken to improve the quality and efficiency of services. Although the GSC is the immediate cause for the development of this instrument, the monitoring system must be applicable in any situation where the governmental service provision is changed, whether or not a GSC is involved. By means of the measurement instrument "Quality Monitoring System" the quality and the efficiency of the services provided will be studied (Schouten 1992).

The quality audit stems from the direct contact between the public and the government. Three contact situations will be considered:

• the customer who visits the local authority;
• the contacts by telephone;
• the contacts by mail.

Client contact will be divided into three parts:

• the expectations of the client with regard to quality service;
• the quality of the product provided;
• the perception of quality service.

The service provision process can be divided into nine parts. These are described in Figure 8.

The "Formulation of demand" stage focuses on the client's perception of the problem that caused him to go to the local authorities. "Accessibility" focuses on the (perception of) distances, the availability of parking space, ergonomics, effective signposting and opening hours. "Waiting time" is the time a client has to wait before he is being served. "Treatment" stands for the way the client is approached, talked to (friendly/unfriendly manner, use of language and clarity) and the time spent on each per client. "Approachability" is the amount of influence the client can exert on decision making during the interaction with the government official. This includes the possibility for the client to tell his story and the willingness of the official to really listen and understand. "Lead time" is the time it takes to produce and provide the service. "Service provision" stands for the service or product which is provided by the government. With regard to quality, the legitimacy of the service is important here. With "Referral" we mean the adequacy, the clarity and the number of referrals in the case of multiple contacts. Finally, the "Costs" are concerned with the price the client has to pay in order to receive the requested product.

The different elements of this matrix are listed for each type of client contact, so that the questionnaires for the telephonic contacts will cover all these elements. However, it will not always be possible to include all elements in the separate questionnaires. In an interview which measures client expectations, a product has not actually been provided yet, and so the lead time or the demand provision cannot be measured.

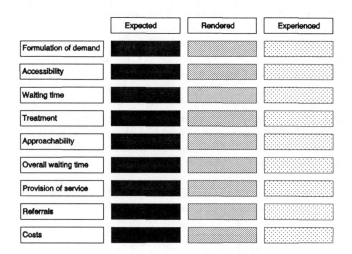

	Expected	Rendered	Experienced
Formulation of demand			
Accessibility			
Waiting time			
Treatment			
Approachability			
Overall waiting time			
Provision of service			
Referrals			
Costs			

Figure 8. The service provision process

The Efficiency of Services

Efficiency of the governmental service provision is defined as the provision of a given product against standardized costs. In the measurement instrument, efficiency is divided into two parts. Every part brings a specific element in view: first, the efficiency of the product. **Product efficiency** focuses on whether or not a product is provided as efficiently as possible. This part excludes the efficiency of a division, or that of the total organization. After all, it is possible that the efficient production of one product leads to the inefficient production of another product. It is also possible that products are made very efficiently, but that the way the government officials spend their time is inefficient. Therefore, it is also necessary to measure the **efficiency of the separate divisions**. Specifically, this part tries to answer the question whether or not the government officials can provide a certain number of services within a given time period and under certain conditions.

Product efficiency is measured by using the so-called 'logbook' method. The production process for a certain service is registered by the official involved. The efficiency of the division is measured by making an inventory of parameters of the production units. This part of efficiency is studied by means of mutual comparison between divisions of separate municipalities.

Conclusion

The research conducted up until now has considerably increased the knowledge about governmental service provision processes. Also, the municipalities involved are enthusiastic about the results and use them and the instruments developed in a way that best fits their own unique situation.

The analysis framework has proven useful for municipalities in visualising the service provision process and taking measures in order to improve the service provision.

The GSC concepts developed help the municipalities to oversee the consequences of the organizational decisions they make with regard to the design of a government service centre. Most municipalities do not choose one concept, but a combination of the three. The experiments conducted have to show which specific model fits a certain type of situation best.

The quality monitoring system on government services has been completed and is available for government organizations. The audit has been developed as a 'self-service' instrument, enabling organizations to perform the audit by themselves. When necessary, they can ask for assistance when doing so.

References

In 't Groen, J. and M. Konings, Failure to Take Up Social Security among Tilburg National Assistance Clients (in Dutch), Tilburg, Katholieke Universiteit Brabant, 1989.

Masselink R. and Sprecher R., *De organisatorische aspecten van dienstencentra van de overheid*, Den Haag, 1991.

Post, J., *De (On-)mogelijkheden van Service Centra van de Overheid*, Den Haag, 1991.

Robbins, S.P., *The Administrative Process*, Prentice Hall, Englewood Cliffs, New Jersey, 1976.

Rosenthal U., M.P.C.M. van Schendelen and A.B. Ringeling, *Openbaar Bestuur, Organisatie, Politieke Omgeving en Beleid*, Samson H.D. Tjeenk Willink, Alphen aan den Rijn, 1987.

Schouten, R., *The Public Service Quality Monitoring System*, B&A Group Policy Research and Advice BV, The Hague, 1992 (available in English).

SGBO, *Kwaliteit van Dienstverlening 2*, Den Haag, 1992.

12

Activity-Based Costing in Service Management

Md. Mostaque Hussain and Sören Kock

Introduction

During the last two decades we have witnessed substantial changes in the service sector as new competitors have emerged as a result of deregulation, which has also given the companies greater freedom in setting prices and determining the mix of products offered. Well-managed service firms with a good understanding of their markets, customers and information technologies can become much more profitable in a deregulated, more competitive environment. In manufacturing companies, functions such as marketing, selling, distribution, service, research and development and general administration have become more significant expense categories than in the past. Traditional costs accounting systems, with their emphasis on cost accounting for inventory valuation, have neglected the flourishing investments and expenses in organizations' service functions. Moreover, conventional cost systems are not able to accurately assign the costs of non-volume-related overhead activities. Assigning overhead costs by using only volume as a basis can supply the management with a wrong picture of how costs are created. In addition, the product costs can be distorted if the non-volume-related overhead costs are a significant proportion of total overhead costs. ... solution to this problem in service firms as well as in manufacturing firms ... ment activity-based costing (ABC). The purpose of this paper is to d... works in service organizations and how the management car... plementing ABC.

Service Management and Activity-Based Costing

Traditional accounting systems are developed for goods, because services[1] have only been seen as a small part of the total problem solution offered to customers. Today, many marketing researchers state that services are as important as goods, perhaps even more important, and that it is difficult to distinguish services from goods. Gummesson (1987) questions whether it is useful at all to talk about service and manufacturing industries. He concludes that it would be more reasonable to talk about service activities and manufacturing activities, irrespective of the kind of firm they appear in. Giarini (1990) goes even further and claims that without services most goods produced within the industrial sector cannot contribute to to-day's economic wealth.

Service production must be based on a consumer perspective. It must recognize all the aspects of a service that customers perceive when consuming a service. The way in which customers perceive the interactions with the service provider could be called functional quality, and what the customers receive could be called technical quality. Both of these as well as the impact image and communication must be taken into account when evaluating customers' total perceived service quality (Grönroos 1990b). In service firms, it is almost impossible to distinguish consumption from production. Furthermore, the relations between the employees of the service firm and the customers are a source of quality in both service firms and manufacturing firms (Holmlund and Kock 1992).

According to Whitt and Whitt (1988), management accounting systems are needed in professional service firms for two reasons; (i) increased competition demands improved planning and control, and (ii) professional service firms have grown in size and organizational complexity and now need systems comparable to those used by manufacturers. These systems must be applicable to service firms. Management accounting is beginning to reject standard cost systems, traditional variance analysis and the sole use of financial accounting for internal decision making. Instead, non-financial measures are supplementing traditional financial measures in evaluating performance. Additionally, the current pace of technological and economic innovation in the financial markets illustrates the critical need for information as an aid for sound decision making in financial institutions. Financial problems and failures in banks and other institutions are no longer considered unique, and yet the production orientation of traditional cost accounting methods has led many observers to conclude that these methods are not useful for financial institutions that must cope with this new environment. In the results of their survey among the 70 largest banks in the world Gardner and Lammers (1988) show that the most important goals are: 1) product development and pricing, 2) achieving cost reductions, 3) performance evaluation, 4) industry cost comparison.

Understanding the cost and value of service activities is a requirement of the 1990s. Markets demand services that often force up business expenses without a

---

According to Grönroos (1990 b), the characteristics of services are: a) Services are more or less intangible, b) Services are activities or series of activities rather than things, c) Services are produced and consumed simultaneously, d) The customer participates in the production process to some extent.

corresponding increase in revenue. Businesses that understand and that can quantify these costs are in the best position to control them. The objective is to minimize the cost rather than the service through the elimination of non-value-added activities[2]. Only few companies have information that provides managers with a clear understanding of which customers and markets profitable. As services become a more significant part of companies' competitive advantage and cost structure, the management tools must respond. The effective use of customer profitability information will greatly enhance a company's ability to detect the right customers. The goal is to increase customer satisfaction and in that way achieve greater returns (Howel and Soucy 1990).

Activity-based costing is useful as a decision-making framework for economic analysis when developing new products and improving existing products. ABC is also a powerful tool in achieving competitive advantages and to provide operational and discretionary project cost data. The approach further provides a more factual basis for decisions involving changes of the service or good option offered, which at present are probably being made incorrectly and intuitively in many cases. In addition, as a result of the emergence of activity-based costing, the accuracy of product costing is receiving new emphasis. This emphasis is also extended to performance reporting using multiple cost drivers, allowing for more accurate budget calculations and, thus, for a more meaningful comparison of actual and budgeted costs. Operational measures, however, are increasing in importance in the production environment because there increasing emphasis is placed upon real-time feedback together with operational measures. This emphasis also influences quality performance and, as a result, management must be seen as a total organizational approach focusing on customers' total perceived quality. However, ABC is useful for the management to find (i) hidden profits, and (ii) hidden losses in relationships with customers.

How Does Activity-Based Costing Work in Service Management?

Activity-based costing works in two stages in both service and manufacturing organizations:

In the first stage of ABC, overhead costs are divided into homogeneous cost pools (Johnson and Kaplan 1987). A homogeneous cost pool is a collection of overhead costs for which cost variation can be explained by a single cost driver. Overhead activities are homogeneous whenever they have the same consumption ratios for all products. Once a cost pool has been defined, the cost per unit of the cost driver is computed for that pool. This is the pool rate. Compu͟ ͟ ͟ ͟ ͟the pool rate completes the first stage. Consequently, the first stage of͟ comes; (i) a set of homogeneous cost pools and, (ii) a pool

In the second stage of ABC, the costs of each overhead p͟ This is done by using the pool rate computed in the fir (the quantity of the cost driver used by each product) o

---

2   If an activity adds value to a customer, it might achieve ͟ that do not add value and a reduction of resources spent on take place.

consumed by each product. The overhead costs assigned from each cost pool to each product are computed as follows:

$$\text{applied overhead} = \text{pool rate} \times \text{cost driver units used}$$

The total overhead cost per unit of products is obtained by first tracing the overhead costs from the pools to the individual products. This total is then divided by the number of units produced. The result, i.e., the unit overhead cost + the per unit overhead cost to the per unit prime cost[3], yields the manufacturing cost per unit. In service firms, the most important cost is the labor cost for personnel. Direct labor costs are traceable to the service rendered. In service organizations, the most important cost would be the professional labor involved in producing the services, i.e., the direct labor cost must be traceable to the service rendered. In addition to the labor cost, various types of overhead costs will occur in any type of business. In a service firm the overhead costs usually occur when offering a service. Consequently, they are classified as service overheads, and can be compared with factory overhead in a manufacturing firm. Professional labor costs are considered service overheads rather than period costs (non-inventorial costs are deducted as expenses during the current period without having been previously classified as costs of inventory).

Studies have revealed that activity-based cost systems need two sets of activities —batch and product-sustaining —to explain the demands that individual products place on resources (Cooper and Kaplan 1991). Batch-related activities, i.e., setting up a machine to produce a different product, are performed each time a batch of goods is consumed. If more batches (production runs) are produced, more set-up resources will be consumed. However, it is important to note here that the resources consumed are independent of the number of units produced. Another example is processing purchase orders.

Product-sustaining activities are performed to enable individual products to be produced and sold. The expenses of these activities are independent of the number of batches or units produced. In addition, one more category might be needed: facility-sustaining expenses that occur in production facilities. Many of these activities are administrative, i.e., managing personnel and plant, taxes, housekeeping, landscaping, maintenance, security, lighting. These activities are necessary for providing a building where the production can take place, but they are not related to the volume and mix of individual products.

According to Grönroos (1990b) the production system in service organizations is divided into a totally invisible part and a line of visibility. The invisible part consists of such parts as systems support, management support and physical support. The visible part is more or less visible for the customer who usually participates in the production process. In the invisible or interactive part, interactions between the service firm's contact persons and customers take place. The augmented service offer includes the service process and the interaction between the organiza-and its customers. Because services are activities or processes in which con-

---

st = Direct Material + Direct Labor + Direct Expenses, are traceable to specific prod-

sumption is partly inseparable from production, the service production is a dynamic phenomenon by definition. The service exists as long as the production process goes on. Hence, any model of services, such as the augmented service offering and the creation of such products, must include a dynamic aspect, where the basic package facilities' services and goods and support products have to be planned according to the service concept. A service that, both in the elements of the basic package and in the accessibility, interaction and customer participation aspects of service production and delivery, includes the desired features which in turn creates the benefits that customer seek. Therefore, facility-sustaining expenses are best dealt with if they can be treated as an expense of operating the facility for the period and not allocated to products.

The process of developing activity-based cost systems for factory expenses are carried out (Cooper and Kaplan 1991) first by identifying the major activities performed; second, by classifying the activities into unit, batch, product-sustaining and facility-sustaining categories; and, finally, by attributing to individual products, the expenses of the unit, batch, and product-sustaining activities using bases that reflect the underlying behavior of the products' demands for these activities.

When applying activity-based costing to service organizations we must distinguish the different services that the organization produces. In a firm producing professional services it is probably easier to implement ABC, as the costs are not so difficult to trace to different activities. In an accounting firm, the customers are limited and the accountants and support people can quite easily keep record of the amount of time and material they use when dealing with a specific customer. Other professional services include consulting services, education services, or legal services. For example, a consulting firm providing educational services, which is likely to give courses in service marketing, will have more or less the same costs for giving the course irrespective of how many persons are attending. Unit level costs will probably be rather low, consisting of copies and similar materials distributed during the course. Most of the costs can be traced to batch level costs, i.e., cost for teachers and rents. Costs for planning, marketing and other similar activities for a specific course can be traced to product level. Costs on facility level can, for example, be general administration and support. At a school the library would belong to this category.

If the service firm produces common services, the possibilities to trace costs to activities used are more complex. Assume that a restaurant is implementing ABC. When a customer comes into the restaurant to eat, then he/she 'consumes' certain activities. The problem is that different customers consume different activities. For example, one customer may wish more advice about what to eat and drink, while another customer decides what to eat and drink all by him/herself. On the other hand, the first customer may be a fast eater and leave quickly, while the second customer may stay longer, use all available services and spill food on the table and the floor so that cleaning is needed afterwards.

When analyzing production expenses in service organizations, the demand for support resources arise from product volumes and mixes. In a lot of service firms, including financial institutions such as banks, some expenses are driven naturally to products, e.g., checking accounts, savings accounts, commercial loans, home mortgages, etc. A great deal of expenses for service functions are caused by differences in customers' preferences, even though they are using the same service. The analysis starts by examining the expense structure of each operating department and proceeds by determining the factors that create the demands for the functions performed by the department. The objective of analysis is therefore to discover the nature of the demand and quantify it. The basic goal of the analysis is to obtain the unit costs for processing transactions from products and customers. The following equation is used to calculate product unit cost:

$$\text{Product unit cost} = \text{hourly cost} \times \text{product unit cost}$$

The hourly cost is calculated by dividing the operating expense budget for the department by the total number of available hours. For labor-paced operating departments, the available hours are measured by the total number of hours that people are available to work in the department, reduced by allowable time for holidays and breaks. For automated departments, the available hours can be estimated by the number of machines that can perform the function and their available processing time. Both types of departments may require adjustments for capacity utilization, i.e., the total quantity that could be produced if all of the machines were kept running continuously.

In the following example we can see different costs that can be generated within a service firm. Assume that the loan department of a bank wants to determine the total costs incurred in processing a typical loan application. They have been asked to compute the cost of processing a normal home loan application (Anderson, Needles and Caldwell 1984). The necessary information concerning the processing of a loan application is given in Table 1.

Table 1.
The information concerning the processing of a loan application
(Source: Adopted from Anderson, Needles and Caldwell 1984, p. 60)

Direct professional labor:			
Loan processors monthly salary		USD	12,000
(4 employees earning 3.000 USD each)			
Indirect monthly loan department overhead costs:			
Chief loan officers salary		4,500 USD	
Telephone expenses			
Depreciation	750 "		
Building	2,800 "		
Equipment	1,750 "		
Automobiles	1,200 "		
Legal advice	2,460 "		
Legal forms/supplies		320 "	
Customers relations		640 "	
Credit check function		1,980 "	
Advertising	440 "		
Internal Audit Function		2,400 "	
Utilities expenses	1,690 "		
Clerical personnel	3,880 "		
Miscellaneous		290 "	13,100
Total overhead costs		USD	25,100
			========

In addition, the department discovers that all appraisal and title search activities are performed by people outside the bank and that their fees are treated as separate loan costs. One hundred loan applications are usually processed each month. The loan department performs several functions in addition to the home loan application tasks; roughly one half of the department is involved in loan collection activities. After determining how many of the processed loans were not home loans, they concluded that only 25% of the overhead costs of the loan department could be attributed to the processing of home loan applications.

A calculation for the cost of processing one home loan application is:

Direct processional labor cost: USD 12,000/100	120.00 USD
Service overhead cost: USD 25,100 x 25%/100	62.75 USD
Total processing cost per loan	**182.75** USD

The estimate of the product unit time is a more complex calculation, involving work measurement processes. Work is measured for each activity in a department that contributes to processing a transaction, i.e., a check, a deposit, or a cash payment on a loan. The unit times are calculated by first asking the employees to keep track of the time spent on various activities and then measure the output produced during the specific time interval. The activities of professional and managerial employees, who are not performing repetitive activities, are measured by asking these employees to estimate the percentages of the available time they spend on each activity.

Once the unit times for processing each product type in each department have been calculated, the two quantities can be multiplied and added up across all the activities to obtain the cost of processing the transaction for a given product, i.e., the total cost of processing a check or a deposit, granting a loan. With this information, the bank can calculate the profitability of its various services like the monthly profit of one service, reduced by the expenses associated with handling all the transactions associated with a check, a deposit, or a cash payment on a loan. The information helps the organization to retain and define highly profitable segments and to transform unprofitable segments into profitable ones through actions on pricing, product features, operating improvements, technology introduction, etc.

One of the qualitative differences between cost systems for services and goods is the need to model customers' behavior when analyzing the source of demand for service functions. With the exception of this, there is no essential difference between the analysis of operating expenses in manufacturing support departments and performing the same tasks for the operating units of service organizations. The activity-based production expense analysis provides an estimate of the production cost of the service and supplements this with the specific expenses associated with a particular order, for instance the cost of processing and delivering the order, the salesperson's commission and design costs. The production cost and the order-specific costs are subtracted from the selling price to obtain a profit or loss on the individual order. The profit or loss on the individual order can then be aggregated into several branches such as product line branch, customer branch, profit branch[4].

Profitability and Activity-Based Costing

For a manufacturer of goods, conventional managerial thinking includes three rules of thumb to follow in order to strengthen the competitive edge of the firm and increase profitability. First, decrease the costs of production and administration in order to gain a decreased unit cost of the goods. Secondly, increase the budget for marketing efforts such as advertising, sales and promotion to make the market buy produced goods. Finally, strengthen the product development efforts. Other strategic management elements can also be included. The cost of production can be decreased, lower prices can be offered or higher margins can be obtained. The quality of goods produced is the same, because the output of the production process does not change, although different more cost-efficient technology or processes are used. Moreover, more marketing efforts will usually have a positive effect on demand. Continuing product development is of vital importance to manufacturing as well as to services.

In manufacturing, such decisions can improve profitability. In a service context, internal efficiency, the ways in which the firm operates and the productivity of labor and capital are more important means when aiming at increased profitability. The internal efficiency of a service firm can be measured by using the unit cost of production. For external efficiency, the customers' total perceived quality and the output of the firm can be used.

Customer profitability has become an issue of great importance in recent years. In marketing, the costs for maintaining and developing customer relationships have come into focus (Grönroos 1990a, Reichheld and Sasser 1990, and Storbacka 1993). An interesting question is how to find out which customers are profitable for the service provider and which are not. In other words, some relationships may look profitable now, but when all activities needed to produce a specific product are carried out, the relationships may not be profitable at all. For other relationships we may find the opposite. For example, one manager that we talked to explained that the implementation of ABC in his firm had been stopped because he thought that it would be difficult to get some customers to accept the increases in prices that ABC indicated for certain products. On the other hand, a firm cannot, at least in the long run, continue to do business with a loss. Therefore, it is essential for a company to know which customers are profitable and which are not. In respect of this decision-making task, ABC can be used by the management to discover (i) hidden profits and (ii) hidden losses in relationships with customers. Additionally, profitability seems to increase when long-term relationships are established (Reichheld and Sasser 1990).

Kaplan (Cooper and Kaplan 1991) describes in a case (Kantal) how a Swedish firm implements a cost-accounting system for cutting down activities that create losses

---

4   For a more extensive discussion, see Cooper and Kaplan 1991, pp. 470-473.

and increasing activities that generate profits. In the new accounting system each cost category was analyzed to determine whether it was related more to the volume of sales and production, or to handling individual production and sales orders. Empirical findings were gathered by personal interviews in each department to establish the hours worked in each order and the volume-related activity. The hours worked for all activities within each cost center were added, and the percentage of total costs related to order and volume-related activities were determined. From a sample report for a group of domestic customers they could see that the profit orders on individual orders ranged from –179% to + 65%. Only 40% of the customers were profitable and they generated 250% of realized profits. The truth was that 5% of the customers generated 150% of the profits and 10% of the customers lost 120% of the profits. In addition, two of the most unprofitable customers were among the three largest buyers according to sales volume. The reason was that they had implemented JIT and, consequently, forced their suppliers to assume responsibility for the inventory. Moreover, one of them was using the supplier as a backup supplier for small special orders of a low-priced item when the main supplier could not deliver. The supplier had always welcomed the orders from these two large suppliers. Now they realize how expensive it had become to satisfy them.

Conclusions

Activity-based costing is a tool that helps the management in service firms to get a more accurate picture of costs caused by different services. In service firms, overhead costs often constitute a substantial part of the total costs and it is essential to derive them to the activities causing costs when producing a service. By using ABC the management in service firms can distinguish profitable customers from non-profitable customers. In other words, the management has a tool that helps them to allocate resources to activities that generate profits. Activities causing losses will consequently receive fewer resources. However, it is important to constantly focus upon customers' total perceived service quality and how to maintain long-term relationships to profitable customers. ABC can then be accepted as a new way of thinking. However, we must keep in mind that management in organizations has certain beliefs, derived from their education and past experience. Implementing ABC might give them a totally new picture of their business that does not correspond to their present beliefs.

In spite of the advantages of ABC the management must be aware that activity-based costing does not solve all the problems involved in decision making. If the management focuses too strictly on ABC it might overlook the fact that other basic analyses are needed, for example, customer adaptation, flexibility and economies of scope. If the management forgets to focus on customers' needs and to adapt the products to their needs, the customers will be unsatisfied and turn to ~ competitor. Similarly, too much focus on costs leads to production systems with ity and no advantage of economies of scope, which has often been manufacturing industry. The assumption of ABC is that all costs ca specific products. However, when we are dealing with economies be difficult to analyze how the production of one component aff tion of other components. In that case it might be an important consideration to implement ABC in service organizations as well as in manufacturing industries.

References

Anderson, H.R., B.E. Needles and J.C. Caldwell, *Management Accounting*, Houghton Mifflin Company, Boston, 1984.

Cooper, R. and R.S. Kaplan, *The Design of Management Systems*, Prentice-Hall Inc., Englewood Cliffs, New Jersey, 1991.

Gardner, J.M. and E.L. Lammers, Cost Accounting in Large Banks, *Management Accounting*, April 1988, pp. 34-39.

Giarini, O., Notes on the Concept of Service Quality and Economic Value, In: S.W. Brown, E. Gummesson, B. Edwardsson and B. Gustavsson (eds.), *Quality in Services: Multidisciplinary and Multinational Perspectives*, Lexington Books, Massachusetts/Toronto, 1991.

Grönroos, C., *Facing the Challenge of Service Competition: Costs of Bad Service*. Swedish School of Economics and Business Administration, Helsingfors, 1990a (unpublished).

Grönroos, C., *Service Management and Marketing*, Lexington Books, Massachusetts/Toronto, 1990b.

Gummesson, E., The New Marketing - Developing Long-Term Interactive Relationships. *Long Range Planning*, no. 4, 1987.

Holmlund, M. and S. Kock, *Quality-Based Service as an Establishing Strategy in Business Networks*, Working Paper No. 249, Swedish School of Economics and Business Administration, Helsingfors, 1992.

Howel, A.R. and R.S. Soucy, Customer Profitability - As Critical as Product Profitability, *Management Accounting*, October 1990, pp. 43-47.

Johnson, H.T. and S.R. Kaplan, *Relevance Lost: The Rise and Fall of Management Accounting*, Harvard Business Press, Boston, 1987.

Reichheld, F.F. and W.E.Jr. Sasser, Zero Defections: Quality comes to services, *Harvard Business Review*, 71, March-April 1993, pp. 64-73.

Storbacka, K., *Customer Relationships Profitability in Retail Banking*. Swedish School of Economics and Business Administration, Research Report No. 29, Helsingfors, 1993.

Whitt, S.Y. and J.D. Whitt, What Professional Service Firms Can Learn From Manufacturing, *Management Accounting*, November 1988, pp. 39-42.

Authors Index

Authors Index

Abstracts

Chapter 1
Quality-Positioning in the Austrian Banking Industry: A Benchmark Case Study

Gerhard A. Wührer

As problems shift, problem-solving instruments must also shift. Long used marketing research instruments such as the FMDS (Finanzmarkt-Datenservice) in Austria, which emphasizes image criteria, have only limited information power for positioning banking institutions as service-oriented enterprises. It was for this reason that a major Austrian banking group wanted to develop a research instrument that could measure service quality, provide information about service orientation of competitors, make available representative figures about nation-wide key benchmarks concerning quality differences among banks, allow comparisons of the quality standards in the country of Carinthia and, finally, help to develop a programme for a stronger quality-oriented strategy in service. A process approach combining qualitative and quantitative marketing research will be developed and some major research findings and conclusions are presented.

CHAPTER 2
Measuring Service Quality: The Results of a Longitudinal Study in Further Education

Sabine Haller

This article is based on a longitudinal study that was conducted in the sector of further education, evaluating a postgraduate programme. The underlying assumption is that perception of service quality varies over time, because the importance that the customer attaches to some criteria possibly changes during the service process.

The results show that service evaluation changed over a time period of one year. Process-oriented criteria gained relevance during the service delivery process, but then became less important towards the end of the course. However, students did emphasize the importance of certain outcome-oriented criteria throughout the course.

A different methodological approach was taken in the study: In addition to the longitudinal focus, both importance and perceptions of the criteria were evaluated. The "importance-performance-analysis" reveals strengths and weaknesses of the evaluated programme. This type of presentation is advantageous to the institute offering the programme as a means of setting priorities for the process of improvement of service quality.

Abstracts

CHAPTER 3
The Retail Service Encounter: Identifying Critical Service Experiences

Kitty Koelemeijer

Research on services marketing mainly concerns so-called pure services. In this chapter the critical incident technique is used to gain insights into the nature of consumer experiences causing extreme satisfaction or dissatisfaction for a variety of retail encounters. Two main groups could be distinguished, which were respectively named "physical product/instrumental service performance" featuring incidents triggered by performance of the physical product or instrumental services, and "employee-customer interactions" in which incidents triggered by service personnel behavior are represented. Within each group three categories were distinguished. Significant relationships were found between type of outcome (dissatisfying or satisfying) and incident group, store and group, and store and type of outcome. Stores selling (standardized) goods were relatively highly represented in the employee-customer interaction group, indicating the significance of search attributes as information useful in avoiding critical incidents. Several attributional characteristics of the reported critical incidents were tested in order to investigate whether the full range of possible causes for (dis)satisfaction was covered. Critical incidents appeared to be attributed to relatively external, controllable, and unstable causes. In addition, differences in the degree of mutual understanding were found between satisfying and dissatisfying experiences.

CHAPTER 4
The Relation Between Service Quality, Satisfaction and Intentions

Veronica Liljander and Tore Strandvik

In the context of quality management in services, the measurement of service quality has been the subject of academic debate since the publication of the SERVQUAL model in 1985 by Parasuraman, Zeithaml and Berry. The disconfirmation model has been proposed as a foundation for both service quality and customer satisfaction. Expectations are assumed to be an important component in these studies. This SERVQUAL study included measures of direct disconfirmation, overall satisfaction, overall quality and intentions to repurchase. The results showed that perceived performance plays a major role in overall satisfaction, quality and intentions to repurchase. The inferred disconfirmation measure (SERVQUAL score) was found to be related to satisfaction, overall quality, and intentions, due to the effect of the performance component in the measure. The results of the study imply that more research should be directed towards different specifications of the expectations component. Another implication, from a managerial perspective, is to pay attention to the performance component.

CHAPTER 5
Quality Marks: Prospective Tools in Managing Service Quality Perceptions

Henk Roest and Theo Verhallen

Managing quality perceptions is of vital interest in services. Quality Marks, as informational beliefs, are a potential tool in this process for service organizations as well as customers. The study focuses on the usage of Quality Marks by customers and on a comparison of actual quality factors controlled by Quality Mark institutions and the quality factors customers expect to be included in the Quality Marks. The study of a sample of N=156 customers included two different Quality Marks: the Benelux hotel and the Michelin star classification. The first is an overall (input and output) Quality Mark and the second a partial (input)

Quality Mark. From the study we may conclude that Quality Marks are often used in quality decision processes and that the service quality attribute expectations associated with the Quality Marks are not fully guaranteed. For three out of the distinguished eight quality factors, more than half of the sample of customers has wrong expectations for both Quality Marks concerning the content of the Quality Mark. This may lead to potential service quality problems as these wrong customer expectations are not being met. Managing service quality perceptions requires that these problem s must be recognized and solved by the service Quality Mark institutions by either adapting the Quality Mark to the expected quality factors or by communicating the content of the Quality Mark and the quality factors accounted for.

CHAPTER 6
The Impact of Cross-Cultural Dimensions on the Management of Service Quality

Audrey Gilmore and David Carson

Modern ferry travel has experienced many changes over the years of this century from sailing ships to modern ro-ro car ferries via a variety of elaborate passenger liners. Customer expectations have also changed dramatically as economies have developed and consumer expectations have become increasingly sophisticated.

This article focuses on the products and services available on ferry travel and passenger reaction to these services. It addresses the issue of whether cultural differences affect customer responses to marketing activity on board by using a study of some major UK and Scandinavian-operated ferries. A description of a comparative study undertaken to examine and compare British and Scandinavian passengers response to the variety of products and services offered on board these two nations ferries is given.

Distinct variances in Scandinavian and British consumer behaviour on board are discussed with respect to the implications for Stena Sealink's future marketing management planning and activity.

CHAPTER 7
Managing Service Recovery

Colin G Armistead, Graham Clark and Paula Stanley

There has been increasing discussion about the link between customer retention and profitability. Customer retention is proposed to be associated with the capability of a service company to deliver consistent quality and to be able to recover well when things do go wrong. The ability for a service firm to compete on the promise of unconditional guarantees probably rests with competence in the delivery of service quality and capable service recovery. The role of front-line personnel is perceived to be integral in the process.

The chapter presents the findings of a survey of UK service managers across a spectrum of service sectors to investigate current attitudes and approaches to service recovery. The findings from the survey are discussed with reference to a model for considering the empowerment of service front-line staff.

CHAPTER 8
Service Implications as Drama: Quality Implications and Measurement

Raymond P. Fisk and Stephen J. Grove

This article is based on the metaphor that behavior is drama (Burke 1945; 1950; 1968; Goffman 1959; 1967; 1974; Perinbanayagam 1974, etc.). Similar use of metaphors to comprehend complex and/or unfamiliar phenomena is quite prevalent in marketing (e.g., "wheel of retailing", product "life cycle", and marketing "warfare"). The drama metaphor was first applied in the marketing literature to services marketing phenomena (Grove and Fisk 1983) and has recently been applied in broader terms to marketing in general (Deighton 1992; Stern 1990). While various services marketers have noted that specific services features have drama counterparts, the metaphor is developed to its fullest in the works of Grove and Fisk (Grove and Fisk 1983; Grove and Fisk 1989; Grove, Fisk and Bitner 1992).

This article discusses the theatrical nature of services, focusing in particular upon the service performance as a theatrical production. In this regard, emphasis is placed upon the ability of the drama metaphor to capture the dynamic and complex character of service performances. Attention is given to the various managerial implications offered by such an approach. In particular, strategies are offered for using drama concepts to improve service quality. Finally, arguments are made for the efficacy of observational research techniques as an appropriate means of assessing service quality when services are considered to be theatrical performances.

CHAPTER 9
The Limits of Internal Marketing

Mohammed Rafiq and Pervaiz K. Ahmed

Existing formalizations of internal marketing appear to suggest that functions traditionally regarded as being in the domain of human resource management (such as attracting, developing and motivating staff) should be subordinated to marketing. This chapter explores the limits of the internal marketing concept and attempts to define the boundaries between marketing and the human resource management function. It further examines the usefulness of marketing concepts and tools such as the marketing mix, segmentation and marketing research when applied to internal markets. For instance, there are problems with the definition of product. What are internal customers buying? How are they paying? Can employees really be treated as customers? This is especially pertinent as the key difference between internal and external customers is that internal customers can be 'coerced' into 'buying' because of the contractual nature of employment. It is suggested, therefore, that a clear understanding of the nature and scope of internal marketing is essential for its effective implementation.

CHAPTER 10
The Service Encounter as a Learning Process

Hans Chr Garmann Johnsen and Harald Knudsen

The aim of this study is to present a conceptual theory in which we address the service encounter as a learning process. We look at two aspects of the learning process. First, there is the process of learning within the organization: How do individuals learn and how is this encouraged by organizational learning? Related to the issue of service, one could exemplify the question as: Why is it that some organizations improve their service performance, while others fail to do so? One could also ask what are the preconditions to stimulate individual learning in the service encounter within the organization. The challenge facing the organization is both to improve its service performance and to learn from mistakes and avoid repeating failures. Both these processes involve learning. In the present model we do not exclude the application of technical tools. The main concept, however, is to facilitate meta-cognitive experiences and theory building in practice, to make the work day an act of discovery, and to facilitate innovative thinking - not by copying textbook and research solutions or by imitating companies of excellence - but by merging the experience of the excellent with that of one's own company to formulate new concepts, new theories in practice.

The second aspect of the learning process addressed in this chapter is related to the operation of the market in which the organization participates. What sort of learning takes place in the market and how does this affect the operation of the organization? The organization operates in a learning environment. What constitutes this learning process, how can the organization and its individuals participate in this process and draw advantages from it? This is exactly what we have tried to do by presenting the learning model. It is our main argument that the quality of the service development, its benign tendencies, which in our context means the same as improvement in service performance, depends on the quality of the learning process and of the learning arena.

CHAPTER 11
Government Service Centres: Three Models in Practice

Robbert Masselink, Jan Post and Rob Schouten

For a number of years now the Dutch government, specifically the ministry of Home Affairs, has tried to stimulate initiatives in order to improve the quality of services offered to its citizens. Much research has been conducted and at this moment experiments are conducted in order to test models of service concepts. The results of the research and the experiments provide valuable information for the 650 municipalities in The Netherlands, many of which are taking initiatives to improve the provision of services to the public.

We think that the cycle of studies on governmental service quality in The Netherlands conducted in the past two years provides interesting insights for managers active in the field of governmental services who are coping with similar developments. We have the feeling, and some of the research performed confirms this, that the Dutch situation is unique with respect to the field of Government Service Centres, where many different governmental services are offered to the public at one counter or one location.

CHAPTER 12
Activity-Based Costing in Service Management

Md. Mostaque Hussain and Sören Kock

In service management, activity-based costing (ABC) can be used as a powerful tool for planning, control and decision making. The management's need for accounting information has increased during the last two decades or so as the competition in the service sector has become more fierce. ABC traces costs to activities rather than products, which provides a more accurate and correct picture of the cost consumption. Furthermore, ABC uses a larger number of cost drivers instead of one or two volume-based cost drivers in a traditional cost system. The use of ABC in service firms differs from ABC in manufacturing firms as the most important costs are professional labor costs and not material costs. A more general problem in service firms is that overhead costs are extensive and that it is difficult to derive costs to specific services. ABC helps the management to provide new services, service improvements and strategies to achieve competitive advantages.

Curricula Vitae

Pervaiz K. Ahmed is a Lecturer in Strategic Management in the Department of Economics and Management at the University of Dundee, UK. He has also held posts of Senior Lecturer in Business Policy at the University of Huddersfield and as Lecturer in Marketing Research at the University of Wales College, Aberystwyth. His main research interests are in globalization strategies, strategic issues in the implementation of TQM, and corporate culture.

Professor **Colin G. Armistead** PhD BSc PhD Cert Ed is the Royal Mail Chair of Business Performance Improvement Group at Bournemouth University. Colin was previously head of the Operations Management Group at Cranfield School of Management, where he was also Research Director for the Centre for Services Management and the joint Director of the Service Operations Research Club. Colin's research interests are in the formulation of operations strategy, the design of service delivery systems and the re-engineering of service business processes, and the management of capacity, quality and resource productivity in service organisations. Colin is past chairman of the Operations Management Association (UK).

David Carson PhD MBA DipM is Professor of Marketing in the Faculty of Business and Management, University of Ulster. He teaches and researches in marketing management. He has wide practical marketing experience over a number of industries operating in international markets. His research interests are in marketing strategies for small businesses and quality of marketing in service industries.

Graham R. Clark BSc MSc DIC FBPICS MIMgt was trained as a Mechanical Engineer with J. Lucas Limited. A period as a Development Engineer was followed by a Master's Degree in Management Science and 12 years in Manufacturing Management. He joined Cranfield School of Management in 1986, where he has carried out research in After Sales Service, Quality Management, and Service Operations Strategy. He is co-director of the Service Operations Research and Development Club and is co-author (with Colin Armistead) of Customer Service and Support (Financial Times/Pitman Publishing). There are two more books in progress.

Dr. **Raymond P. Fisk** is Associate Professor of Marketing at the University of Central Florida. His Ph.D. is from Arizona State University. His publications include articles in the Journal of Marketing, Journal of Retailing, Journal of the Academy of Marketing Science, Journal of Health Care Marketing, Journal of Professional Services Marketing, and Marketing Education Review, and others. He has been teaching and conducting research in services marketing for over 10 years.

Audrey Gilmore is a lecturer in Marketing in the Faculty of Business and Management, University of Ulster. She teaches and researches in marketing management, quality in marketing and customer care. She is currently carrying out research in the travel trade.

Dr. **Stephen J. Grove** is Associate Professor of Marketing at Clemson University. His Ph.D. is from Oklahoma State University. His publications include articles in the Journal of Advertising, Journal of the Academy of Marketing Science, Journal of Public Policy and Marketing, Journal of Health Care Marketing, Journal of Marketing Education, Journal of Business Ethics, and others. He has been teaching and conducting research in services marketing for over ten years.

Dipl.-Kffr. **Sabine Haller** was born in Reinbek/Hamburg, West Germany, in 1956. After graduating from the *Gymnasium* in 1975, she spent a year in Columbia, South America, studying the language. Returning to Germany, she worked for the German airline *Hapag Lloyd Flug GmbH* for eight years. In 1985 she returned to school, studying Business Administration at the *Freie Universität Berlin*, where she graduated in 1989 with a degree in *Diplom-Kauffrau*. She started working on her Ph.D. in 1990. The topic of her dissertation is the evaluation of service quality. Sabine Haller gives lectures on marketing and business strategy at various institutes and companies. Presently, she works as an associate lecturer and researcher at the *Fachhochschule für Wirtschaft* (technical college) in Berlin.

Md. Mostaque Hussain is a Ph.D. student of Accounting at the Swedish School of Economics and Business Administration in Vasa, Finland. He is also an associate researcher at the Research Institute of the same School. He has completed his master of Commerce in Accountancy with honors in 1992, from the University of Dhaka.

Hans Char Garmann Johnsen is senior researcher at Agder Research Institute. He has studied business administration and political science, and has obtained a Cand Polit degree from the University of Bergen, Norway. He had an eight-year experience in business administration before he joined the Agder Researcher Institute. He also lectures organization theory at Agder State College in Kristiansand, Norway.

Dr. **Harald Knudsen** is Professor of Management at Agder College, Kristiansand, Norway. He studied business administration and has obtained a Ph.D., from the University of Oregon in 1972, majoring in business policy. He has been involved in lecturing and research at the University of Bergen and the Norwegian School of Business and Economics, Bergen, Norway. Since 1976 he has worked at Agder College, initially as associate professor, in 1980-1983 as College President. Since 1984, he has particularly focused on issues of internationalization, strategic management and organizational learning.

D.Sc. **Sören Kock** is an Associate Professor in Marketing at the Swedish School of Economics and Business Administration in Vasa, Finland. His research interests are in business networks, strategies, services marketing, relationship marketing. Sören has published and/or presented several working papers at international conferences such as the Industrial Marketing and Purchasing Conference, European Academy and Nordic Management Conferences. He has worked as visiting scholar at SCANCOR, Stanford University (USA), Uppsala University in Sweden, and FICSM (Arizona State University in the USA). Sören lectures in industrial marketing, international marketing and strategic management.

Kitty Koelemeijer is assistant professor in Marketing and Marketing Research at the Department of Business Administration at Tilburg University, The Netherlands. Her main research interests concern services marketing, distribution channels, and quantitative research methodology. She is currently preparing a Ph.D. thesis on distribution services on which a number of articles have been published and other articles are being prepared for publication. Part of the research for the chapter published in this book was carried out at Wageningen Agricultural University.

Veronica Liljander works as a researcher at the Swedish School of Economics and Business Administration in Helsinki, Finland. Her main research interests are service management and measuring service quality. She has published articles in the International Journal of Service Industry Management and the Journal of Consumer Satisfaction, Dissatisfaction and Complaining Behavior. She was co-organizer of the Workshop on Quality Management in Services III, 1993, in Helsinki.

Ing. **Robbert Masselink** MBA is a management consultant at MIM, a consultancy firm active in the field of Services. Specialized in service quality and as such involved in projects concerning the development of Government Service Centres (GSC).

Drs. **Jan E. Post** works at the Ministry of Home Affairs as secretary of the Project Group on Government Service Centres (GSC).

Dr. **Mohammed Rafiq** is a Lecturer in Retailing and Marketing at Loughborough University Business School, UK. His current research interests are in strategic retail marketing, leisure and services marketing and ethnic entrepreneurship.

Henk Roest is a faculty member within the Department of Business Administration at Tilburg University in the Netherlands. He studied Business Economics and Law and graduated in Marketing in 1987 (cum laude). Since 1988 he has held the position of assistant professor in Marketing and Marketing Research. His research interests are in the management of service quality expectations, on which he is preparing a Ph.D. dissertation. He has published a number of articles on this topic. Other fields of interest are the managerial aspects of brands and service industrialization.

Drs. **Rob Schouten** is a partner of B&A Group Policy Research & Consultancy, a firm active in the field of Strategic Research and Consultancy. As project leader responsible for projects concerning the development of GSC models and the quality audit on government services

Paula Stanley BA MPhil is Senior Research Officer for the centre for Services Management at Cranfield School of Management, and a member of the Operations Management group. Paula's research interests in the area of services management include: service quality in public services, service recovery and service pledges and charters. She also has an interest in criminology; in particular offender/professional relationships in the criminal court sentencing process. Paula is a member of the Operations Management Association, the British Academy of Management an the British Society of Criminology.

Tore Strandvik is (acting) professor at the Department of Marketing, Swedish School of Economics and Business Administration in Helsinki, Finland. His main research interests are service management, service quality, qualitative and quantitative research methods and management cognition. He has published articles in the International Journal of Service Industry Management and the Journal of Consumer Satisfaction, Dissatisfaction and Complaining Behavior. He was co-organizer of the Workshop on Quality Management in Services III, 1993, in Helsinki.

Theo M.M. Verhallen has held the position of Professor in Marketing and Marketing Research at the Department of Business Administration and CentER at Tilburg University since 1991. He studied economics and psychology, and was associate professor in economic psychology until 1985. He then became the research director of Research International in Rotterdam, as from 1988 combined with a research professorship in marketing research at Tilburg University. His publications include articles in the Journal of Economic Psychology and the Journal of Consumer Research on marketing research methodology and consumer psychology.

Dkfm. Dr. **Gerhard A. Wührer** is Assistant Professor at the University of Klagenfurt, Austria. He teaches at the School of Economics and Business Administration, Department of Marketing and International Management and obtained his Ph.D. at the University of Stuttgart, Germany. Before his current position at the Business School he worked as a marketing research analyst and project manager at Roland Berger Consultants in Munich, Germany. At present is lecturing on Marketing Research and Euro-Marketing within the study of "Applied Business Administration" at the University.